From Fascism to Populism
in History

From Fascism to Populism
in History

Federico Finchelstein

With a New Preface

UNIVERSITY OF CALIFORNIA PRESS

University of California Press, one of the most distinguished university presses in the United States, enriches
lives around the world by advancing scholarship in the
humanities, social sciences, and natural sciences. Its
activities are supported by the UC Press Foundation and
by philanthropic contributions from individuals and
institutions. For more information, visit www.ucpress.edu.

University of California Press
Oakland, California

© 2017 by Federico Finchelstein

First paperback edition 2019
ISBN 978-0-520-30935-7 (pbk. : alk. paper)

The Library of Congress has cataloged an earlier edition
as follows:

Names: Finchelstein, Federico, 1975– author.
Title: From fascism to populism in history / Federico
    Finchelstein.
Description: Oakland, California : University of
    California Press, [2017] | Includes bibliographical
    references and index. |
Identifiers: LCCN 2017006846 (print) | LCCN 2017014268
    (ebook) | ISBN 9780520968042 (Epub) | ISBN
    9780520295193 (cloth : alk. paper)
Subjects: LCSH: Fascism. | Populism.
Classification: LCC JC481 (ebook) | LCC JC481 .f518 2017
    (print) | DDC 320.53/3—dc23
LC record available at https://lccn.loc.gov/2017006846

Manufactured in the United States of America

25 24 23 22 21 20 19
10 9 8 7 6 5 4 3 2

A Gabi, Luli, y Laura

CONTENTS

PREFACE TO THE PAPERBACK EDITION

We are living in a new era of populism, one that is more xenophobic, intolerant, and authoritarian than all previous populisms in history. It is also more successful, especially in Europe and in the United States. But how much of this is really new? To be sure, more extremist populists are now in power in many countries of the increasingly illiberal Northern Hemisphere, but this has happened only after many decades of populist regimes in the Global South.

While it is true that new populist governments emerged after the spectacular coming to power of Donald Trump in 2016, Trumpism remains a recent and unusual chapter in a long history. How and why we can explain in terms of history what is new and what is not in the current moment is the main subject of this book. In the present time, we are witnessing not only a new range of populisms but also a gargantuan expansion of populism studies, accompanied by an explosion of new books on the topic. These works owe much to the fact that populism has suddenly become a "trendy" topic, inspiring many scholars in the social sciences to turn their attention to it. Many of these new experts have bought into the notion, promulgated by populists themselves, that what is going on in the world is an entirely new type of political event that is not rooted in history. They simultaneously claim that the cases they write about are unique and that the challenges of the current moment are entirely new. The peculiar result of this amalgamation is a proliferation of new experts, who perceive the new actors as unique and whose books are devoid of history. They talk about populism as if nothing important had previously been written on the topic.[1] This is not one of those books. My book is in dialogue with decades of research on fascism and populism. The ideas and interpreters of fascism and populism are addressed, criticized, and explained in its pages. Many scholars, and I am but one member of this group of "veterans" of populist and fascist studies, dealt with these issues long before populism and fascism became the current fashion. In my case, I have worked on fascism and populism for the past twenty years. I did not become a researcher of fascism and populism because it has only now become a topic of global concern or a preoccupation of the northern regions of the world. In other words, Trumpism is not the reason I decided to write this book.

I have been studying these phenomena from the perspective of the Global South, especially in terms of the historical correlations between fascism and populism. And yet, it is not only in the South that democracy has often been threatened in history. Nor is it only in Latin America, Africa, or Asia that democracy has often died and been reborn. As far as global history goes, democracy has encountered moments of radical change but also deep continuities with the past. These processes of change and continuity need to be mutually addressed when thinking through the manifold contextual paths from fascism to populism on a truly international scale.

These transatlantic and global connections to authoritarianism are not recent phenomena of study. And yet when I left
Argentina (where I was born and raised) and went to the United
States to do my PhD in the early 2000s, one general idea in the
American academy was that these things could happen only in
Latin America, or maybe in Southern Europe (Italy was often
cited), but not in Northern Europe or the United States. Even at
the time, that view was probably already a bad reading of the
radically changing global context. The new right-wing populism that is dominant in the present did not come out of the blue,
and it has a long history. For many observers, especially in
Europe and North America, the extreme and scandalous nature
of Trumpism is something they have never experienced before,
but for scholars of the Global South, there are only a few new
things about Trumpism.

My own trajectory is that I previously studied the transatlantic connections between Argentine and Italian fascism. At the
end of my book *Transatlantic Fascism* (2010), I was already talking
about Peronism as a form of postfascism. For my book on *The
Ideological Origins of the Dirty War* (2014), I included a chapter analyzing the issue of populism and dictatorship in Peronist Argentina.[2] In both books, I explored what happened to fascism after it
was defeated internationally in 1945, and how and why a new
understanding of politics came to power in the South. That former fascists created a new political regime is of no minor importance in the history of modern politics. Just as studying the
actions of Hitler and Mussolini shows that fascism was not only
about aesthetics and discourse but also about ruling the nation,
the same is true with populism. In the late nineteenth and early
twentieth centuries, populists were a form of opposition in Latin
America, Europe, the United States, and beyond. Populists

gained power only after 1945, first in the Global South—more precisely, in Latin America. The study of power regimes matters. By focusing on these first, populist Latin American regimes, we can better understand what this type of politics means, not only when it is part of the opposition, but also when it rules.

Populism is much more than a popular critique of the elites. It is also a conception and a practice of how democracy should work. When populists are in power, they govern with the idea that the people and the nation need to be ruled by an overpowering leader, who speaks and acts in their name. Observers who ignore Latin American history and see populism as appearing first in, for example, Europe in the 1980s or in America under Trumpism are taking a myopic view. One needs to study populism globally, not through the egocentric lens of nationalism or regionalism. This is why it is problematic to ignore Latin American populism and other histories of the Global South, which often preceded European or North American events and experiences. Those who argue, but never explain why, that Latin America doesn't need to be included in the global history of populism do not fully understand the facts and demonstrate an unwillingness to engage with them. Often, they lack curiosity about what has happened outside of their own worlds. In disregarding the history outside of Europe and the United States, as well as banking on an image of Europe or the United States as distinctly modern and democratic compared with Latin America (or Africa or Asia), these observers privilege stereotype over global historical inquiry. Their opinions result from either a conscious or an unreflexive prejudice, which takes as axiomatic the differences between the Global North and South, rather than being formed on the basis of a serious assessment of historical similarities and differences. Latin Americanists, Asianists, or

Africanists are generally trained in European and American historiographies, but the opposite is not necessarily true. Europeanists and Americanists would gain insights about their centers by learning about their margins. As I address it in this book, this argument is never explained as such and the Global South has just been ignored in many recent takes on populism. But actually Trumpism, Salvinism, Orbanism, Bolsonarism, and other recent populist cases show how connected these histories are.

In the following pages of this preface to the paperback edition, I will briefly analyze populism in light of what has happened during the less than two years since publication of the first edition in 2017.

I

Just a few years after the rise of Trumpism to power, are we living in a new era—a new political epoch, which the American leader himself has immodestly called "the age of Trump"? Should all recent political histories be explained as genealogies or effects of the Trumpian moment? After the triumph of Trumpism, new populist extremisms came to power globally in countries like Austria, Brazil, and Italy.[3] And to be sure, extremist populists such as Matteo Salvini in Italy or Jair Bolsonaro in Brazil are often presented, respectively, as the "Italian Trump" or the "Trump of the tropics." But a Trump-centered view of recent history is deeply limited, as is Trump's influence and novelty. The example of Trumpism is often more important than that of a Salvini or Bolsonaro, but this does not mean that Trumpism is the source of European or Latin American developments. While many Americans sound the alarm about the threat that Trumpism poses to constitutional democracy at home, it also has a dangerous impact abroad. But not in the ways many pundits think.

Trumpism is not responsible for the spread of illiberalism to Europe, Latin America, and other places in Asia and Africa. It is certainly not responsible, for example, for Italy's right-wing turn to populism. Italian developments preceded Trumpism. In fact, the emergence of Silvio Berlusconi some decades ago prefigured Trump. In recent years, democracy has been recurrently undermined by populist leaders, and Italian politics has been at the forefront of this trend. The same is true for other countries. Marine Le Pen in France, Viktor Orban in Hungary, and, to provide an example outside of Europe, Rodrigo Duterte in the Philippines were all in place well before Trump's rise to power. At most, Trumpism represents a key confirmation of the illiberal politics wielded by these leaders. Rather than serving simply as a role model for right-wing populists, Trump influences those conservative politicians who outwardly distance themselves from him but nonetheless recognize the political appeal of his style and politics. They have subtly—and dangerously—embraced his appeals to racism and state violence to shore up their support, sanding off Trumpism's roughest edges, so that their illiberal tactics go undetected.

European and American pundits constantly repeat the notion that Trumpism is the template for populists worldwide and has inspired the rise of right-wing parties in France, Italy, Germany, and beyond. It's a view they have been even more prone to trumpet since former Trump chief strategist Stephen K. Bannon's many European tours—to Italy, of course, but also to France, where he appeared before Le Pen's National Front and touted the rise of a "global populist movement." Especially in a country like Italy, which was the cradle of fascism and where right-wing populism has thrived for years, Bannon is treated not only as the creator of Trump but also as an exporter of Trumpism. But while Trumpism and other populist movements share a genealogy, this is not a stereotypical export-import situation. Rather, the rise of these movements across Europe, the United States and Latin America reflects a shared crisis of democracy and a widespread sense that there is a crisis in political representation. People do not see their concerns being addressed by their governments, and growing economic and social inequality are fueling more radical and nationalist politics.

The populists present themselves as the solution to these problems of democracy, but in general, their proposals simply exacerbate the current unrepresentative dimensions of government and economic inequality, while also weakening democratic institutions. They rely on intolerance as a way to deal with those who are (or appear) different or who think differently. Even when populists represent large electoral groups, those who criticize their leaders are delegitimized, presented as traitors, terrorists, and antinational enemies of the people, who don't deserve to have their views reflected in government policy.

In adopting this approach, the new populists are building on a long tradition—but adding a modern twist that the success of Trumpism has incentivized. Populism first came to power in countries such as Argentina and Brazil as a way of overcoming fascism while also offering an alternative model to liberalism and socialism. In other words, Latin American populists in power created a new form of authoritarian democracy. This democracy was antiliberal (against existing models of constitutional democracy), but it wasn't dictatorial and racist as fascism had been. And that's what is new—or rather, what is old—about today's right-wing populisms, including Trumpism, Bolsonarism, and Salvinism.

They don't reflect a desire to replicate the totalitarian fascist regimes, but they want to return to precisely what classical populism opposed: fascist violence and racism. Trump expresses his hatred of his political enemies in mostly racist terms, which is something he shares with the right-wing movements in Europe. The new right-wing populism in America, Italy, and other countries, such as France, Austria, Spain, Poland, Germany, and Hungary, tends to conceive of "the people" as an ethnically and religiously homogeneous body. This represents a return to the interconnected right-wing histories of populism and fascism, and Trump is invoked as evidence of the appeal of their politics.

Trumpism has had a far more significant global impact, however, on conservative or even social democratic leaders in Europe and Latin America. They want to leverage the appeal of Trumpist positions on both "law and order" and immigration restrictions while avoiding being charged with populism and racism. To be sure, right-wing politicians worldwide have adopted these positions for a half century, but by demonstrating the appeal of this old model in the world's most powerful country, Trumpism has legitimized these views and helped to bring them into the political mainstream.

Many of the politicians who are learning a political lesson from Trumpism have no plans to embrace Trump's rhetorical style or to present themselves as populists. Conservatives leaders like Mauricio Macri in Argentina, Mark Rutte in the Netherlands, Sebastian Kurz in Austria, or Sebastián Piñera in Chile are notable examples of this phenomenon. In fact, they are populists on a diet, which means that the media and many voters are dangerously ignoring the impact Trumpism is having on them. They are not interested in condoning Bannon or the Ku Klux Klan, but they do hope to build support by excluding immigrants and celebrating the unrestrained violence of law enforcement. As they distance themselves from Trump publicly, they work to quietly leverage what they understand as his appeal. Like Trump, these "antipolitical" leaders enjoy pillorying politics as usual, claiming they are doing the work of politics while keeping themselves free from the political process.

These importers of Trumpism-lite are fusing antipolitics and a technocratic government of managers, adding in a large dose of paranoia and xenophobia against immigrants. In Germany, as part of the conservative attempt to attract xenophobic, extreme-right AFD voters, "populism light" prompted one minister of the interior to declare that "Islam does not belong to Germany." These "moderates" often call themselves antipopulist—to distance themselves from the extreme right wing—but they nonetheless advance their own measures of xenophobia and discrimination. They avoid focusing on structural problems of inequality and underemployment by sporadically stressing hatred of the immigrant and others who look different or don't speak like them. They are ready to celebrate police repression for political gain.

This is Donald Trump's real export. Right-wing populists like Salvini, Le Pen, or the almost-fascist Bolsonaro have been around for decades. But they are mainstreaming Trump's ongoing racist and repressive legacy, legitimizing each other along the way—and on a global scale.

II

The world is undergoing a historic transformation: populism meets fascism again. This drift toward the extreme right has multiple national roots, but its implications are global. The Italian case is exemplary in this regard. In the country where fascism was born, populism does not reject its predecessor but, rather, aims to form political fronts that also include the aims and ideas of the fascists. Or, to put it another way, fascists and populists share an objective: fomenting xenophobia without neglecting political violence. The new populism mainstreams violence, making it fashionable again. Fascist assassins and populist politicians maintain common goals. In the United States, it is not surprising that people whose ideology aligns with Trump's engage in political violence, from harassing immigrants on the streets or in restaurants to actually sending bombs to those demonized by the American president as "evil" opponents and "enemies of the people." This is so even if the government doesn't appear to have any direct relationship, and in that sense the United States is still far from fascism. But Trump does bear a moral and ethical responsibility for fostering a climate of violence. In 2018, in a warning to the antifascist movement, Trump said, "[Antifa] better hope that the other side doesn't mobilize ... Because if you look, the other side, it's the military. It's the police. It's a lot of very strong, a lot of very tough people. Tougher than them. And smarter than them." According to Trump, the groups that stand against antifascism "are sitting back and watching and they're getting angrier and angrier." For Trump, their mobilization would mean that "antifa's going to be in big trouble. But so far they haven't done that and that's a good thing."[4] By validating violence against antifascists as an expression of legitimate actors whom he likes but does not necessarily control, the American leader acts as an ideological enabler of violent behavior by members of his "base." This potential move from theory to practice by some of the followers represents worrisome evidence of the curtailing and bastardization of democracy that the new populism especially represents from the top.

As Bernard Harcourt put it, "President Trump makes constant use of the language and logic of the 'new right,' a toxic blend of antebellum white supremacy, twentieth-century fascism, European far-right movements of the 1970s, and today's self-identified 'alt-right.'" This imbrication between extreme right-wing populism and fascism is not exclusive to the United States.

The new president of Brazil, Jair Bolsonaro, campaigned more as a fascist than a populist, and time will tell whether his government will leave populism behind. In Brazil, racism has again become a key tool of populism. For Bolsonaro and other postfascist populist leaders around the world, Trump is an icon of success, a projection of their most extreme political desires. In 2017, Bolsonaro identified with Trump's self-portrayal as a victim. He said, "Trump faced the same attacks I am facing—that he was a homophobe, a fascist, a racist, a Nazi—but the people believed in his platform, and I was rooting for him." Bolsonaro has certainly embraced the violence and exclusionary politics that define this generation of postfascist populist politics. He often argued during his campaign that criminals should be summarily shot rather than face trial. During his political life, the former military man has bluntly defended dictatorship and has made several racist and misogynist statements. For example, he accused Afro-Brazilians of being fat and lazy and defended the physical punishment of children to prevent them from being gay. Bolsonaro is especially obsessed with sexual difference. He argued in 2002 that "I'm not going to fight or discriminate, but if I see two men kissing in the street, I'm going to hit them." Like Trump, Bolsonaro defends sexual aggression against women, telling a representative in congress that he "would not rape her because she did not deserve it." Also like Trump, Bolsonaro has several times defended the use of torture, has advocated for the murderous Brazilian dictatorship of the 1960s and 1970s, and has even said that the dictatorship's big mistake was it only tortured rather than killed. Bolsonaro claims to be a man of the people who is restoring law and order in Brazil. The new global populist politics of hatred were at the center of his presidential bid.

The enabling example of Trumpism cannot be put aside when assessing this new populist Latin American right. Like the Trumpists, Bolsonaro believes religion is intrinsic to politics. He has received strong support from the powerful evangelical sectors of Brazil. He also promised tax cuts, investor-friendly austerity measures, and deregulation as economic solutions. This mix of economic neoliberalism and authoritarianism is not new, but Bolsonaro is so far its most extreme champion in the region.

Neoliberal economics has previously coexisted with dictatorships, such as the ones of Augusto Pinochet in Chile and the Dirty War military junta in Argentina in the 1970s. In the 1990s, a blend of neoliberalism and populism was put forward by right-wing leaders like Peronist President Carlos Menem in Argentina and Fernando Collor de Mello in Brazil. These populists were not postfascists in the way Trump and Bolsonaro are. In fact, in many ways, Bolsonaro and Trump might be closer to the likes of the dictatorial Pinochet and the Argentine generals, rather than to their populist predecessors.

Like Trump and his European counterparts, Bolsonaro wants to bridge the historical gaps between fascism and populism.[5] Similarly, Italian populists cannot be absolved of fueling the fascist right. But like its counterpart in the United States, the populist government in Italy claims to have no "direct relationship" to violence. It is important to remember what happened some days before the Italian elections of 2018, which brought Italian populists to power. At that time populism, neofascism, and violence were distinctly connected when Luca Traini, a criminal wrapped in an Italian flag, started shooting people in the streets of Macerata. He chose his victims (African immigrants) for the color of their skin, and when he was captured he held his arm high in the fascist salute, doing so in front of a monument to the fallen that Mussolini himself had honored one morning in the fall of 1936. Traini, who had been a candidate of the populist and xenophobic Lega, became one more example of a new context, in which political alliances and combinations between fascists and populists are constantly occurring. Fascists can follow populist leaders and these leaders, in turn, can enable, condone, or minimize fascist violence. In modern, democratic Italy, a country whose constitution is explicitly antifascist, fascism has been rehabilitated by populist politicians, who see fascists and racists as potential or real allies.[6] Fascists and populists share common themes and talking points. In this context, we have witnessed the emergence of domestic terrorists like the Norwegian Anders Breivik, the 2011 mass murderer who killed seventy-seven people whom he regarded as defenders of Islam, feminism, and multiculturalism; or of Robert Bowers, the anti-Semitic shooter who in Pittsburg, in late 2018, committed the deadliest anti-Semitic attack ever to take place on American soil. Like Brevik, Bowers portrayed his act of terrorism as "a defense" of his people. Sharing his concerns about a "migrant caravan" that had previously denounced by Trump, Bowers wrote, "I can't sit by and watch my people get slaughtered. Screw your optics. I'm going in." He then assassinated eleven people in cold blood. Also in 2018 was an equally significant American example of the links between fascist terrorism and populism in "MAGA [Make America Great Again] bomber" Cesar Sayok, who mailed pipe bombs to President Trump's enemies in the political opposition and the press. It is not surprising that people whose ideology identifies with Trumpist obsessions and conspiracies would commit extremist acts like killing and bombing, even when Trumpism itself is not practically connected to these acts. These attacks could have happened in the United States only within the context of Trumpism in power. In the context of the midterm elections of 2018, Trump mobilized American troops to the border and warned that US soldiers would shoot at the supposedly violent migrants. Trump also promoted an ad that dubiously linked Democrats to "murders carried out by a man twice deported to Mexico." The ad also linked "the man's murderous behavior to the supposed threat posed by all migrants." *CNN* called this ad racist. Writing in the *Washington Post,* Ishaan Tharoor declared the ad was symptomatic of a broader pattern—"This overt turn toward white nationalism is perhaps the dominant theme of Trump's time in office."[7]

In light of all this, it is rather surprising that some observers on the left overlooked this problem, expressing faith in the ephemeral nature of Trumpism. More generally, during the first years of American populism in power, progressive and left-wing voices in America have struggled over the question of how broad and deep Trumpism goes, and how dependent Trumpism is on the figure of Trump himself. By many traditional standards—legislation passed, polling of public support, media endorsement—Trump's is a presidency in constant crisis. But these critics have confused crisis (and scandals) with precariousness. Trumpism is not a benign form of populism but an extremist one. Populism thrives in crisis, instability, and polarization. In fact, as of early 2019, Trump still commands a potent movement (one potentially capable of reelecting him, given the peculiarities of America's Electoral College and the strikingly high tolerance among a broad section of those who voted for him in 2016 for Trump's racism and sexism, as well as for his calls for repression). The actual character of the presidential office changed with the rise of populism to power. The president uses the White House, quite literally, as a bully pulpit. By also using his post as a branding opportunity to enrich himself, his family, and the Trump organization, the president is guilty of serious conflicts of interests.[8] Moreover, as Trump uses and abuses realms of Executive Power, typified by Executive Order and invocations of national security, his presidency is proving to be extremely consequential. And yet, the picture that emerges from these views is that of a weak presidency. There is a precedent for this minimization of the effects of the Trumpist mainstreaming of violence and discrimination in the historiography of German fascism. Some few German historians also insisted many years ago that Hitler was a "weak" dictator. Needless to say, this assessment could be believed only by ignoring the extent of the suffering of Nazism's victims. The idea that Trumpism is a weak political movement is far from how the main victims of this authoritarian presidency—migrants and minorities—experience it. For these targets of Trumpism, the caudillo and his conservative enablers are not weak at all. Explaining these contrasting assessments, which are not motivated by a need to justify or condone populist policies, always comes down to perspective. In other words, it is a matter of the interpreter's subject position.

The center and the margins have different experiences of realty, which are often antithetical. Erosions of basic rights do not affect everyone in the same way, from the rich North to the southern deserts. In fact, some observers on the liberal left argue that freedom has actually increased in Trumpist America. How is it possible to reconcile this idea of "freedom" with the caging of young immigrant children, which has become a symbol of Trumpism? Things look and are experienced differently in different parts of the same country. Far from the seminar room, and at the border, global histories of racism, persecution, and incarceration are especially connected. The same can be said for the interconnected histories of fascism and populism that this book analyzes extensively.[9]

All over the world, extreme right populist leaders, who are not themselves fascists, enable fascist acts by following the fascist playbook. In countries such as France, Austria, the Netherlands, and Germany, common ground is often found among them. Racist stances against immigrants are ·at the center of these elective affinities between fascists and populists. However, as Nadia Urbinati suggests, the question of immigration marks a great difference between old fascism and new populism, because this issue blurs all parties' borders. For a member of the moderate center-left interested in exploring the populist ways of the right, it becomes difficult to be humanitarian if humanitarianism entails more tolerance of new immigrants. This is why, especially in Europe but also in the United States, it is hard to understand the calls for a New Left populism. To be sure, the demands for a new populism are often the result of a terminological confusion about the difference between popular and populist movements and politicians. Like liberalism, socialism cannot be equated simply with populism. But standing up for popular demands and a more extensive participation, being against technocratic elites, or adopting a more egalitarian position does not make politicians or movements populist.

In the United States, where this confusion abounds, Bernie Sanders, Elizabeth Warren, and Alexandria Ocasio-Cortez are often misrepresented as populists. In fact, they make specific egalitarian demands for distinctive constituencies, and they do not pretend to mirror the people in their own image. In practice, they are opposed to authoritarianism and antipluralism and do not promote the idea that those who disagree with them are enemies of the people. They act as more traditional representatives and do not claim to exclusively represent the popular will. In contrast, for populists, delegation replaces representation, and the voice of the people is identified with that of their leader.

The model of left populism that theorists like Ernesto Laclau and Chantal Mouffe have been conjuring is not the most significant leftist response to right populism in the United States, in Brazil, and in many other places. On the other hand, in countries like Argentina, France, and Spain, Laclau's and Mouffe's work has been taken up by political actors. All in all, most calls for a populism of the left insist on the need for a leader like Hugo Chavez in Venezuela (1999–2013), who would also become the living symbol of a homogenized popular will and the artifice of the fights against the enemies of the people. They insist such a leader would bypass institutional channels and effectively create a more direct form of democracy. But in the current context, is this New Left populism going to have an infallible leader, who in impersonating and ventriloquizing the voice of the people also caters to nationalism and the current ethnic intolerance of diversity? Those on the left who espouse these populist desires want to forget not only the Latin American authoritarian precedents of this populism but also the more recent xenophobic resentment of the traditional voters of the left, especially in Europe but also in the United States. They somehow forget that in the name of leaving ideas and political programs behind and in embracing political myth, the left ends up being oblivious to its antifascist past.[10]

III

One of the things that I argue against in this book is ahistorical definitions—they are in fact Platonic definitions—that ignore the longstanding historical patterns behind the current phenomenon. Instead of a definition, I propose a historical understanding of what has constituted populism in history. In the long history of populism, its latest chapter—which is defined in terms not only of Trumpism but also of the Lega, of Le Penism, of Bolsonarism, of Afd in Germany, of Vox in Spain, and others— is more racist and antidemocratic than before.

As I elaborate in the book, when populism first reached power in 1945, in its different Latin American cases, it was a recalibration of fascism for democratic times. In other words, central to populism early on was the continuance of some authoritarian trends, at the same time that it rejected fascist political violence and racism. With the passing of time, populism adopted different forms all over the world, from more left-wing permutations, which included Kirchnerism and Chavismo, to neoliberal ones in places like Italy under Berlusconi, Argentina under Menem, and Brazil under Collor de Mello. For many of these forms, the populist idea of the people was far removed from the fascist idea of the people. It is not the same situation with Trump, Salvini, Orban, Bolsonaro, and other new populist caudillos of the present.

For the fascists, the people are not only defined as a *demos* but are also conceived of as an *ethnos*. There is a radical distinction between that fascist notion of the people and early populism in power. As authoritarian as the early populists were—in the sense that if you were not with them you were considered an enemy of the people (of the antipeople, not the people—their definition of the people was rooted in the notion of the *demos.* If you wanted to support the regime, you would quickly switch from the antipeople to the people. In contrast to fascism, under populism these antipeople are demonized rhetorically as the antithesis of the people but are almost never extensively attacked physically. In addition, their political rights are not substantially destroyed. In other words, under populism they are enemies of the people who lack legitimacy, but they are still allowed to exist and lose elections. They are not entirely persecuted or banned, even though they are merely tolerated.

When we move to more recent chapters in the history of populism—the most important being Trumpism because he came to power in the most powerful country in the world—we see a conflation of the idea of the people as a demos with the originally fascist idea of the people as ethnos. Racism has again become of key importance to this authoritarian tradition, but we have not come full circle. We are not seeing a return to fascism, but one of the paradoxes of the present is that after many decades of populism's original reformulation of fascism, populists are returning to a notion of the people that is based not only on the demos but also on the ethnos. It is increasingly or, in the case of Trumpism fully, racist.

This is why today's tendency to confuse populism with fascism is attributable in part to the fact that the current populism sounds much more fascist than the original postwar populism. Under the new populism, from the United States to Italy and beyond, the people are defined in ethnic terms and the antipeople are often defined in antireligious or racist terms. And yet these enemies of populism are not fully persecuted or eliminated, as the enemies of fascism were. In other words, while populism *sounds* like fascism, practically it is not.

From its beginnings after the end of World War II, populism already implied a move away from fascism. As postfascism, populism led to the refoundation of democracy in authoritarian but not in racist or totalitarian terms. It tried to transpose the authoritarianism of yesterday into a plebiscitarian key—in practice separating itself from the fascism from which it originated. More practically, it often separated the fascists from their politics. The fascists, General Perón famously said, were not good political allies for achieving broad and successful electoral victories. He did not want to form coalitions with them. And he certainly did not consider them part of his base.

The logic of classic populism is no longer typical of the new times, in which Trumpism in the United States has generated a coalition that includes right-center Republicans, populists, racists, and neofascist fellow travelers. This is a new fact in the history of populism in power. In their history, the populists always governed in the name of the majority, excluding or even demonizing the electoral minorities. But in the case of Trump, it is the minority that demonizes and excludes the will of the majority. Trumpism exploits these systemic flaws and bastardizes even more a democracy that is becoming increasingly formal and therefore less and less substantive. In these times, American democracy serves as a negative example for the rest of the globe.

European countries like Italy or Hungary also represent this new experience of populism in power. And Latin America has seen an extension of these new populist experiments with the victory of Jair Bolsonaro in Brazil in 2018. The "new populism" in power today is closer to fascism than ever before, and this fact should be a wake-up call for all of us, and especially for those who remain silent.

New York, May 5, 2019

PROLOGUE

> It is known that personal identity resides in memory,
> and the annulment of that faculty is known to result
> in idiocy.
>
> Jorge Luis Borges, *History of Eternity* (1936)

Some months before Donald Trump became the president of the United States, I found myself in Dresden surrounded by a mix of German neo-Nazi and xenophobic populist demonstrators. I had come to the city with my family to lead a seminar on fascism and populism at the city's university. As fate would have it, we arrived on Monday, the day that the Patriotic Europeans against the Islamization of the West (Pegida) held its weekly demonstration. Racist flags and angry faces encircled us. Literally, one of the most extreme examples of current populism was now standing between the hotel and us. At this point, my eldest daughter, who was eight years old at the time, asked "Are these the Nazis that killed Anne Frank?" We had visited the Anne Frank Museum in Amsterdam the previous year, and she had been quite affected by her story. No, I answered, they are not her killers, but these neo-Nazis are happy she was killed. The identification of extreme right neo-fascists and populists with past movements has reformulated the dictatorial legacy of fascism for different democratic times and is central to understanding the connections between the past and the present. With soothing words, and in Spanish, I assured my daughters, Gabriela and Lucia, that nothing was going to happen to us because in a democracy there are limits to what violent partisans can do. I trusted that these xenophobes would not dare to move openly from their populist rhetorical demonization to fascist physical aggression. But as the history of populism shows, they would nonetheless undermine tolerance and eventually democracy. My daughters were born in New York, and the conditions would be ok there too. Was I right? Having lived under a military dictatorship in Argentina when I was their age, I remember that it would have been too dangerous to pose similar questions to my parents in public. And certainly my family and I would not have been able to walk and talk freely in the midst of military profascist demonstrations. As a young boy, I had been interested in the history of the Holocaust and in Hitler's persecution of the Jews, but the connection between those in power and fascism was not a topic that a child from a middle-class Jewish family openly talked about in Argentina.[1] Too many people had been "disappeared." But like many other citizens, I am asking them now, when populists occupy the global stage.

The first modern populist regime was born in Argentina, not the United States, but lately the world's greatest power is the one brandishing its populist might to the rest of the globe. This is something many Americans, including most social scientists, had previously deemed impossible. Having lived in the United States since 2001, I have often been told that neither populism nor fascism could ever set foot north of the Rio Grande. But especially now that populism has taken hold in the United

States, the global histories of fascism and populism offer key lessons that we should bear in mind as we enter a new era of populism in America and beyond.

If we return populism to its global history, the apparently unexpected can be better understood. This book examines the historical connections between fascism and those in power in the context of populist democracies.

Like other historians who have dedicated their academic lives to the study of fascism and populism, I have always thought studying the past could illuminate the present, and for the last two decades, my work has looked backward to understand the problematic relationships among fascism, populism, violence, and politics. Now the question of fascism and power clearly belongs to the present.

Crisis, xenophobia, and populism characterize our new century. But these traits are not new nor were they simply reborn in our present. To understand the apparent rebirth of populism is, in fact, to comprehend the history of its adoption and reformulation over time. This history starts with fascism and continues with populism in power. If this century has not left behind the history of violence, fascism, and genocide that was so central to the twentieth century, dictatorship, and especially fascistic dictatorships, has nonetheless increasingly lost legitimacy as a form of government. Inflated metaphors of Munich and Weimar aside, we are not witnessing the return of fascism as it existed before. The past is never the present. Yet the current expressions of neofascism and populism have important histories behind them, and the passage from fascism to populism over time has shaped our present. This book argues not only that contextual public and political uses of fascism and populism are key to understanding them but also that studying how these histories have been conceived and interpreted will refresh our awareness and increase our understanding of the current political threats to democracy and equality. Contexts and concepts are key.

This book counters the idea that past and present-day experiences of fascism and populism can be reduced to particular national or regional conditions. It argues against dominant American and Eurocentric views. Especially in light of the historical turning point of Trump's populist victory, tales of American democratic exceptionalism have finally been put to rest. This new age of American populism shows clearly that the United States is like the rest of the world. Similar arguments can be made for French or German democratic culture. We now have no excuse to allow geopolitical narcissism to stand against historical interpretation, especially when analyzing ideologies that cross borders and oceans and even influence each other.

I present a historical take on populism and fascism but also offer a view from the south. In other words, I ask what happens to the center when we think about it from the margins.[2] Neither populism nor fascism is exclusively European, American, or Latin American. Populism is as American as it is Argentine. By the same token, fascism also took hold in Germany and in India. In the United States and in Europe, too many scholars explain the past and present of fascism and populism by narrowly emphasizing the American or European dimensions of what is in fact a global and transnational phenomenon. Decentering the history of fascism and populism does not mean adopting a single alternative explanation for their origins. All histories are important.

What is *fascism* and what is *populism?* These questions were first asked by some fascists, antifascists, populists, and antipopulists to validate, criticize, or distance themselves from the perceived common features associated with the terms. Their supporters, and some of their staunchest critics, have repeated them ever since.[3] Then and now, actors and interpreters alike have agreed that both terms have been counterposed against liberalism; that both involve a moral condemnation of the liberal democratic order of things; and that both represent a mass response advanced by strong leaders in the name of the people, and against elites and politics as usual. But beyond these affinities, and moving past ideal types and the limits of generic interpretations, how have fascism and populism been connected historically and theoretically, and how should we address their significant differences? This book provides historical answers to these questions. While fascism and populism are at the center of political discussions, and are often conflated, they actually represent alternative political and historical trajectories. At the same time, fascism and populism are genealogically connected. They belong to the same history.

Modern populism was born out of fascism. In the same way that fascist mass politics moved popular engagements beyond democratic premodern agrarian forms of populism such as the Russian Narodniki or the American People's Party, and was also radically different from protopopulist formations such as Yrigoyenismo in Argentina or Battlismo in Uruguay, the first modern populist regimes in postwar Latin America moved away from fascism while keeping key antidemocratic features that were not as predominant in prepopulist and protopopulist movements before World War II.

A new populist modernity was born with the defeat of fascism. After the war, populism reformulated the legacies of the "anti-Enlightenment" for the Cold War era and for the first time in history became complete, that is, it achieved power.[4] By 1945, populism had come to represent a continuation of fascism but also a renunciation of some of its defining dictatorial dimensions. Fascism put forward a violent totalitarian order that led to radical forms of political violence and genocide. In contrast, and as a result of the defeat of fascism, populism attempted to reform and retune the fascist legacy to a democratic key. After the war, populism was an outcome of the civilizational effect of fascism. The rise and fall of fascisms affected not only those like General Juan Perón in Argentina that have been close to the fascists but also many authoritarian fellow travelers such as Getulio Vargas in Brazil, or many members of the American populist right that had not experienced or agreed full heartedly with fascism in the first place. In order to reach power, postwar populism renounced its interwar, pro-dictatorial foundations but did not leave fascism entirely behind. It occupied the place of fascism as it became a new "third way" between liberalism and communism. However, unlike fascism's supporters, its proponents wanted populism to be a democratic choice. This populist intention to create a new political tradition that could rule the nation but was different from fascism, and its eventual success in doing so, explains the complex historical nature of postwar populism as a varied set of authoritarian experiments in democracy. To be sure, modern populism incorporated elements from other traditions, but the fascist origins and effects of populism after the defeat of Hitler and Mussolini shaped its postfascist constitutive tension between democracy and dictatorship.

In history, populism can be a reactionary force leading society into a more authoritarian mode, but in its progressive variants, it can also start, or advance, democratization in a situation of inequality while also undermining the rights or legitimacy of political minorities to its right and to its left. Especially in terms of the left, and particularly in the context of left populist's claims to represent the left as a whole, one should not meld together mass citizen participation and popular egalitarian social and political demands with a populist situation. Pundits often ahistorically confuse social democracy, progressive politics, and populism. One of the objectives of the book is to be clear in situating populism historically, and to be equally focused on the ethicopolitical need to make a distinction between populism and other democratic and emancipatory forms that are too often dismissed as populist. If populism uses xenophobia to turn society backward, as it often does in its right-wing versions, in its leftist formations populism turns society's attention to unequal social and economic conditions. More recently this has meant questioning even the dogmas of neoliberal austerity measures and the supposed neutrality of technocratic business-oriented solutions.

In all cases, populism speaks in the name of a single people, and it does so in the name of democracy. But democracy is defined in narrow terms as the expression of the desires of the populist leaders. Populism cannot be simplistically defined by its claim to exclusively represent the entire people against the elites. It is not only that populists want to act in the name of all the people, they also believe that their leader *is* the people and should be a surrogate for the citizens in making all decisions. The global histories of populism show that it has generally had a constitutive beginning when the leader becomes the people. But though the leader in theory personifies the people, in practice he or she represents only his or her followers (and voters), which populists conceive as the expression of an entire people. The leader replaces the people, becoming their voice. In other words, the voice of the people can only be expressed through the mouth of the leader. It is in the persona of the leader that the nation and the people can finally recognize themselves and participate in politics. In fact, without a conception of the charismatic and messianic leader, populism is an incomplete historical form. Understanding populism without its authoritarian notion of leadership and its aim of reaching power through electoral means, therefore, is difficult. These absolute claims on people and leadership encapsulate not only the populist understanding of how populists in the opposition and campaign modes should severely question the state of a democracy but also how that democracy should be ruled when populists reach power. Ultimately, and in practice, populism replaces representation with the transfer of authority to the leader. From left to right, this constitutes the ideology of populism, which is the need for a more direct and authoritarian form of democracy. In other words, when a populist wins the will of the circumstantial electoral majority, its will is conflated with the desires of the leader, who acts in the name of the "real" people.

As Andrew Arato, a leading scholar of political and social theory, explains, in populism, the part becomes the whole. That is, a fictional united people is invented to be led and incarnated by authoritarian leaders. "The people," in fact, is a concept that accounts for many diverse peoples living in a nation. Its translation into a single united people embodied in a leader is a key historical recurrence in populism. This historical process, by which the people created from a section of the citizens first become One, then are appropriated by a movement, and finally are incarnated in the authoritarian leadership of a constructed subject (the united and undifferentiated people) that does not actually exist, has clear undemocratic effects. But for the populists, it is the enemy that is against democracy, not them.[5] From the Argentine populist left to the populists on the French and German extreme right, populists have argued that they are defending the people from tyranny and dictatorship. For populists, dictatorship is viewed not so much as a past form of government but as a metaphor for the enemy in the present. This allows them to equate democracy with populism while neatly associating its opposite (tyranny or dictatorship) with the political foe, be it anti-Peronism in Argentina, imperialism in Venezuela, or the European Union in France and Germany. To be sure, all of these actors have, or have had, authoritarian dimensions, but they are not part of the populist caricaturization of the political enemy. Populists are not greatly concerned with the subtleties of empirical observation but instead direct their attention toward reworking, even reinventing, reality in accordance with their varied ideological imperatives. Living inside the populist bubble allows leaders, regimes, and followers to present everything they dislike as lies of the media and as internal and external conspiracies against the people, the leader, and the nation. Here populism relates directly to fascism's classic refusal to determine the truth empirically.[6]

A distinction between populism and liberalism, as well as between populism and socialism, is that liberalism and socialism must empirically confront their failures, which they typically, though not always, do. Populists think differently. Everyone opposing them is turned into a tyrannical entity. In this context, democracy and dictatorship are just designations for the self and the other. They become images of the populist vision and are no longer categories of political analysis. This transformation of concepts into images is a key dimension of populism's take on a similar fascist trait, long ago noted by Walter Benjamin—namely, the aestheticization of politics. This emphasis on politics as spectacle accompanies populism whenever it shifts from an opposition movement to a regime.

If important, even essential, differences exist between the manifold populisms of the left and the right, populism generally presents a stark contrast when it moves from the opposition to take on the quite different role of the regime. In opposition, populism appears as a protest movement and makes clear the limits that governing elites have in representing important segments of society, but it also claims that it represents society as a whole. As a regime, populism sees no limits on its claims to popular sovereignty, identifying the votes of electoral majorities who support the regime with the structural, transcendental desires of the people and the nation. As the opposition, populism often contributes to an understanding of the frustrations but also to the outing of the long-held prejudices of large elements of the population. As a regime, populism claims the full representation of an entire people and often translates this into the idea of full delegation of power to the leader. In this context, the leader claims to know what the people truly want better than they do.

Unlike fascists, populists most often play the democratic game and will eventually cede power after losing an election. That's because populism, though similar to fascism in conflating itself with the nation and the people, links these totalizing claims of popular national representation to electoral decisions. In other words, populism projects a plebiscitary understanding of politics and rejects the fascist form of dictatorship.

Populism is an authoritarian form of democracy. Defined historically, it thrives in contexts of real or imagined political crises, wherein populism offers itself as antipolitics. It claims to do the work of politics while keeping itself free from the political process. Democracy in this sense simultaneously increases the political participation of real or imagined majorities while it excludes, and limits the rights of, political, sexual, ethnic, and religious minorities. As noted above, populism conceives the people as One—namely, as a single entity consisting of leader, followers, and nation. This trinity of popular sovereignty is rooted in fascism but is confirmed by votes. Populism stands against liberalism, but for electoral politics. Therefore, we can better understand populism if we think of it as an original historical reformulation of fascism that first came to power after 1945. Populism's homogenizing view of the people conceives of political opponents as the antipeople. Opponents become enemies: nemeses who, consciously or unconsciously, stand for the oligarchical elites and for a variety of illegitimate outsiders. Populism defends an illuminated nationalist leader who speaks and decides for the people. It downplays the separation of powers, the independence and legitimacy of a free press, and the rule of law. In populism, democracy is challenged but not destroyed.

As I finish this book, a new populism has taken the world's reins. Once again, the electoral success of a narcissistic leader has come with offending, and downplaying the value of, others. Intolerance and discrimination have opened the way for a definition of the people that relies simultaneously on inclusion and exclusion. As in the past, this new, recharged populism challenges democracy from within, but history teaches us that democratic institutions and a strong civil society can forcefully challenge populists in power. In short, we can learn from historical instances of resistance.

When modern populism emerged, the Argentine writer Jorge Luis Borges stated that, having been thrown out of Berlin, fascism had migrated to Buenos Aires. The regimes of Germany and Argentina advanced oppression, servitude, and cruelty, but it was even "more abominable that they promote[d] idiocy." Even if he problematically conflated fascism (a dictatorship) and populism (an authoritarian electoral form of democracy), Borges acutely revealed why and how they both endorsed stupidity and the absence of historical thinking. They ignored lived experiences and affirmed crass mythologies. If in his elitism he was not able to recognize why the new populism was an inclusive choice for people who felt unrepresented, Borges still clearly noted its defining "sad" monotony. Diversity was replaced with imperatives and symbols. In this early analysis of populists in history, Borges stressed how their leaders turned politics into lies. Reality became melodrama. They twisted everything into fictions "which can't be believed and were believed." Like Borges, we need to remember that fascism and populism must be faced with empirical truths, or, as he put it, we need to distinguish between "legend and reality." In times like this, the past reminds us that fascism and populism are themselves subject to the forces of history.[7]

New York, May 2, 2017

Introduction

Thinking through Fascism and Populism
in Terms of the Past

Representing a historian's inquiry into how and why fascism
morphed into populism in history, this book describes the dictatorial genealogies of modern populism. It also stresses the significant differences between populism as a form of democracy
and fascism as a form of dictatorship. It rethinks the conceptual
and historical experiences of fascism and populism by assessing
their elective ideological affinities and substantial political differences in history and theory. A historical approach means not
subordinating lived experiences to models or ideal types but
rather stressing how the actors saw themselves in contexts that
were both national and transnational. It means stressing varied
contingencies and manifold sources. History combines evidence
with interpretation. Ideal types ignore chronology and the centrality of historical processes. Historical knowledge requires
accounting for how the past is experienced and explained
through narratives of continuities and change over time.

Against an idea of populism as an exclusively European or
American phenomenon, I propose a global reading of its historical

itineraries. Disputing generic theoretical definitions that reduce populism to a single sentence, I stress the need to return populism to history. Distinctive, and even opposed, forms of left- and right-wing populism crisscross the world, and I agree with historians like Eric Hobsbawm that left and right forms of populism cannot be conflated simply because they are often antithetical.[1] While populists on the left present those who are opposed to their political views as enemies of the people, populists on the right connect this populist intolerance of alternative political views with a conception of the people formed on the basis of ethnicity and country of origin. In short, right-wing populists are xenophobic.

Emphasizing the populist style rather than its contents, most historians have rejected the most generic, transhistorical dimensions of the many theories of populism that minimize historical and ideological differences. By questioning definitions of populism as either exclusively left or right, I stress how populism has historically presented a range of possibilities, from Hugo Chávez to Donald Trump, maintaining essential social and political distinctions between left and right but without losing its key illiberal attributes in its varied historical manifestations. And against the commonplace idea of populism as a new political experience without a deep history—namely, a new formation that was born out of the turn-of-the-century fall of Communism—put forward a historical analysis of populism as equally rooted in the three other global moments of the past century: the two world wars and the Cold War.[2]

From the European right to the United States, populism, xenophobia, racism, narcissistic leaders, nationalism, and antipolitics occupy the center of politics. Should we brace ourselves for an ideological storm similar to the one fascism precipitated when it first appeared a little less than one hundred years ago? Some actors and analysts of world politics believe so, and the recent surge of racist populist politics in the United States, Austria, France, Germany, and many other places around the globe seems to confirm it. But few agree on what fascism and populism actually are, and scholars of fascism and populism have often been reticent about entering the public discussion about the uses of the terms. By absenting themselves from public debates, they have left the uses of fascism and populism basically devoid of historical interpretation. Whereas fascism and populism seem to be all over the place, many current actors and interpreters are not aware of their actual histories.

THE USES OF FASCISM AND POPULISM

Fascism, like populism, is often used to denote absolute evil, bad government, authoritarian leadership, and racism. These uses of the terms take away their historical meanings. The problematic belief that history merely repeats itself has traveled the Global North and the Global South, from Moscow to Washington, and from Ankara to Caracas. After the Russian annexation of Crimea in 2014, and the connected Ukrainian crisis, Russian officials referred to the government in Ukraine as the outcome of a fascist coup. Hillary Clinton, secretary of state at the time, described Russian president Vladimir Putin's actions with respect to Ukraine as something like "what Hitler did back in the '30s." Far from the Black Sea, the Venezuelan president, Nicolás Maduro, that same year used the threat of fascism to justify his imprisonment of an opposition leader. The same problematic claims were, and are, made by those opposed to Latin American experiments with populism. Similar epithets are commonly used for the Middle East and Africa. In 2017,

Turkish President Recep Tayyip Erdogan described Europe as "fascist and cruel." Almost identical characterizations of both government and opposition as fascist crisscross the Global South and North from Argentina to the United States, where Donald Trump faced this very serious accusation during his successful 2015–16 presidential campaign and where he himself as President-elect accused intelligence agencies of having engaged in Nazi practices against him. Trump symptomatically asked, "Are we living in Nazi Germany?"[3]

Like the term *fascism,* the term *populism* has been abused equally as a condensation of extremes from right to left. It has been inflated or conflated with anything that stands against liberal democracy. For example, politicians like Mexican president Enrique Peña Nieto or the former British prime minister Tony Blair (notably, after the British "Brexit" of 2016) charged that populism was standing against the neoliberal status quo that they so passionately represented. In fact, this tendency to paint populism as an unproblematized negative take on democracy reveals a simplistic, and often self-serving, identification of democracy with neoliberalism. These positions replicate the us versus them totalizing views of populism. Moreover, these views void democracy of any emancipatory potential. In this context, when confronted with its neoliberal enemies, sectors of society (from right to left) that feel they have been left aside by technocratic elites find populism even more appealing. Populism and neoliberalism can be seen as equally undermining democratic diversity and equality, but neither is a form of fascism.

Populism and neoliberalism do not enable meaningful political decision making by citizens. Nonetheless, they are part of the democratic spectrum, and especially after 1989 they have been causally connected and have often succeeded each other.

On a global scale, populism is not a pathology of democracy but a political form that thrives in democracies that are particularly unequal, that is, in places where the income gap has increased and the legitimacy of democratic representation has decreased. As a response, populism is capable of undermining democracy even more without breaking it, and if and when it does extinguish democracy, it ceases to be populism and becomes something else: dictatorship.

Historically, the populist responses to these contexts (right or left) are distinctive and have been framed within varying national situations and political cultures, but they generally go in the direction of authoritarianism. This is mainly because populism, like fascism before it, understands its own position as the only and true form of political legitimacy. The single truth of populism is that the leader and the nation make up a whole. For populism, the singular will of the majority cannot accept other points of view. In this regard, populism is like fascism in being a response to liberal and socialist explanations of the political. And also like fascism, populism does not recognize a legitimate political place for an opposition that it regards as acting against the desires of the people and that it also accuses of being tyrannical, conspiratorial, and antidemocratic. But this refusal to recognize the opposition's legitimacy does not generally go beyond the logic of discursive demonization. The opponents are turned into public enemies but only rhetorically. If populism moves from this rhetorical enmity to practices of enemy identification and persecution, we could be talking about its transformation into fascism or another form of dictatorial repression. This has happened in the past, for example, in the case of the Peronist Triple A during the beginning of Argentina's Dirty War in the 1970s, and without question it could happen in the future. This morphing of populism back into fascism is always a possibility, but it is very uncommon, and when it does happen, and populism becomes fully antidemocratic, it is no longer populism. While fascism celebrates dictatorship, populism never does so. Fascism idealizes and practices raw forms of political violence that populism rejects in theory and, most often, in practice. Talking about populism and fascism as though they are the same is thus problematic, as the two are significantly different. Populism is a form of authoritarian democracy, while fascism is an ultraviolent dictatorship. The terms are genealogically but usually not conceptually or contextually connected. Properly historicized, populism is not fascism.

Why then are populism and fascism used without reference to their histories? Are we really witnessing the return of fascism, the ism that marked the first half of the twentieth century with steel and blood? Generally, fascism is not approached as a specific historical experience that had very traumatic outcomes but is, rather, considered an insult. Thus, populist parties and leaders that generally represent authoritarian understandings of democracy, but ultimately are not against it, are wrongly equated with fascist dictatorial formations. After 1945, for the first time in its history, populism finally morphed from an ideology and a style of protest movements to a power regime. This was a turning point in its conceptual and practical itineraries, and the historical relevance of this turning point cannot be stressed enough. Likewise, fascism became truly influential only when it transitioned from ideology and movement to regime. In this sense, as the first populist leader in power, Perón played a role similar to the one enacted by the fascist leaders Mussolini and Hitler. When populism became a regime, it finally crystalized as a new and effective political form for ruling the nation. In doing so, populism reformulated fascism, and to that extent, as in the famous case of Argentine Peronism, it became a fully differentiated ism: one that was, and is, rooted in electoral democracy at the same time that it displays a tendency to reject democratic diversity.

FASCISM RETURNS

Fascism as a term has the uncanny ability to absorb any new event in a way that obscures its meaning and history. We are not far from the time when US president George W. Bush presented Al-Qaeda as an Islamo-fascist entity. Fascism is part of our political vocabulary, but has it really returned from its 1945 grave? Has it returned as populism? Significant differences exist between fascism as discursively invoked and its more bifurcated continuities in the present. As a regime, fascism never returned after the end of World War II, and in fact the absence of fascist regimes defined the second half of the last century. Liberalism and communism united to defeat the other ism of modern politics. Once they defeated fascism, they often fought and competed against each other, creating the Cold War. Modern populism as we know it today emerged in this new context. Many historians agree that the Cold War was in fact very hot in the Global South (from Vietnam and Indonesia to the Guatemalan genocide and the Argentine Dirty War), but it never reached the record global "hotness" levels of the fascist violence that led to the Holocaust and World War II. In any case, after 1945, most actors believed that fascism had been defeated for good. From then on, few antidemocratic politicians, from Juan Perón to Marine Le Pen and Donald Trump, associated themselves with terms such as *fascism,* but this does not mean they were fully disassociated from fascism in theory and practice. *Populism* is the key term for understanding the fascist soundings of events and political strategies that reformulated the legacies of fascism for new democratic times.

In the guise of postfascist forms of antiliberal democracy, fascism continued its legacy through various combinations of populism and neofascism. The truth is that, despite the predominance of populism, many neofascist groups remained and continue to exist. Actual neofascist movements that, unlike the populist ones, want to flatly invoke and replicate the fascist legacy are on the rise in Europe. Countries like Greece, with its extreme right-wing movement Golden Dawn, or Norway, where a solo, fascist mass killer, fed by transnational neofascist readings, slaughtered seventy-seven people in 2011, have provided these societies with measured doses of fascist political violence and death that exemplify what neofascism stands for. Sometimes neofascists are fellow travelers of populism. Populists differ from neofascists in their desire to reshape democracy in authoritarian fashion without fully destroying it, but like the neofascists, right-wing Euro-populists identify "the people" with an ethnically conceived national community. In Germany, the Alternative for Germany (AFD), and especially the Patriotic Europeans against the Islamization of the West (Pegida) Movement straddle right-wing populist authoritarianism and the neo-Nazi legacies of German fascism. These populists reduce democracy to the predominance of a majoritarian ethnic group and claim that this type of democracy is being attacked by outsiders. Similarly, populist movements in France and the Netherlands are partly rooted in a xenophobic reclamation of the fascist past, at the same time that they reject it.[4] In Ukraine, the street protests of 2014 were crowded with Ukrainian radical rightists, but this does not mean that fascism is ruling Ukraine or that France or Germany are at risk of witnessing a fascist resurgence. The same pattern goes for the European populism of the right and extreme right as a whole, as well as for North American populism.

TRUMPISM IN HISTORY

During the 2015–16 US presidential campaign, Donald Trump, and significant sectors of the American right, featured populist forms of racism, especially against Mexican immigrants, and discrimination against religious minorities as key parts of their programs. These forms of populism were also supported by neofascist groups like the Ku Klux Klan and others, but this does not mean that Trumpism was a form of fascism. As in Europe, neofascist fellow travelers supported what in fact was a constellation of right-wing populisms that defined the Trumpist campaign.[5] As a result of the predominance of xenophobic moments in the campaign, including some cases of violence against critics and protesters, a new legitimacy for these views emerged. The extreme right-wing side of Trumpism at the white supremacist "alt-right" website, *Breitbart*, argued in its famous "A Manifesto for the 60 Percent: The Center-Right Populist-Nationalist Coalition" that the politics of populism stood between national salvation and a new civil war. Only a "strong and far-seeing leadership" could save America from a war from within. Electoral decisions were part of this populist formula, but they were linked to the idea of Trump as representing what the people wanted even before they voted. As the American populists argued, "That's populism in a nutshell, taking the people's side against the power elites who clearly do not have our best interests at heart." They claimed "populism" made "a resurgence in America and indeed in increasingly significant pockets across Europe because it puts our people first, FIRST. That is why it is winning. That is why the elites hate it so much, and it's ultimately the root of why they hate Donald Trump." The former CEO of Breitbart Steve Bannon, who was also one of Trump's closest advisors and the CEO of his campaign, especially stressed the populist nature of the rise of Trump in American history. His alt-right, white supremacist supporters stated that Trump belonged to the tradition of American populism, which they differentiated from fascism.[6]

From a historical perspective, Trump clearly sounded like a fascist, and he bridged the gap between what he represented— namely, a radical extremist populist candidacy—and what fascism has stood for. But he was still inscribed in the postwar authoritarian ways of populism rather than in "classical" fascist politics. Like many other populist leaders, from Juan Perón in Argentina to Silvio Berlusconi in Italy, Trump repeatedly stated that he acted in the name of the people, while he also pushed the limits of democracy. Even though he introduced himself as the "law and order" candidate, he questioned respect for the rule of law and the separation of powers. Trump was especially antidemocratic in his attempts to downplay the autonomy of the justice system. He used race as a political tool to attack the judiciary when he accused an American judge of acting against him because of that judge's Mexican heritage. In the campaign, Paul Ryan, the Republican speaker of the house and the second most powerful Republican politician at the time, characterized Trump's comments about the judge as "the textbook definition" of racism. In turn, Trump resorted to the populist playbook, declaring his candidacy was the unspoken expression of what "the people" wanted: "The people are tired of this political correctness when things are said that are totally fine."[7] Trump saw himself as the unrepressed voice of the people's desires. In turn, he saw his opponent, Hillary Clinton, "as running against all of the American people and all of the American voters." Trump believed he represented the people of the entire country, and Clinton was antithetical to the American people and the nation. Fascist-sounding conspiratorial views abounded in Trump's authoritarian message. He said that Clinton had met "in secret with international banks to plot the destruction of US sovereignty." Having won his own party's primaries, Trump understood that he had received a "mandate from the people," which justified his antagonistic populist style, but he remained far from fascism's dictatorial ways.[8]

The ideas presented in the Trump campaign had clear fascist and racist undertones. As noted historian of fascism Robert Paxton argued, while there are significant differences between the interwar context that gave rise to fascism and the present day, "echoes of fascism" could be heard in Trump's themes in 2015 and 2016, especially in the candidate's concern for national regeneration and fear about decline, as well as in his "style and technique." However, he concluded that Trump was not a fascist. Paxton referenced Trump's xenophobic proposals, which clearly linked the candidate with Hitler and Mussolini, and identified Trump as a protofascist in the making. He represented "a sort of populist quasifascism" that had not yet developed into fascism.[9] If Paxton as a historian used populism as a prefascist stage to historically analyze the fascist soundings of Trumpism, other interpreters of fascism and populism refused to view Trump through the lens of fascism. Stanley Payne, a famous conservative historian of fascism, stressed that Trump was not a fascist but a reactionary. Violence and nationalist revolutionary trends were absent in Trump, who was part of a "right-wing populist movement." Similarly, for Roger Griffin, a renowned historian of fascist studies, "You can be a total xenophobic racist male chauvinist bastard and still not be a fascist." Griffin did not see in Trump the fascism that he identifies with his own theory of fascism: "There has to be a longing for a new order, a new nation, not just a reformed old nation." For Griffin, Trump was not yet fascist: "As long as Trump does not advocate the abolition of America's democratic institutions, and their replacement by some sort of post-liberal new order, he's not technically a fascist."[10]

These scholars did not stress the historical links between fascism and populism.[11] Mostly absorbed with the West, neither significantly considered the transnational dimensions of these phenomena. In other words, their Euro–North American approach to fascism and populism did not meaningfully place Trump in a global context beyond the United States and Europe. At best, global examples acted as mere additions to what was and is for them basically a North Atlantic story. What sounded like echoes of the past were part of the historical explanation of the present. In contrast with these arguments, I would argue that fascism and populism, while linked in history, belong to different contexts and became very different historical global experiences. Fascism and populism are different chapters in the same transnational history of illiberal resistance to modern constitutional democracy. Trumpism is part of that history. From fascism to populism, many things changed in the world, including the fact that fascist regimes were left behind in the dividing waters represented by the allied victories in 1945 and the subsequent Cold War between them. Fascist regimes were part of the past, but populist regimes thrived after the defeat of fascism. While there are important links between fascism and populism, one historical experience cannot be subsumed under the other. Hitler and Mussolini were indeed different from Perón and

Trump, but historically meaningful connections exist between Peronism, or American populism, and fascism.

All in all, most of these populist movements and persons distanced themselves from classical fascism, but they nonetheless were often labeled as such. Most historians, myself included, are allergic to these generalizations. These public uses of fascism and populism need to be confronted, not simply denied or ridiculed. Presently, pundits and politicians use fascism to loosely describe not only populism but also authoritarian regimes, international terrorism, or repressive stances by the state, or even street protests by the opposition. This laxity is historically problematic, as such careless uses of fascism demonize populism but don't account for its historical causes. The conflation of fascism and populism often leads to proffering the status quo as the only alternative to populist choices.

In Latin America, for example, these ahistorical uses of populism and fascism often conflate populist leaders (either in the government or the opposition) who aggressively used mass politics with the dictatorial leaders who used criminal means to suppress them. They collapse essential distinctions between the populism of the left and the right, when in fact populism can be distinctively leftist or rightist or an amalgamation of both. They also conflate democratically elected regimes or democratically engaged citizens with military dictatorships that destroy democracy. In conceptual terms, the use of the adjectives fascist and populist is a serious problem. In light of the way the terms *fascism* and *populism* have been used and abused, the time has come to place both in their historical contexts. Only then can we assess the movements and situations presently taking place in Latin America, Europe, Africa, the United States, and elsewhere. The present cannot be understood in isolation from its many genealogies, and fascism and racism are clearly among them. Fascism is not only a blurry ghost from the past but also a once-defeated historical ideology that has clear populist and neofascist repercussions today. Overall, this book provides a contextual reading of primary sources, historiography, and political theory that is highly attentive to how and why fascism often turned into populism. It offers a historical critique of the pathways from fascist to populist ideologies, movements, and regimes. Moving away from the public uses of the terms, this book studies how and why fascism and populism emerged in history.

FASCISM AND POPULISM IN HISTORY

After Mussolini and the Italian fascists adopted fascism as the name for their antidemocratic revolution, and especially when fascism became a power regime in 1922, the word *fascism* became a global marker of a renewed anti-Enlightenment, antidemocratic tradition. Going beyond national contexts and restricted Eurocentric theories, I put forward a historical understanding of fascism as a traveling political universe, a radical nationalism affected and, to some extent, constituted by transnational patterns.[12]

In history, fascism was a political ideology that encompassed totalitarianism, state terrorism, imperialism, racism, and, in Germany's case, the most radical genocide of the last century: the Holocaust. Fascism in its many forms did not hesitate to kill its own citizens, as well as its colonial subjects, in its search for ideological and political domination. Millions of civilians perished across the world during the apogee of fascist ideologies in Europe and beyond.

In historical terms, fascism can be defined as a global ideology with national movements and regimes. Fascism was a transnational phenomenon both inside and outside Europe. A modern counter-revolutionary formation, it was ultranationalist, antiliberal, and anti-Marxist. Fascism, in short, was not a mere reactionary position. Its primary aim was to destroy democracy from within in order to create a modern dictatorship from above. It was the product of an economic crisis of capitalism and a concurrent crisis of democratic representation. Transnational fascists proposed a totalitarian state in which plurality and civil society would be silenced, and there would increasingly be no distinctions between the public and the private, and between the state and its citizens. In fascist regimes, the independent press was shut down and the rule of law was entirely destroyed. Fascism defended a divine, messianic, and charismatic form of leadership that conceived of the leader as organically linked to the people and the nation. It considered popular sovereignty to be fully delegated to the dictator, who acted in the name of the community of the people and knew better than they what they truly wanted. Fascists replaced history and empirically based notions of truth with political myth. They had an extreme conception of the enemy, regarding it as an existential threat to the nation and to its people that had to be first persecuted and then deported or eliminated. It aimed to create a new and epochal world order through an incremental continuum of extreme political violence and war.[13]

In my own work, I propose analyzing fascism as a transnational ideology with important national variations. A global ideology, fascism constantly reformulated itself in different national contexts and underwent constant national permutations.

Fascism was founded in Italy in 1919, but the politics it represented appeared simultaneously across the world. From Japan to Brazil and Germany, and from Argentina to India and France, the antidemocratic, violent, and racist revolution of the right that fascism presented was adopted in other countries under different names: Nazism in Germany, *nacionalismo* in Argentina, *integralismo* in Brazil, and so on. Fascism was transnational even before Mussolini used the word *fascismo,* but when fascism became a regime in Italy in 1922, the term received worldwide attention and acquired different meanings in local contexts. This is not to say that the Italian (or the French or later the German) influences were not important for transnational fascists. But there were few imitators. Transnational fascists tailored fascist ideology to fit their distinct national and political traditions. As the Brazilian fascist Miguel Reale argued, "fascism is the universal doctrine of the century," and as such it transcended Mussolini's Italian version insofar as from the beginning "The creature was bigger than its creator." Reale concluded that fascism in Brazil was superior to that in Europe. Similarly, Argentine fascists claimed that theirs was better precisely because it was not restricted by European problems.[14]

Across the globe, fascists conceived of political violence as the source of political power. Against a shared liberal and communist idea of power as being the result of the state's monopoly on violence, fascists equated power with the exercise of political violence, not its suppression. Fascists believed that unleashing violence created and increased their power. They envisioned violence as the source of a new authoritarian society in which nationalism, racism, and (centrally planned) capitalism could be integrated. Fascists saw the state's restrictions on violence as being opposed to political power. They also believed that a free press and an open public sphere acted against their interests. In fascist regimes, civil society had no place. Dissent was not permitted. Fascism identified the pacification of national and international spaces with political weakness. At the same time, fascists conceived of their own violence as "sacred." Nationalist myths inspired and legitimized violence as a key dimension of the fascist political religion. According to fascist ideology, these myths preceded and transcended historical time. Central to this conception was the messianic leader as a warrior who would lead the people into holy contests against internal and external enemies. Brute force was deemed fundamental to opposing those who were perceived to be against the fascist trinity of people, nation, and leader. On a global scale, this fascist brutalization of politics created and legitimized the conditions for extreme forms of political repression, war, and genocide. Fascism theorized an existential enemy that it would subsequently identify and repress. To recapitulate, fascism proposed dictatorship, a mythical idea of the leader, a social-nationalist take on capitalism, and a radical idea of the enemy as the foundation of modern politics.

These historical features of fascism, especially the stress on the mythical leader of the people and his authoritarian rule, the third way between liberalism and socialism, and the idea of an enemy that must be responded to with total war have clear continuities with the right-wing forms of prepopulism that preceded fascism. Like previous forms of racism, xenophobia, and imperialism, this prepopulist side of fascism cannot be ignored. In turn, fascist ideas of the community of the people, the leader, and the nation have been foundational elements of modern populism since World War II, but populism often reformulated or even at times rejected these features, especially those related to fascism's extreme political violence and its totalitarian over-throw of democracy.

Fascism came in different colors that carried different meanings. As the historian of Japanese fascism Reto Hoffman observes, fascism was "donning a rainbow of shirts"—steel gray in Syria, green in Egypt, blue in China, orange in South Africa, gold in Mexico—and these variations spoke volumes about the distinctive national adaptations of what clearly was a global ideology.[15] To this connection between ideology and fashion, one could add the now classic brown in Germany and, of course, black in Italy, blue in Portugal and Ireland, and green in Brazil. As a global rejection of universal democratic values, fascism displayed an ideological palette clearly located on the extreme right of the political spectrum. In contrast, populism was shirtless. As epitomized in Argentine Peronism, the first populist regime in history and thus one of the more significant cases of modern postwar populism, the lack of shirts of the followers (the *descamisados*) explicitly rejected fascism and established populism as postfascism.[16] The historical example of the lack of coloration in populism also works as a metaphor for the ideological crossings of populism and explains why populism, unlike fascism, was not a united front against liberalism. Linking, once again, extreme nationalism with social concerns and an intolerance of the people, modern populism did not restrict itself to the political right. This expanded populism's reach but voided a transnational, ideological consensus on its anti-Enlightenment meanings, as had been the case for global fascism. In different historical postwar experiences, in which even the rejection of liberal forms of democracy took a democratic form, populism contested both liberalism and fascism. The existence of a previous fascist regime was not a necessary precondition for the rise of postwar populism. Populist movements and regimes emerged without national fascist interludes in countries like Brazil, the United States, Peru, or Venezuela, but a central tenet of these new populisms was that fascism was no longer an option for global authoritarians. Along these lines, in the United States, Senator Joseph McCarthy's post-1945 populism was very different from the interwar fascism espoused by a fellow traveler like Father Charles Coughlin. And the authoritarianism of Getulio Vargas in Brazil changed when his dictatorship ended in 1945. It had undergone a populist transformation by the time Vargas was elected president in 1951. More important than the global impact of Peronism after 1945, or Varguism later on, was the way each exemplified how democracy and authoritarianism could coexist. To these and other global authoritarians, populism provided a successful example of a new electoral road to power. After fascism and its constellations of fascist-like coups, anticommunist dictatorships were no longer viable political options in most of the world. In this new context, and especially in Latin America, populists engaged with the world of constitutional democracy, polluting its foundations but not causing them to crumble. As populism struggled with the fascist and liberal pasts, it adopted elements of both and mixed them with other popular traditions from the left and the right.

This new modern populism's ascent to power after World War II was the unintended result of fascism. In a new age of liberalism, it replaced fascism as the most significant challenge (besides communism) to liberal democracy. Like fascism, populism was and is hard to pin down. Even more than fascism, postwar populism created coalitions that crisscrossed the traditional boundaries of the political spectrum, incorporating sectors that had hitherto been opposed to each other. This history explains why conventional categories and schemes do not explain its different looks. Is it right? Is it left? Echoing the title of historian Zeev Sternhell's major book on fascism, *Neither Right nor Left*, I find that populism is conceptually neither.[17] But I would say that historically, as an intolerant understanding of a democracy in which dissent is allowed but is portrayed as lacking any legitimacy, it has been both. More often than not, the differences among populisms have been immense in the ways they push and combine forms of participation and exclusion. In fact, a defining characteristic of modern populism is the fluidity of its transitions from right to left and vice versa.

Populism is an ideological pendulum, but some central features nonetheless remain constant: an extreme sacralizing understanding of politics; a political theology that considers only those who follow an illuminated leadership to be the true members of the people; an understanding of the leader as being essentially opposed to ruling elites; an idea of political antagonists as enemies of the people, who are potentially (or already) traitors to the nation but yet are not violently repressed; a charismatic understanding of the leader as an embodiment of the voice and desires of the people and the nation as a whole; a strong executive branch combined with the discursive, and often practical, dismissal of the legislative and judicial branches of government; continuous efforts to intimidate independent journalism; a radical nationalism and an emphasis on popular or even celebrity culture, as opposed to other forms of expression that do not represent "national thought"; and finally an attachment to an authoritarian form of antiliberal electoral democracy that nonetheless rejects, at least in practice, dictatorial forms of government.[18]

Despite the recurrence of academic references to the volatility of populism as a concept and experience, populism is no mystery to historians reading the sources. In fact, I would argue that it is not that we lack clarity in defining the term, but rather that our theories of populism lack history. Needless to say, the reverse is also true. Historians often neglect the contributions of theoretical approaches to populism. The result is a lack of understanding between history and theory.

A new understanding of populism needs to address the postwar democratic context for the emergence of the first modern populist regimes in history—namely, that populism was originally reconstituted in 1945 as a postfascist response to liberalism and to the left. However, it was not a radical break with the past, and populism was not engendered outside a historical continuum. From the end of the nineteenth century to the interwar years, pre- and protoforms of populism emerged in places as far apart as the United States, Russia, Mexico, Argentina, Brazil, and France. These movements and leaders spoke in the name of the people as one single entity. From the left and the right, they opposed oligarchies and elites, but they did not generally contest liberal democracy tout court.

The contestation of democracy came after World War I, when fascism fused prepopulist tendencies of left and right with a radical antiliberal and anticommunist ideology that led even some noted historians to talk about fascist-populist dictatorships. After 1945, in a radically changed context, modern populism returned to its prefascist roots, but without forgetting the lessons it had learned from fascism. For historians this historicity is clear, but outside the field, populism is often regarded as a transhistorical phenomenon. In other words, it is viewed as happening without a historical context. As postfascism, populism emerged as a form of authoritarian democracy for the Cold War world: one that could adapt the totalitarian version of politics to the postwar hegemony of democratic representation. This transformation was first predominant in Latin America, after the global fall of fascism, and much later became widespread in Europe after the fall of real socialism.

Populism started with the recognition that fascism was now part of the past rather than the present. For General Perón, the leader of the first modern populist regime in history, fascism was "an unrepeatable phenomenon, a classic style to define a precise and determined epoch." As much as Perón mourned the loss of Mussolini and his fascism, he did not want to imitate the defeated past. He wanted to free Peronism from the charge of fascism, and the result was a postfascist, authoritarian, and anti-liberal version of democracy.[19] Many years later, Italian neofascists arrived at a similar conclusion. Thus, Gianfranco Fini, the Italian leader of the neofascist Movimento Sociale Italiano, in attempting to morph it into a populist formation, argued in 1993 that fascism was irreversibly consigned to the past: "Like all Italians we are not neo-fascists, but post-fascists."[20]

Similar moments of recognition first occurred in Latin America in the 1940s and 1950s and much later in other European contexts, where, for example, Lepenism started its ambivalent transition from neofascism to populism in the 1980s. While Bolivian and Ecuadorian populists renounced their links with fascism during the early part of the Cold War, Austrian neofascists practically did so when they became part of a government coalition in 2000. This situation generated outrage and repudiations in Europe, but Italian postfascists had preceded the Austrians when they formed their first power coalition with Silvio Berlusconi in 1994. In the Berlusconi coalitions that followed, postfascist leader Fini subsequently became deputy prime minister, foreign minister, and later president of the Italian chambers of deputies. In a spectacular U-turn, Fini even said in 2003 that Mussolini's participation in the Holocaust meant that "fascism was part of absolute evil."[21]

Though populism often curtailed political rights, it at times expanded social rights while limiting the more radical emancipatory combinations of both. This specific postfascist historical dimension of populism is often lost in the various theoretical reconfigurations, including those approaches that favor or oppose the populist phenomenon.

As a contemporary concept and case, populism has a specific modern history. In other words, it is not a concept outside history. The nonhistorical view of populism reduces it to a transhistorical metaphor for something else, whether it be the constitutive problems of representative democracy, the empty or filled spaces of the political, technocracy, or politics as such. In sharp contrast with those views, I propose viewing populism as the outcome of a modern historical process, in other words, as part of an ongoing history in which the limitations and intrinsic problems of formal democracy meet the interwar and postwar history of democracy being contested from within and without. This book stresses the place of fascism and its legacy in the foundation of modern populism.

By exploring the intimate historical and theoretical links between the fascist and populist experiences, this work analyzes the centrality of global practices, styles, and concepts, and of the postwar memories of political violence for thinking through these connections. Fascism and populism are forms of nationalism, but they also present supranational links and commonalities.

Part of a new transnational trend in the study of fascism and populism, this book expands the understanding of both by way of their transatlantic, and global, repercussions in the postwar period, especially the populist rejection of fascist violence. Violence, its conception and more importantly its practices, divides the waters between fascism and populism. Violence, and its legacy of repression and extermination, defines the contrasting global experiences of fascism and populism as ideologies, movements, and regimes. as well as their subsequent reformulations in our new century.

Focusing on the legacies of fascist violence allows us to better grasp fascism's historical global implications after 1945. I want to overcome the opposition between antitheoretical approaches to fascism and populism and those focused solely on the theoretical dimensions of fascist and populist phenomena. The emphasis on fascist violence on a comparative and cross-national scale overcomes the dichotomy between history and theory. My main point is that fascism's emphasis on political violence, repression, and genocide has remained a significant dimension of its place in the memories of fascists and antifascists, and of populists and antipopulists, after 1945. This traumatic memory of violence has also engendered both neofascist movements and postfascist forms of populism. Thus, this book's perspective integrates the fields of conceptual history and political theory, especially with respect to European and Latin American history but also to instances of fascism and populism in Africa, Asia, and beyond. The interconnected histories of global fascism, populism, and political violence offer particularly meaningful cases for the analysis of the interactions among ideology, antidemocracy, and politics

MAPPING FASCISM AND POPULISM

Overall, the emphasis here is on the transnational and national dimensions of historical experience at the center and at the periphery, but thinking comparatively about the ideology and politics of modern antidemocratic practices across contexts and beyond historical and theoretical commonplaces is also important. Fascism and populism are two historical formations that are contextually connected, and the fact they are not generally analyzed together by historians and theorists is puzzling. This introduction, like the book as a whole, reconnects and analyzes histories and theories of fascism and populism. Chapter 1 provides a conceptual and historical working explanation of fascism and stresses the central role violence and genocide play in fascist ideology and practice, especially in its global dimensions. It establishes a dialogue between different historical interpretations that often avoid talking to each other. In this context, I insist on the need to analyze the history of fascism as a form of political violence that contrasts sharply with populism, in order to contextualize the key distinctions between the two. The chapter also addresses how historians have interpreted fascism, from an early focus on its national variants to one emphasizing generic theories of fascism that downplay national distinctions. I critically engage with these historiographies, especially with their refusals to study fascism outside Europe. Against a Eurocentric view of fascism, I stress the contributions of the new transnational turn in its history. Overall, the chapter forwards a reading of fascism as a critical subject of global history (from Europe to Latin America to Asia and beyond), at the same time that it deals with fascism's ultimate and most extreme realization, the Holocaust.

Most historians of the Holocaust have rejected the notion of fascism as a causal explanation for its origins. At the same time, many historians of fascism present the Holocaust as a particular event that is not central to fascist historiography. Chapter 1 underlines how the Shoah, when viewed in a global rather than national context, poses significant challenges to the transnational history of ideology and politics. Finally, this chapter addresses the "populist" dimensions of fascism in history and theory. The chapters that follow analyze how these dimensions affected the novel postwar experience of populism in power, precisely because it marked an ambivalently democratic rejection of the legacies of fascism, genocide, and dictatorship.

Chapter 2 deals with the emergence and development of modern populism. Eurocentric and US-centered versions of the populist phenomenon prevail in the analysis. Against these ethnocentric tendencies in history and theory, and the challenge they pose to theories of populism as a sort of pure form of democracy, I put forward a more global and critical reading of populism, taking a critical stance toward contemporary interpretations that use history merely to illustrate theory. I provide a working definition of populism in history, and show what historians and theorists can gain by considering populism in regard to fascism. In short, the chapter presents a historical explanation of what populism is, from the early populisms of Russia and the United States to the protopopulisms of Mexico, Argentina, and Brazil. While the former were incomplete populisms, in the sense that they were only opposition movements and not regimes, the latter were in power but were not fully engaged with the populist fusion of antiliberalism and electoral democracy. The chapter also explores the adventures of populism from the "classical" postwar populists in power to neofascist, neoliberal, and left-wing, popular-nationalist forms of populism, especially in Latin America and Europe but also in the United States, Africa, and Asia.

Populism stands in clear opposition to the fascist version of dictatorial rule that preceded the Cold War, decolonization, and different transitions to democracy on a global scale. In other words, populism has been a form of antiliberal democracy that reproduced, but also often reformulated and at times even rejected, the political antinomies of fascism. Populism was and is defined by its contextual postwar rejection of fascist dictatorship and extreme violence, while it continues to reflect some of fascism's ideological premises.

Dictatorship is one of the historical foundations of modern populism. Yet populism is not dictatorship. In fact, in the context of the early Cold War period, modern populism represented a democratic renunciation of dictatorship. In this context, chapter 3 argues that "mass dictatorship" is central to the genealogy of populism. More specifically, the fascist dictatorial experience was one of the reasons behind the emergence of the first populist movements and regimes, but it also helped define them in opposition to their dictatorial origins. Later on and in other contexts, especially in its Southern European, African, and Latin American left-wing variants, populism took on forms of nationalism that explicitly rejected fascism, imperialism, colonialism, racism, and dictatorial rule. This rejection has historically been more ambiguous in right-wing and extreme right-wing cases of populism, which sometimes adopted neoliberal forms.

In dialogue with, but also in contrast to, a literature that makes a binary distinction between fascism and populism, I stress the need to understand the ambivalent, democratic nature of the authoritarian populist experience, including the more recent issues of the new media landscape, "macho-populism," and "Islamic populism."

Born out of the dictatorial defeat of fascism, postwar populism historically became an authoritarian form of democracy. Yet nothing prevents its future relapse into its past fascist foundations.

Few but significant historical examples of the relapse of populism into fascist violence range from neofascist Peronism in the 1970s to the Golden Dawn in Greece and to other European movements of the extreme right. Even if it does not renounce electoral democratic procedures, populism as a movement becomes neofascism when it transitions from a homogenizing conception of the people to one that posits its ethnic identification with the national community, while simultaneously switching from a more or less generic rhetoric of an unidentified enemy (the elites, traitors, outsiders, etc.) to the articulation of an identifiable racial or religious foe who is met with political violence. Similarly, as a regime populism becomes dictatorship (fascist, neofascist, or nonfascist) when it voids its association with its defining democratic features. To put it differently, when elections are finally banned or are no longer free, when the intimidation of the independent press leads to its suppression, when dissent is not only deemed illegitimate by those in power but is also prohibited and punished, when undermining the separation of powers morphs into unifying them under the leader, and last but not least when the populist logic of polarization is translated into actual political persecution, populism loses its historical elements and, in many ways, ceases to be populist. In these cases, the populist tendency to corrupt constitutional democracy leads to its elimination. If populism reverts fully to its classical, dictatorial, and antirational roots, it is no longer populism—a resolution of the populist ambivalence between dictatorship and democracy that is always possible, but historically has not been the most common one. More generally, populism as an antiliberal democratic response to modern politics straddles these two opposing poles. This foundational historical tension in populism emerged in the early Cold War and was reinforced after the fall of the Iron Curtain and the rise of new twenty-first-century nationalisms. In 1919, in 1945, and in the early years of our new century, the contexts were very different. While fascism was born in 1919 out of the interwar crisis of liberalism, and was then reinforced by the deep economic crisis of the 1930s, modern populism emerged in 1945 out of the crisis and defeat of fascism. It did so in the context of the world powers' economic recovery. The new surge of contemporary xenophobic populism is happening in a context that is more similar to the 1920s and 1930s, the period that witnessed the rise of fascism. In this new century, in the context of the Great Recession, democracy is confronting challenges that are similar to those it encountered during the Great Depression.[22] We are witnessing a new global slump and a new crisis of representation in which democracy is once again being tested by populist forces.

History does not repeat itself, but genealogies are important for understanding the present. The new populism of the right is very different from that which accepted the torch from the fascists after World War II. In fact, it is directly related to the affirmation of neoliberalism in Europe and in the rest of the world after 1989. As neoliberalism solidified after 1989, Europe, West and East, saw the rise of invigorated nationalisms, which often looked to the interwar authoritarian past as a precedent for the liberal triumph over communism. Nationalism worked in tandem with neoliberalism. As opposed to claims that the new populisms of the right and the extreme right are unidimensional products of 1989, and thereby have no significant links with the past, connecting these populisms to their authoritarian genealogies both inside and outside Europe is important. Populism and neoliberalism are parts of the same process that the leading political theorist of populism Nadia Urbinati suggests is a disfigurement of democracy.[23] This new American and European populism in many ways is less defensive about its nationalism and racism. It remains close to the interwar past, offering old, undemocratic solutions to new problems.

Globally, populism is particularly attractive for sectors that have perceived of themselves as excluded from the political system, and as unrepresented by existing democratic institutions. Populist leaders equate their desires with the needs of the people and the whole nation. They stand for a homogeneous society that never existed. Populists push nationalist proposals intended to exclude the other and to integrate followers, while remaining deeply suspicious of difference.

As in the past, contemporary populism offers authoritarian answers to the crisis of democratic representation. Populism constantly changes, but the fundamentals remain. Since its postwar ascent to power, populism has asserted a democratic third way between liberalism and socialism. In that context, fascism became populism in history.

ONE

What Is Fascism in History?

The word *fascism* derives from the Italian word *fascio* and refers to a political group (such as the political group led by Giuseppe Garibaldi during the times of Italian unification). Fascism also refers visually and historically to a Roman imperial symbol of authority. Its birthplace as a modern political movement was northern Italy, the year of its birth was 1919, and its founder was Benito Mussolini. Thus, *fascism* as a term as well as a political movement originated in the Italian peninsula. Its ideological origins, however, predated its name. Because its antidemocratic realities were global and existed under different national names, its effects were both national and transnational. Knowing that fascism was born as a global ideological contestation of the pre–World War I liberal order before its explicit emergence as a movement is central to any understanding of fascism. The ideology of radical nationalism that made it possible was part of a larger intellectual reaction to the Enlightenment,[1] a tradition that was both European and "non-European." Ideologically, fascism was conceived as a reaction to the progressive revolutions of the long nineteenth century (from the French revolution of 1789 to the American and Latin American revolutions of 1776 and the 1810s, respectively, to the Paris commune of 1871 and the Cuban War of independence that started in 1895). Fascism represented a counter-revolutionary attack against political and economic equality, tolerance, and freedom.

Rooted in the ideology of the anti-Enlightenment, fascism was not only a reaction against liberal politics and a rejection of democracy. Fascism did not oppose the market economy, for example, and often put forward a corporatist organization intended to promote the accumulation of capital. Equally important, fascism was a philosophy of political action that ascribed absolute value to violence in the political realm. This ascription was boosted by one radical outcome of the Enlightenment: Soviet communism. The triumph of Bolshevism in 1917 was both opposed and emulated on a global scale. By presenting themselves as the opposite of communists, fascists took advantage of this widespread rejection and fear of social revolution while also incorporating some of its dimensions.

A new age of total war, rather than the Soviet experiment, is what ultimately provided the context of fascism. In fact, fascist ideology first emerged in the trenches of World War I. As the Italian historian Angelo Ventrone argues, the war provided a "reservoir" for fascist ideology.[2] This war ideal, and its related notion of the militarization of politics, transcended European borders and circulated in places such as India, Iraq, and Peru. Adolf Hitler and Benito Mussolini openly stated that war constituted their most meaningful personal experiences, and after World War I, these two former soldiers found violence and warfare to be political elements of the first order. When this ideology of violence fused with extreme right-wing nationalism, imperialism, and non-Marxist antiparliamentarian leftist tendencies of revolutionary syndicalism, fascism as we know it today crystallized.

The moment of fascist crystallization was not exclusively Italian or European. In Argentina, former socialist intellectuals like the poet Leopoldo Lugones soon understood the political implications of this fusion. Fascism permutated in different national contexts. As General Eoin O'Duffy, the leader of the Irish Blueshirts argued, the recent history of Italian fascism had a "striking similarity" to the Irish situation but "This is not to say that Ireland can be rescued only by Fascism, but we would be fools were we to shut our eyes to the fact that behind fascism in Italy, and responsible for its phenomenal success, is the same spirit which is now making the Blueshirt movement the biggest political movement that Ireland has ever known."[3] The Argentine fascists admired the Irish Blueshirts, but they saw them as part of their kin, not as models to copy. Sharing the same spirit did not mean imitation; as the Portuguese fascist João Ameal maintained, Italian fascism as it existed in Italy could not be reproduced outside the country. Portuguese fascism could not be a "sterile copy." Fascism was rooted in each nation but was related in transnational revolutionary ways: "It is not the case that it is a reproduction. It is about equivalence. The Italians did their revolution of order. We are starting ours."[4]

Like Lugones and Ameal, the Brazilian fascist Miguel Reale saw fascism as the expression of a universal transnational ideology of the extreme right: "After the Great War, in Brazil as in China, in India as in France, there is no place for a nationalism without socialism. In other words, there is no place for nationalism lacking the elements of profound social revolution." Like their transnational partners, Brazilian fascists believed they represented "a powerful renewal" of the practices of "individual and collective life." Reale claimed that "the revolution" was no longer done in the name of a class: "The revolution is the sacred right of the nation, of the totality of its productive forces." Similarly, Spanish fascists assumed fascist movements existed in countries as far from each other as China, Chile, Japan, Argentina, or Germany because fascism was an agglomeration of right-wing "nationalist" movements. This cluster of fascism was going to "save" each country by constituting "a true new international of civilization against barbarism." Fascism represented a new foundation for the world, "a civilization of unity, universality and authority."[5]

At the end of the war, young Adolf Hitler, a disenfranchised war hero, began to give political expression to his basic violent tendencies. And he did it in the new trenches of modern mass politics.[6] Hitler first adopted, and then shaped, the ideology of a small German party of the extreme right, soon to be called National Socialism. Hitler early on recognized his debt to the thought and practice of Mussolini, but both leaders shared a more extended belief that the world as they knew it was in crisis. Above all Hitler felt illuminated by Mussolini's road to power. The epochal dimension of the fact that fascism had become a regime cannot be more stressed. As the prominent historian of Nazism Richard Evans argues, "Hitler looked admiringly to Mussolini as an example to follow."[7] Hitler and Mussolini, shared fierce anticommunist and antiliberal stances that were widely disseminated among global counter-revolutionaries at the time. This antidemocratic modernism combined modern politics with technological innovation, aesthetic ideas, and a discourse of war.

The modernity of fascism has preoccupied major thinkers over the course of the last century. Whereas Sigmund Freud saw fascism as the return of the repressed—namely, the mythical reformulation of death and violence as a source of political power—Theodor Adorno and Max Horkheimer in their *Dialectic of the Enlightenment* presented fascism as modernity's worst outcome.[8] Although I agree overall with their arguments, they are nonetheless limited to European developments. Grasping the global and transnational dimensions of fascism requires an understanding of its history, first as it is formulated on the national level, and second, as that manifestation of fascism relates to intellectual exchanges across the Atlantic Ocean and beyond.

Like Marxism and liberalism, fascism was a global phenomenon that assumed many national variations and political interpretations. Also like them, fascism never had a closed ideological apparatus. Its ideas changed over time and only now, with the benefit of hindsight, is it possible to conceive of its major ideological patterns. Most fascists perceived fascism as a new political ideology in the making. It was radically opposed to traditional democratic politics, what they disdained as western "electoralism."[9] Its creator, Benito Mussolini, argued that only decadent and old-fashioned ideologies had a closed body of knowledge. For Mussolini, ideas were useful when they had a practical value, that is, when they confirmed his own confused intuitions about social regeneration and the rebirth of nations, the leading role of men like himself in guiding the people, politics as an art, and more generally his noted antihumanitarianism. In short, for the creator of fascism, ideas were useful when they legitimized short-term political goals.[10]

Mussolini was a strategist who believed political needs should determine theoretical formations. Many historians have concluded that this belief made Mussolini a kind of antitheorist and that fascist theory was not important to the movement. For these historians, fascist theory is simply not significant.[11] To be sure, Mussolini at some moments of his career had antitheoretical biases, but all the political needs that shaped Mussolini's strategic view of fascism were informed by a set of unarticulated thoughts and aims. His ideas about power, violence, the internal enemy, and empire, and his own expectation of being the virile, messianic leader of his people, drove Mussolini's political practice over the years. These ideas were abstract enough to inform his political priorities, and practical enough to be considered by transnational fascist politicians, who often wanted to avoid conceptual complications. Antonio Gramsci, an astute antifascist Italian observer and theorist, preferred to stress the "concretism" of Mussolini as a defining characteristic of the fascist leader and, perhaps, of fascist ideology at large.[12] Mussolini's concretism was related to the idea of the primacy of politics over "rigid dogmatic formulas." With some wishful thinking, Mussolini himself argued that "theological" or "metaphysical" discussions were foreign to his movement. Fascism was not dogma but a "special mentality." In typical anti-intellectual terms, Mussolini usually merged his concretism—namely the fascist preference for violent "immediate action"—with a simplistic understanding of reality. Early on, Mussolini posed his "heretic" realism against the "prophecies" of liberalism, socialism, and communism. In other words, Mussolini defended the "reactionary," "aristocratic," and yet "antitraditional" character of fascism by juxtaposing it with the "orgy of the revolution of words."[13]

Fascism was essentially modern. Nevertheless, it was a "reactionary" form of modernism.[14] Acting against emancipation in order to create a new totalitarian modernity, fascism saw itself as a child of the present and even as a "primitive" dimension of the future. Past causes, past theoretical formations, and even past experiences were not as important to Mussolini as present political "action." However, present strategies could for him only be manifest acts of a significant whole, a set of meaningful formations that constituted the basis from which political strategies could emerge. The search for a symbiosis between this common ground from which fascist practices emanated, and various theoretical justifications for these strategies, constituted the most dynamic element of fascist ideology, and also revealed its most obvious limits to full canonization. At the end of the day, the creation of a fascist canonical corpus was an endless task for fascists. They tried to combine various short-term strategies with a long-standing basic preconception of the world. The fascist synthesis was based on this impossible transition from the politics of daily life to dogma. Fascist interpreters across the world had to articulate the often-tense relationship between fascist practice (strategy) and ideal (theory). These ideas about the divine, race, the people, empire, and a mythical past were constantly adapted to the particularities of the very different realities of East and Southeast Asia, Europe, the Middle East, and Latin America. In India and the Middle East, fascist ideas served the purpose of rethinking an authoritarian variant of postcolonialism, whereas in Japan they were used to rethink the modernity of the empire. In Republican, postcolonial Latin America, fascism often presented itself as having continuities with the prerepublican Spanish empire, but also as the primary way of putting forward an authoritarian form of anti-imperialism. In all these places, as elsewhere with fascism, aesthetics were a key dimension of its politics.

Yet fascist theory was not only about aesthetics. In this regard, although it is important to pay attention to antifascist conceptions of fascism, my emphasis does not rely much on Walter Benjamin's aesthetic notion of fascism. For Benjamin, "The logical result of Fascism is the introduction of aesthetics into political life."[15] As historian Robert Paxton argues, Benjamin clearly saw that war was the most extreme aesthetic experience of fascism. The fascist leader wanted to elevate the people into "a higher realm of politics that they would experience sensually." This substitution of "reasoned debate" with the intimacy of shared sensorial experiences substantially altered contemporary politics.[16] To be sure, fascist aesthetics played a central role in how fascism showed itself to the world, but fascism as a political ideology could not be exclusively encompassed by aesthetics. Fascism needed to balance its static ideal of the perfect world with a deeper articulation of its political ideas that could account for and justify a constantly changing strategy. Ultimately, fascist practice was not related to mundane day-to-day politics, or to aesthetics, but rather was focused on a set of political rituals and spectacles aimed at objectifying fascist theory and grounding it in lived experiences. These practices presented fascism as something that could be seen and involved active participation and contact with others, turning ideas into reality.[17]

Fascist theory never became an articulated system of belief. It was always a changing set of tropes and ideas. In this sense, Mussolini considered fascism to be unique "within the forest of 'isms.'" He personally disliked systems of belief because he considered them to be by definition dysfunctional. If economics or art were elements that the Duce deemed irrelevant to a person of his stature, he considered fascist ideology or fascist theory to be subordinated to practice and thereby capable of worldly adaptation. But behind or above adaptation there was something more grandiose: the definition of fascism as an epochal turning point, a mythical and sacred revolution of the nation, the leader, and the people. Indeed, despite his contempt for theory, Mussolini believed in the existence of high theory—the master narrative that represented immediate intuitions about the world—namely, a belief in the primacy of fascist basic meaning over the external word. Intentional, self-affirmative violent meaning was thereby the hardcore attribute of fascist ideology. Above all fascism put forward a radical form of political subjectivity. Fascism's inner meaning represented the fascist matrix, its sacred founding dimension. This conception of an unconscious, prerational intuition expressed the supposed purity of the fascist ideal, the "fascist feeling" that kept the fascist universes of people and specific ideas tied together.[18] Tellingly, even as early as 1919, Mussolini had represented the different groups that formed fascism as sharing the same "unique soul." Fascism, he claimed, may have been "distinctive in form but it is fused and confused in substance."[19] To borrow a Saussurean metaphor, fascism was to be understood as a specific code, a language of political interpretation and action that had a changing set of signifiers attached to a less malleable signified. Mussolini called this more rigid aspect of fascism the "fondo commune," or the "common denominator." It was the meaningful nucleus, the core contained within the less coherent changing dicta or set of fascist signifiers. The common denominator was a master cursor, a point of orientation. It was, in short, the fascist core that contained the most basic premises of fascism, what was relatively constant in fascist ideology as opposed to variable forms of fascist expression. The "fondo commune," the fascist primal notion of the world, was more important than its contextual practices or strategic presentations. The latter were the externalized manifestations of fascism in particular contexts, the strategic instantiations of a more stable "substance of fascism." As Mussolini put it in an uncanny moment of full disclosure, "Each of us has his own temperament, each has his own susceptibility, each has his own individual psychology, but there is a common denominator through which the whole is equalized."[20]

For the Duce, this equalized whole, the fascist matrix, was the most basic level, or core, of fascist notions about politics and the world. It was a set of master tropes, distorted values, and feelings about violence; war; the trinity of leader, people, and nation; myth; the sacred; and the abject. For some present-day interpreters, it may be difficult to make sense of the sheer charge of irrationality and instinctual force that fascism embodied, what Antonio Gramsci had earlier presented as a fascist embrace of the "mysterious" coupled with a "psychology of war."[21] Although fascists in the past often understood this psychology in mystical or even esoteric terms as being imbued with unsignifiable, or unrepresentable, hidden meaning, its main components can perhaps be defined by historians in the present.

The fascist matrix was constituted by traditional binaries such as "us versus them" or "civilization versus barbarism," and the people versus its enemies, among others. But the fascist importation of this notion of the other as a total, existential, enemy provided a central dimension to its ideology. Thus, fascism also had central victimizing dimensions, that is, negative drives that represented what it stood against as opposed to what it stood for. My historical working definition of fascism as a global mythical ideology with distinctive national movements stresses the connections between these binaries and fascism's modern, counter-revolutionary, ultranationalist, antiliberal, and antisocialist features, which took shape in the perfect storm of the interwar years: the dual crises of capitalism and liberalism. In this scenario, the primary aim of fascism was to destroy democracy from within and create a totalitarian dictatorship. Destroying democracy would in turn destroy civil society, political tolerance, and pluralism. The new legitimacy of the fascist order was rooted in the power of the leader, the people, and the nation. Fascism was formulated on the basis of a modern idea of popular sovereignty, but one in which political representation was eliminated and power was fully delegated to the dictator, who acted in the name of the people.

This dictatorship of the people, with its will to create a new man and a new world order, relied on its dialectical other, the existential enemies, the antipeople. These links among the enemy, the dictatorship, and the people were central to fascists around the globe. Fascism's methods against the enemy were persecution and elimination. As the Argentine fascists put it, "The day of final reckoning is close in the future, we will make disappear all the unworthy for the sake of the Patria."[22] In his famous "prophecy" speech of January 1939, Hitler had, just a few months before he himself started World War II, similarly, and equally explicitly, addressed the world as follows:

> In the course of my life I have very often been a prophet, and have usually been ridiculed for it. During the time of my struggle for power it was in the first instance the Jewish race which only received my prophecies with laughter when I said that I would one day take over the leadership of the State, and with it that of the whole nation, and that I would then among many other things settle the Jewish problem. Their laughter was uproarious, but I think that for some time now they have been laughing on the other side of their face. Today I will once more be a prophet: If the international Jewish financiers in and outside Europe should succeed in plunging the nations once more into a world war, then the result will not be the Bolshevization of the earth, and thus the victory of Jewry, but the annihilation of the Jewish race in Europe![23]

For Hitler, sacrifice and violence worked in tandem with believed lies and the imagined actions of the enemy of the people. The notion of sacrificial violence in the name of the prophetic leader and the people concerned not only the enemy but also the fascist self, as Mussolini often repeated and Hitler personally embodied with his suicide in 1945. Fascist racism and anti-Semitism were the consequences of the continuous search for the ideal public enemy, who was becoming increasingly dehumanized from 1919 onward.[24] However, fascism was not made up only of "anti," or negative, dimensions. The more "positive" elements of a definition of fascism included a messianic "religious conception,"[25] which stressed the centrality of a dictatorship embodied in the persona of Mussolini, for whom violence, war, and the accumulation of power were the categorical premises for a desired turning point in national and world history: the fascist empire. In fascist ideology, violence and aggression were considered the best expressions of power, as embodied in the people's "race" and "normal" masculinity. The clear outcome of this extremely *masculinist* and antifeminist dimension of fascism, was, as historian Richard Evans suggests, "a state in which men would rule and women would be reduced mainly to the functions of childbearing and childerearing."[26]

Fascism represented a particular understanding of the state and its monopoly on violence—namely, totalitarianism.[27] Whereas the Italian antifascists who coined the term *totalitarianism* in the 1920s meant it to denote a modern form of tyranny, with fascism as a contemporary version of absolutism, Mussolini had a different take on totalitarianism. He appropriated the term, changing it from a negative political adjective to a self-assertive concept, and reformulated it to encompass all of fascist ideological imperatives (violence, war, imperialism, and a particular notion of the abject) with respect to the state, the nation, and the people:

The Fascist State is not a night-watchman, solicitous only of the personal safety of the citizens; nor is it organized exclusively for the purpose of guarantying a certain degree of material prosperity and relatively peaceful conditions of life, a board of directors would do as much ... The State, as conceived and realised by Fascism, is a spiritual and ethical entity for securing the political, juridical, and economic organization of the nation, an organization which in its origin and growth is a manifestation of the spirit. The State guarantees the internal and external safety of the country, but it also safeguards and transmits the spirit of the people, elaborated down the ages in its language, its customs, its faith. The State is not only the present; it is also the past and above all the future. Transcending the individual's brief spell of life, the State stands for the immanent conscience of the nation. The forms in which it finds expression change, but the need for it remains.[28]

The state that fascism posited as being above and beyond anything else was not every state but a fascist state personified in the leader of the national people and his ideological imperatives. It was the state that fascism had previously conquered and dominated. This state eliminated the distinction between the public and the private. Moreover, the fascist state swallowed civil society and eventually destroyed it.[29] As many antifascists noted at the time, fascism used democracy, and even democratic alliances, in order to destroy democracy.[30]

The fascist revolution that the state impersonated was supposed to exterminate the bourgeois order once and for all. Fascism advertised itself as the antithesis of gradualism, the "anti-party," the "anti-Europe," that would move Europe and the world to the future.

Fascism was essentially revolutionary in that it created a new political order, but it was less revolutionary in its relationship to capitalism. In fact, it never threatened it. Fascists wanted to reform capitalism in nationalist terms that took social reform away from the left. They put forward a way of ruling society with massive popular support but without seriously questioning "conservative social and economic privileges and political dominance."[31]

Yet while capitalism remained intact, the way most fascists approached capitalism should not be conflated with liberal or neoliberal methods. In the interwar years, transnational fascism put forward corporatism as an economic and social solution, and in this economic sense, it was not that far from other experiments in capitalistic reform like the New Deal in the United States.[32] On the contrary, fascism essentially differed from liberalism politically. In the political sense, fascism was clearly totalitarian.

Like Soviet Russia, fascism eliminated political discussion, tolerance, and plurality. Like "real socialism" it obscured the distinction between the state's legitimate use of power and the use of unlawful violence. In short, in totalitarianism, the state became a criminal that abhorred enlightened normativity. However, if Stalin was totalitarian in practice, he never rejected the legacy of the Enlightenment from a theoretical point of view. This was, of course, the ethical failure of communist ideology.[33] That Nazis could enjoy listening to Beethoven in the midst of Auschwitz stands in contrast to Lenin's incapacity to listen to the German composer in the midst of communist terror. Lenin believed that listening to Beethoven would make him softer while he was engaged in the gruesome repression of political opponents. As we are told in the German movie *The Lives of Others* (2006), for Lenin, Beethoven's music represented reason—namely, the legacy of the Enlightenment. This was a symptom of Lenin's recognition that one could not listen to reason while acting against it.[34]

In contrast, for the Nazis, the German composer represented bare beauty and violence. One may recall in this regard, film director Stanley Kubrick's re-creation of postfascist urban squads leader Alex DeLarge in *A Clockwork Orange* (1971).[35] De Large shared his musical taste with Nazis such as Hitler, Goebbels, and Mengele. Fascist totalitarianism, unlike Soviet Russia, does not spread fear, violence, and death with the sole objective of silencing real and imagined dissent. In fascism, violence ceases to be exclusively a means to achieve political goals and becomes a political end in itself. It is precisely the primacy of violence in fascism and its absence in populism that, as we will see, presents the starkest contrast between fascists and populists. But first we will examine how historians have interpreted fascism, followed by an analysis of the Holocaust and, more generally, the primacy of violence in the name of the people as key examples of the logic that shaped fascism in history.

FASCISM AND HISTORIANS

As a globalized form of political ideology, like Marxism and liberalism, that found followers throughout the world, fascism has always been an object of global study. But more recently, the resurgence of a binary that traditionally put history in opposition to theory as a field of study appears to be working in tandem with a classic division of labor among historians. According to this situation, many "working" historians test the hypotheses developed by groups of historical theorists, the "generic" interpreters of fascism. As a result, highly theoretical notions arrived at aprioristically now shape national considerations of fascism in history. At the same time, a transnational phenomenon like historical fascism has been displaced, obscured, or simply ignored. What occupies its place is a generic definition that homogenizes what fascism is and does not consider important national distinctions. Such an understanding of fascism as a generic phenomenon is not new. Since its inception, "Nazi-fascism" was theorized in political and global ways that were easy to understand and useful to combat it. This simplicity helped in its defeat but had the unintended result of obscuring its complex historical nature. These first readings, which were antiliberal, anticommunist, or both, stressed fascism's surrogate role as a global puppet of capitalism or, alternatively, as a borderless replica of communism. However, in the 1960s and 1970s, new comparative historical studies acknowledged that different fascisms shared common structural features even as they also stressed the particularities of a given national incarnation.[36] With these new trends, the centrality of contexts and processes was affirmed, but their transnational effects were lost. Until the 1990s, this was the prevailing tendency among historians, who were mainly working on national cases. Fascism was part of different national histories. Italian historian Renzo De Felice is the most representative example of this approach.

De Felice was a founding historian of fascism studies in Italy. He outlined the idea that fascism was a unitary phenomenon resulting from a dialectical movement among many forces from right and left. A main component of this complex interaction, Mussolini at many times conditioned these forces but at many others he was conditioned by them. Already in 1965, in the introduction to the first volume of his extensive biography of Mussolini, De Felice identified himself with the famous phrase by Angelo Tasca, "per noi definire il fascismo è anzitutto scriverne la storia [for us to define fascism is above all to write its history]." De Felice interpreted it in terms of the need for a new historicization of fascism. He advanced a new historiographical line, in clear opposition to Benedetto Croce and predominant Italian historiography, that claimed fascists were a parenthesis, a historical aberration, and were not a truly causal outcome of Italian history.[37]

Telling the history of fascism involved recognizing the difficulties presented by characterizing (or defining) it from theoretical typologies, since, for De Felice, fascism was not a phenomenon made up of immutable, well-defined characteristics but a reality that was in constant transformation. To be sure, De Felice never suggested that the task of generic characterization was impossible. In fact at the same time that he downplayed the need for a cross-national understanding of fascism, he embraced the comparative concept of totalitarianism. In this context, De Felice's narrative adopted a fierce anticommunist stance, which was reinforced by the early Cold War approach to totalitarianism that equated fascism with communism.[38] This approach converged with that of such historians as Ernst Nolte, François Furet, Stéphane Courtois, and, more recently, Timothy Snyder in propagating a new historical paradigm that tends to conflate fascist and communist forms of violence and repression. Doing so involves reformulating the theory of totalitarianism in terms that remain close to the slogans of the early Cold War.[39] As the Israeli historian Zeev Sternhell argues, "The theory that fascism and communism are twins, accomplices and enemies at the same time, and that Nazism was an imitation of Stalinism, an understandable and even natural response to the Bolshevik danger and a simple product of the First World War, is not only a banalization of fascism and Nazism but above all a distortion of the true nature of the European disaster of our century."[40]

Expanding on the works of George Mosse, Stanley Payne, and the German historian Ernst Nolte in the 1970s and 1980s, a new generic trend emerged in the 1990s and early 2000s. Since then, the historical study of fascism has consolidated into a distinctly global field of knowledge, one that must be founded by consensus.[41] And yet the consensus approach was not totally accepted by all researchers. According to Payne, criticism of the consensus usually took a nominalist perspective. The historian Gilbert Allardyce stood as the emblematic advocate of this position.[42] Allardyce saw no use in the term *fascism* and proposed discarding it as a category of historical analysis.[43] In contrast, most historians promote the need to understand fascism beyond national borders.

Among the most cogent definitions of fascism is Emilio Gentile's. He argues that fascism was typically organized as a militaristic party that held to a totalitarian conception of state politics, an activist and antitheoretical ideology, and a focus on virility and antihedonistic mythical foundations. A defining feature of fascism was its character as a secular religion, which affirms the primacy of the nation understood as an organic and ethnically homogeneous community. Moreover, this nation was to be hierarchically organized into a corporativist state with a vocation for potency, warmongering, and national expansion.[44]

Similarly, Paxton expanded our knowledge of fascism by providing a theory of its developmental stages, from the creation of fascist movements and their presence in political systems to the fascist seizure and exercise of power. The last stage is the moment when fascism is in power and either goes in the direction of self-destruction through war and radicalization or follows the path of entropy and de-fascistization. Paxton made clear that "Most fascisms stopped short, some slipped back, and sometimes features of several stages remained operative at once. Whereas most modern societies spawned fascist movements in the twentieth century, only a few had fascist regimes. Only in Nazi Germany did a fascist regime approach the outer horizons of radicalization." Paxton de-emphasized the centrality of fascist ideology and focused on its practice. Consequently he stressed behavior and function over fascist ideas and rationales. Paxton defined fascism "as a form of political behavior marked by obsessive preoccupation with community decline, humiliation, or victimhood and by compensatory cults of unity, energy, and purity, in which a mass-based party of committed nationalist militants, working in uneasy but effective collaboration with traditional elites, abandons democratic liberties and pursues with redemptive violence and without ethical or legal restraints goals of internal cleansing and external expansion."[45]

Another influential author of current theories of fascism is the German historian Ernst Nolte, who is also famous, or rather infamous, among historians for having generated the *Historiskerstreit*, that is, the debate among West German historians and critical theorists regarding the German character of the Holocaust. Nolte stressed the common genetic nature of fascism and Marxism. This is a position that led him first to minimize fascism as an event that was born not out of right-wing traditions but from Marxism, and second to minimize Nazi extermination policies against the European Jewish population.[46]

Nolte started his treatment of fascism with a definition that became highly influential for later generic historians.[47] Fascism was primarily a dialectical reaction to liberalism, and, more importantly, to Marxism. The latter is for Nolte the consequential culmination of the former. If fascism as anti-Marxism aims to "exterminate its opponent, it cannot be satisfied with the mere political defeat of a recognizable party: it must expose the 'spiritual roots' and include them in its condemnation." In Nolte's view, the Nazis, even in their exterminatory drive, took after the Soviets. Stalin thus inspired Hitler. In short, fascism was a revolutionary reaction against Marxism that aimed to change the world that surrounds it.[48] Nazism was the synthetic form of fascism, something close to its ultimate realization. Nolte defined Nazism as, "the death throes of the sovereign, martial, inwardly antagonistic group; it was the practical and violent resistance to transcendence." *Transcendence* is a term that for Nolte relates to the historical, the transhistorical, and even the metaphysical in probing the "hidden structures of fascism."[49]

Whereas for Nolte, fascism was basically anti-Marxism (in his view a combination of Marx and Nietzsche), Sternhell, an intellectual historian who rejects most generic definitions, is far more suggestive in his approach to fascism. He stresses the anti-liberal nature of fascism, with its proposal for the future, and argues fascism cannot be defined only by what it stood against: liberalism, Marxism, and democracy. Also, he points out, Marxism and liberalism began by challenging the existing ideas and political forces: "Before offering its own vision of the world, Marxism began by opposing liberalism, which a century earlier had risen up against absolutism. The same was true of fascism, which conflicted with liberalism and Marxism and then was able to provide all the elements of an alternative political, moral, and intellectual system."[50]

In contrast to Nolte and other scholars who take a generic approach, Sternhell studies a cultural and ideological phenomenon, the revolt against the Enlightenment that was synchronically developed with it, and was later reinforced in the aftermath of the French Revolution.[51] Thus, for him, the prehistory of fascism is to be found in the anti-Enlightenment. However, Sternhell suggests that it was much later, at the end of the nineteenth century, that this revolt radicalized itself into a massive political phenomenon, as it was during the Dreyfus affair. But

Sternhell sees these two events as catalysts and not prime movers.[52] Sternhell argues that an aristocratic rejection of the Enlightenment was translated into truly popular, revolutionary terms by thinkers like Maurice Barrès and other members of the generation of 1890. Barrès and company radicalized the legacies of thinkers like Edmund Burke, J.G. Herder, Friedrich Nietzsche, Ernest Renan, and Hippolyte Taine, launching a revolt against "ideological modernity, against the 'materialism' of liberalism and Marxism. Thus fascism was a third revolutionary option between liberalism and Marxism that could offer its own vision of the world and create a new political culture."[53]

Sternhell sees the latter part of the nineteenth century, and the period before the First World War, as a laboratory of fascist thought.[54] During this period, the crisis of liberal democracy was a symptom of a broader intellectual crisis critically centered on democratic values. Fascism has two essential components: 1) a brand of antiliberal and antibourgeois tribal nationalism based on social Darwinism and, often, biological determinism; and 2) a radical leftist, antimaterialist (and anti-Marxist) revision of Marxism.[55] Sternhell's work addresses the origins of fascism in the pre-World War I context. The Great War was important insofar as it created favorable conditions for fascism to become a political movement with a broad mass of constituencies. But Sternhell provocatively proposes that the war was not that important in the genealogy of fascism. For Sternhell, "Anyone who regards fascism as no more than a byproduct of the Great War, a mere bourgeois defensive reaction to the postwar crisis, is unable to understand this major phenomenon of the past century. As such fascism represents a rejection of the political culture prevailing at the beginning of the century. It is difficult to find in the fascism of the interwar period, in Mussolini's regime as in all the other European movements, an important idea that had not gradually come to fruition in the quarter century preceding August 1914."[56]

Likewise, Mosse, and later Gentile, has stressed fascism's prewar origins in radical nationalist ideas of the nation, its history, and the people, as well as in political cultures, rituals, and modern aesthetics. According to Mosse, a political and cultural phenomenon such as fascism cannot easily be categorized within the traditional canons of political theory. For Mosse, this type of phenomena was not constructed as a coherent system that can be understood by means of a rational analysis of philosophical writers. Fascism is for him a preeminent object of cultural history.[57] Mosse thinks of fascism as a complex phenomenon that in its different national variants introduced itself as a spiritual revolution made up of hierarchical mass movements. In this way, it could appeal to the past for ways of relating it to a national mystic. Linked to *Romaness* in Italy and to "race" in Germany, and lacking a concrete political or economic program, a specific fascist aesthetics constituted the essence of fascism, which was objectified through its particular mythologies, rites, and symbols and which expressed the general willingness of the movement and the nation.[58]

For Mosse, fascism needed to be analyzed through its own self-understanding. Social and economic factors were important, but they were not as important as its cultural dimensions. Fascism was a civic religion and belief system. It combined extreme nationalism, ideas of regeneration and sacrifice, a mythical mindset, a supreme leader, an expansionist drive, racism and extreme violence, aesthetic ideals of war and masculinity, and revolutionary rites and symbols.[59]

As historian Enzo Traverso argues, "In spite of their differences, Mosse, Sternhell and Gentile converge in their underestimation of a major mark of fascism: anti-communism."[60] Traverso is right in emphasizing the anticommunist dimensions of fascism. But why have so many historians occluded this dimension? An important aspect of this oversight is the extent to which this idea has been exaggerated by conservative historians like Ernst Nolte, the most famous champion of the idea of fascism as anticommunism. But if the Sternhell or the Mosse-Gentile approaches have been truly influential for transnational historians of fascism, Nolte's methodology has been the most important for generic historians, who have thus far dominated recent discussions of what fascism is in history. For them, fascism works as an illustration of the theory that it has previously explained. Thus, in most generic approaches, taxonomic explanations tend to replace more empirically based historical inquiries.

FROM THE "GENERIC CONSENSUS" TO THE TRANSNATIONAL TURN

Generic historians present a European explanation of fascism. When confronted with the non-European fascism of modernizing reactionary traditions, they often resort to tautology. Fascists outside Europe cannot be true fascists because they are not European. This European objection is not apparent in fascist sources, and like other simplistic definitions does not preclude fascism's becoming a diverse reality on European and non-European soils.[61]

For these historians, fascism as a generic object of study becomes a subject only when it is "ideal typed."[62] Examples of this swift and paradigmatic displacement of agency (from how fascist theorists saw themselves to how historical theorists generically defined them) are to be sure quite diverse, and sometimes are even opposed. For Payne, fascism is a radically antagonistic form of revolutionary ultranationalism having a vitalist philosophy and authoritarian conceptions of leadership, war, violence, and mass mobilization. In contrast, Roger Griffin sees generic fascism as essentially focused on national rebirth, what he suggestively calls the palingenetic myth, as a form of historical, modernist resistance to liberalism.[63]

Generally, generic historians tend to displace the peculiar intertwining of fascist theory and practice. Yet this radical connection between action and theory shaped how fascists themselves conceived of the experience of political violence as ideology. Although this connection was not specific to fascism, it was with fascism that it became radicalized in an extremely novel political formation, according to which the primacy of violence was globally explained and practiced through the prism of political myth. I consider this mythical experiential ideology to be one of the most significant aspects of transnational fascism, as it accounts for how and why fascists acted out ideological constructs through extreme forms of violence. Violence became the ultimate form of theory, and the centrality of violence is precisely what these historians tend to situate outside of national and transnational contexts.

Most generic historians of fascism consider their task to be finding the "fascist minimum," a sort of Holy Grail of fascist historiography.[64] Ironically, this view coincides with Mussolini's belief in an essential kernel of fascism that transcends its more national and political connotations. However, generic scholars are not very interested in fascist self-understanding that posits a transnational enemy of the people in politics. They tend to reify important aspects of fascism, such as notions of national rebirth, modernism, and biopolitics, while also omitting the analysis of fascist processes of global circulation, adaptation, and reformulation.

In his important critique of generic historiography, Benjamin Zachariah juxtaposes the "fascist minimum" of generic historians to his proposal for a "fascist repertoire," which he draws from his own research on Indian fascism: "Perhaps it is easier to acknowledge this important presence if fascism is not seen as a specific European import that comes readymade and relatively clearly formed." For Zachariah, "The repertoire tends to include an organic and primordial nationalism involving a controlling statism that disciplines the members of the organic nation to act as, for, and in the organic (or *völkisch*) nation that must be purified and preserved. It is in the service of preserving this organic nation that a paramilitarist tendency towards national discipline is invoked. The coherence of the repertoire is maintained by inciting a sense of continuous crisis and alarm about the potential decay of the organic nation if discipline and purity is not preserved."[65] Zachariah cogently argues for the need to rethink fascist transnational connections as processes of convergent evolution and mutual recognition, rather than as top-down "diffusionist" Eurocentric frameworks. This argument represents a new trend in transnational studies that rethinks fascism as a diverse group of national formations with a distinctive and yet converging set of political ideas and practices.

All in all, major generic historians of fascism like Paxton, Griffin, Mosse, and Payne propose a Eurocentric model of fascism that emphasizes the mimicry and the lack of agency of non-European actors. The same can be said for the few who take the nominalist position that dominated earlier discussions in the field. Going back to De Felice's emphasis on national singularity, Nolte's historicism about an epoch of fascism that had no clear links with its past and its future, and Allardyce's antitheoretical nominalism, these neo-positivist historians deny the possibility of fascism outside of Europe and project great hostility, even irritation, toward both the relationship between history and theory and the idea that analyzing fascism globally is opposed to, that is, not the same as, merely telling its history. These historians dispute that Argentine, Japanese, or Indian fascists were fascists because they stress epochal, national, and specialized disciplinary paths. In this profoundly conservative and anti-intellectual view, fascism deserves no analysis, and its ephemeral nature does not warrant any substantive interpretation. The history of fascism problematically becomes a form of antiquarianism.[66]

Unlike neopositivists, most generic historians turn fascism into a theory that is at the ready when it is needed to catalog fascism according to its different national expressions. To be sure, generic theorists deal with fascism as a universal entity and expect all national historiographies to follow their models. However, most historians of, for example, Italian fascism in Italy, or Latin American, Japanese, or German fascisms have not joined the generic consensus, or they even ignore its success among English readers interested in fascism.

Many studies of fascism go only so far in addressing the interwoven dimensions of fascism on a global scale. As Constantin Iordachi remarks, too often historians of fascism "fell into the trap of reifying geographical labels into historical types." And as Zachariah observes, "Much of the (still meagre) material on 'global' fascism 'outside Europe' still sees Europe as the natural homeland of fascism; it is not clear why this is the case."[67] An outcome of employing this European-centered lens is that fascism outside Europe is regarded as a subject without agency or as having been replaced with stereotypes, such as "Islamo-fascism" in the Arab world or the "caudillo" rule in Latin America. It is rather curious that scholars of European history are open to studying the global circulation of liberalism and Marxism, but when they are confronted with the European participation in fascist global exchanges, they prefer to stress a more Eurocentric view. As bluntly put by Zachariah, "Scholarship on fascism tends to ignore the extra-European writing for reasons of embarrassment, disciplinary specialisation or (in)competence or because it is seen as a secondary part of the history of fascist ideas."[68] When confronted with these positions on fascism, many historians of India, Japan, Syria, Brazil, and other places simply accept them and then treat fascism as a category that is essentially external to their national histories. In some cases, there is even an undercurrent of nationalism in these historical positions. This often unacknowledged nationalist approach stresses the singularity of national history and denies that, for example a country like Argentina could have been polluted by such a problematic "European" ideology. The result of this approach is an essentialist idea of two nations, one being authentically national and the other being a European ideology that was first exported and then adopted by nationals with false consciousness or worse. These readings of fascism that converge in denying it any sort of national dimension are devoid of contextual implications, but paradoxically they first appeared in many contemporary antifascist sources that confronted fascism from the position of a progressive nationalism. For them, fascism simply had no relation to more inclusive national traditions. These antifascist critics offered up an idealized idea of the nation that had no place for fascism. Yet historical explanations still need to address why fascism belonged to the experience of extreme right actors within so many of these national traditions, at the same time that it circulated and was constantly reformulated around the globe.[69]

TRANSNATIONAL FASCISM

When considered globally, in terms of its national specificities but also in terms of ideological transfers and social, cultural, and economic exchanges, fascism becomes less European centered. In contrast with what the leading historian of global history Sebastian Conrad aptly criticizes as a "national container" mentality and a "methodological nationalism," global mobilities, circulation, and transfers are in fact key elements of national history.[70] As a historical approach that focuses on external links that also shaped nations, the transnational perspective leads to better a understanding of the national and supranational workings of geopolitical spaces.

The history of the transnational is not only about transfers but also about those things that were never transferred, or could not be successfully exported because of specific national histories. As Rebekka Habermas suggests, transfer and nontransfer "are two sides of the same coin and therefore must always be viewed together." She argues it is important to look not only on "what was transferred or not transferred but also at the often unintended effects the transfer interaction produced." Processes of transfer are "always accompanied by the shadow of a non-transfer, whether owing to actual ignorance or a conscious decision not to address an issue."[71] In analyzing the clear and shadowy aspects of fascist exchanges, transfers, and nontransfers, the transnational approach to fascism moves it far away from ideal forms and "minimal" definitions. Fascism was a lived experience and, like liberalism and Marxism, it eventually became a global political ideology with significant differences from one national context to another.

Fascism crossed the Atlantic and adopted extreme clerico-fascist dimensions that were not as prevalent in Europe. If this were the case in countries like Argentina, Japanese fascism put forward a distinctive imperial notion of "restoration" of the past. But as in Argentina and elsewhere, Japanese fascism was concerned with modernizing previous forms of national sovereignty. The historian of Japanese fascism Reto Hofmann observes, "The ambiguities of Japan's fascism are a characteristic of fascism itself, reflecting its role as a mediator between revolution and restoration as well as its hybrid nature as a product of global and national history."[72] As a global contestation of liberal democracy and socialism, fascism affirmed nationalism while posing a seemingly paradoxical global challenge to liberal and socialist forms of universalism.

The relationship between fascism and the nation was always ambivalent, since fascism was both a global ideology and an extreme form of nationalism. Most fascists defended a fascist form of internationalism. For the Colombian fascists, the Leopards, there were no "enemies to the right," which for them meant that both nationally and internationally, fascism represented a dictatorial solution to national states of emergency. The fascists of Colombia argued that they "represented a coherent, organized and logical doctrine that has a solution of its own to all the problems in the universe." The Leopards especially stressed how Latin American forms of the extreme right had to be dually rooted in anti-imperialism and Bolivarian ideals. Latin Americans had to be united in order to defend themselves from the "ambitions" of the Anglo-Saxon races that were taking away from their national sovereignty. But if racism were a legitimate solution for a cosmopolitan place like Argentina, the Leopards wanted to defend the internal homogeneity of Colombia as it had grown from the "simple mestizaje of the Spaniard and the Indian."[73] Similarly, José Vasconcelos, a major Mexican intellectual who embraced fascism, presented his country, and Latin America as a whole, as living in colonial conditions. For him, Mexico needed to defend its *mestizaje* and its imperial Hispanic legacies against the northern powers and the "world program" of the "Jews."[74]

While in Brazil some fascists proposed an idea of a multiracial and multireligious totalitarian society, in Mexico fascists often associated fascism with an idealization of both Catholicism and Mexico's Indian past.[75] If in Germany fascists were obsessed with Judaism as the primary enemy of the community of the people, in the Andes, the Peruvian Blackshirts aimed their totalitarian animosity toward Asians, and especially Japanese, immigrants. In what eventually would become India and Pakistan, fascism adopted Hindu or Muslim undertones, while in Argentina, fascists put forward "Christian fascism." Considered from a transnational perspective, fascist entanglements defy standard national histories. Even in Europe, fascism did not always come to power out of an internal crisis such as in the "classical" cases of Germany or Italy. It is true that Mussolini and Hitler were "elected" to power, but it is also true that they reached power as members of party coalitions that they eventually came to dominate and later obliterate. If in Germany and Italy fascism destroyed democracy from within and they became dictatorships, in countries like Spain, fascism came to power with a coup d'état. Desires for civil war in the name of the people's national community predominated on both sides of the Atlantic. Peruvian fascists, for example, called themselves the "children of the people," but in a more adult manner they also stated that they were waging a "holy crusade" as "guerrillas" of fascism. These claims notwithstanding, an actual civil war took place in a few historical cases, notably Spain in 1936–39 and in Italy in 1943–45.[76] Across the world, fascism thrived not only when conservative and authoritarian powers were in decay (Italy, Germany, Spain, and Argentina) but also when other fascist powers helped them. The reasons for fascism were both internal and external. In countries like Romania, Norway, France, and Hungary fascism was "successful" after the German fascist war of occupation. Power and transnational politics were equally important during the Spanish Civil War, which the Spanish fascists won owing to substantial Nazi and Italian fascist support. The same can be said about the Ustasha Movement in Croatia. When this was not the case, the fascists were contested or diminished by authoritarian governments or imperial powers: in Hungary before the Nazi occupation; in Brazil, Colombia, Portugal, Uruguay, and Mexico during the 1920s, 1930s, and 1940s; in British India and British South Africa; and in imperial Japan.

Across the world, fascism contested liberalism and socialism, but it also confronted more moderate forms of the conservative right on a global scale. Most fascists supported forms of corporativism, but they differed in terms of their ultimate and practical applications. Fascism brutalized politics and militarized society. It magnified the political use of violence.[77] The two world wars affected all territories of the world, but in very different ways and with very different outcomes. Countries like Argentina, Mexico, Portugal, and Spain never faced external war during this period, but their politics, fascism included, were substantially affected by international conflicts. England and the United States, on the other hand, experienced the war as combatants but did not face important internal fascist threats. The opposite happened in what is now Ukraine and the Baltic countries, the Middle East, China, Japan, and India, where fascism found an important place in the sun. Later on, the emergence of populism in the Global South was also related, and it became a response to the military events and the genocidal violence that had first originated with fascism in the north.

Political violence through internal and external repression and war remained at the center of transnational fascism. Fascism was a political model that first took power in Italy, but then acquired regional and cross-regional connotations. There were important Mediterranean points of convergence among southern fascisms, and the same can be said about transatlantic fascism, Central European fascisms, and fascism's Asian or Middle Eastern variants.[78]

In contexts of political deterioration, and during periods of economic regression or imperial occupation, fascism proposed an alternative to the perceived crisis of liberal democracy in the interwar and war years. It put forward political violence, racism, and dictatorship as transcendental solutions to epochal problems. Fascism wanted to redefine the relationship between society and the state, but its efforts to do so resulted in very different national permutations. At times, different fascisms (especially but not only Nazism and Italian fascism) competed against each other, and conflict was often at the center of fascist transnational exchanges. Even the study of Nazi Germany is in need of more transnational approaches.[79]

All in all, it would be misleading for historians to study specific cases of fascism without considering others. As Zachariah argues, fascism was

> a family of ideas, with common—though often disavowed—roots, intellectual underpinnings, styles and organisations of movements, and sometimes even a strong overlap of personnel. The phenomenon of fascism in India has not been adequately explored, in part because of a prejudice that fascisms in general are strictly European phenomena and that non-Europeans only produced inade-

quately understood imitations. When and if it is addressed at all, fascism in India is usually attributed (correctly) to the Hindu right, collectively known as the *Sangh Parivar,* but often (incorrectly) only to the Hindu right; however, its history in India is a much longer and broader one.[80]

As in most places, many Hindus in India recognized fascism as both a global and local phenomenon, while Muslims like the fascist intellectual Inayatullah Khan al-Mashriqi not only claimed to have inspired Hitler's own program but also considered his own "Muslim fascism" to be the best version of fascism. If al-Mashriqi claimed that fascism should follow "the shining guidance of the Holy Qur'an," Argentine fascists claimed that their clerico-fascist version was superior to the more secular European versions. In Argentina it was "a Christianized fascism."[81] These views of Latin American fascism were also influential in Europe. A prominent Spanish fascist even stated that European fascists should learn from the Latin Americans:

> It is the case that the Latin American processes of reaction followed an inverse path to that of Europeans. Here [in Europe] it is the nationalist and imperialistic consciousness that initiates the processes, and [European fascists] look for a way to accommodate Catholic principles and the Church. There [in Latin America] the Catholic groups initiate the process and they start looking for collaboration with fascist instruments and styles. Here it is force and violence that, with a decorative intention, later call upon Catholic principles. There, these Catholic principles call upon force in order to defend themselves.[82]

In contrast with this Latin American, and at times European and Southeast Asian, view of the sacred in fascism, Japanese fascists admired fascism's down-to-earthness rather than its god-like features.[83]

Fascism was different and even incompatible in different places. Its causes and effects changed with respect to broader national histories, as well as to changing international contexts, from the Great War to the Cold War and beyond. In my own work, I have studied how in Argentina the clerico-fascism of the 1930s and 1940s was central in the postwar period through Peronism, its populist reformulation, and later in the ideological origins of the Dirty War in the 1970s.[84]

These aftereffects of fascism are often missing from the Eurocentric literature, which downplays fascism's transnational and later its transcontextual connections. For example, in Japan, as in Argentina and in the Arab World, the complex relation between European powers and fascism was a key element in the local attempts to leave fascism behind after 1945. In Argentina and Japan, past fascist connections became inconvenient truths in the new Cold War against communism.[85] After 1945, fascism encountered a certain denationalization of its ideology with the increasing development of pan-European forms in Europe and, often, anti-European forms in Latin America or Asia. As Andrea Mammone, a foremost historian of transnational neofascism argues, "Even what is generally perceived as a narrow nationalism can take a non-national dimension and redeploys at a supranational or international level (even if the main feeling of black shirted comradeship was almost always with their right-wing fellows and with their political and ideological projects)."[86] Neofascists in France and Italy influenced each other and even read their own national contexts in terms of the other. Transatlantic neofascist engagements were continued and often reformulated among Chile, Argentina, and Spain and between Brazil and Portugal. As the Mexican historian of Latin American neofascism Luis Herrán Ávila shows, transnational fascist ideas crisscrossed the Americas from Mexico City and Miami to Buenos Aires and Taipei.[87] Many of these neofascists, earlier in Latin America and the Middle East and later in Europe, would turn to populism as the way to reach a wider antiliberal consensus.

Immediately after World War II, the memories of fascist violence, especially those of the Holocaust, motivated the populist rejection of the past. New forms of postfascist populism created an authoritarian version of democracy, influenced but also firmly rooted in the explicit rejection of genocidal fascist violence.

Modern populism also enforced a notion of popular sovereignty, but this was, and is supposed to be, anchored in an antiliberal electoral democracy and not in the fascist form of dictatorship. Fascism and populism presented clear distinctions in their uses and conceptions of political violence. If fascism understood power as firmly rooted in violence, populism later shared with liberalism a more Weberian, and restricted, notion of violence. In fact, when actual dictatorship in countries like Argentina in the 1970s replaced populist forms of democracy, fascist forms of violence returned. In this case, fascism came back from the past in the form of often-silenced, but at times quite active, memories of and by perpetrators. This was a process in which fascist notions of violent subjectivity returned after they had been repressed. This new take on the perpetrators' memories of violence renewed fascist ideology, in the postfascist and neofascist contexts of the Latin American Dirty Wars but also in other "hot" war contexts of the global Cold War, from the Middle East to Africa and Southeast Asia. Many of these radical dictatorships represented a form of antipopulist ideology, in which violence reigned supreme. In contrast, populism put forward an authoritarian version of democracy that straddled democracy and dictatorship. Turning the page on the Holocaust and other memories of fascist violence, populists tried to close the book of liberal recipes for the nation. Populist postfascism denied the centrality of extreme violence for the authoritarian democracies it constructed in the early postwar period. If many populist regimes were initially founded in order to detach from the fascist past, populists implicitly ignored how much their politics were an effect of this past's radical violence, which the German case epitomized. Because it is at the center of the populist reformulation of fascism, the Holocaust remains a challenge to historians of fascism and populism.

FASCISM AND THE HOLOCAUST

The Holocaust is a paradigmatic fascist transnational experience of genocide, and for this reason still poses, and is symptomatic of, the problems and perspectives opened by a critical global history of fascism. By the end of the Holocaust, Argentine writer Jorge Luis Borges thought of Nazi ideology as a theory of violence. And in 1945, Borges considered violence literally to be fascist ideology. Borges also realized that the victims of this radical form of political violence—the Jewish other in the Holocaust case—were turned into sacrificial objects. For the Borgean Nazi character of the story "Deutsches Requiem," camp commander zur Linde, for example, the fascist body and the national organism are sacrificial objects as well. Moreover, for zur Linde the sacrifice of the fascist self is, in a sense, an even more significant source of ideological self-determination through violence. Moments before his imminent execution by the Allies, zur Linde argues that the memories of fascist violence will remain after the defeat of fascism: "An inexorable epoch is spreading over the world. We forged it, we who are already its victim.

What matters if England is the hammer and we the anvil, so long as violence reigns and not servile Christian timidity? If victory and injustice and happiness are not for Germany, let them be for other nations. Let heaven exist, even though our dwelling place is Hell. I look at myself in the mirror to discover who I am, to discern how I will act in a few hours, when I am face to face with death. My flesh may be afraid; I am not."[88]

In Borges's view, the Nazi idea of the sacrifice of the Jews implied for Hitler's followers an end in itself—namely, bare physical violence.[89] For a fascism that transcended national borders and cultures, the Jew represented absolute darkness. This violence is presented as a naked innate form of authenticity, but according to Borges's interpretation it leads to an ideological maelstrom of destruction and self-destruction beyond fascist regimes.

Fascism ends when it achieves its ideologically sacred imperative of violence. It ends with the sacrifice, the destruction of the fascist self. This was clearly exemplified in Hitler's decisions as his armies began to undergo defeat at the eastern front. He sacrificed his troops regardless of military logic. Fascism is fully entropic. More so than any other ideology, fascism is bound to inevitable decline and harm its own political viability. Entropy leads to the destruction of reason as epitomized in the split between the flesh and the ego in the body and memory of Zur Linde. The killing of the ego is the result of the overdetermination of the forces of desire in politics, the equation of authenticity with victimization, sacrifice, and violence. For Borges, the fascist internationalism that aims to establish violence through victimization as the only politics is a wrong kind of universalism.

Some years before, Sigmund Freud considered Nazi victimization as a central element of global fascist ideology, especially in terms of its stress on myth and the unconscious and of its rejection of reason.[90] Both the Argentine Borges and the Austrian Freud considered the Nazi victimization of Jews an essential element of fascist ideology. To be sure, their view was more sophisticated than the simplistic view shared by the majority of their fellow antifascists. For the latter, fascism was simply an evil, a brute yet silly aberration from normative politics. Fascism had no ideology and was even a surrogate for other ideologies and economic forces.[91] Borges and Freud postulated the opposite view. Fascism was above all a radical ideological event that threatened enlightened civilization. The reasons for this distinctive perspective in the context of antifascism was especially related to the Borgean and Freudian emphasis on anti-Semitism as a central source of ideological fulfillment in Nazi ideology, as well as their inclusion of the latter within a broader fascist mythical notion of the primordial role the unconscious played in politics. The most violent dimensions of this mythical worldview would later be repressed with the defeat of fascism but as Borges indicated, its most damming legacies would remain for future perpetrators as a memory of the overpowering violence of fascist victimization.

It was in the camps that this most violent mythical implication of fascist ideology was first experienced and later interpreted. Jean Améry, an antifascist and a member of the resistance against Nazism, would talk of "real fascism and singular Nazism."[92]

Many other victims felt the same. The tendency to identify fascism with Nazism was widespread during the time of the Holocaust, especially among the victims. In the Warsaw Ghetto, for example, Chaim Kaplan used it to aptly explain the Nazi fascist attempt to create a new world order.[93] For Kaplan, this world order clearly proposed victimization as an ideology of conquest and persecution. In contrast, for historians of the Holocaust, the limits of historiographical notions of fascism and Nazism explained the need to exclude fascism altogether as an analytical tool for understanding the Holocaust. As a result, many historians often overlooked the actual ideological connections between the transnational history of fascism and the historical conditions for the Holocaust.

Primo Levi, who became a member of a fascist youth group in 1924, when he was only five, came to realize the victimizing implications of the Italian variant of fascism. He saw and experienced the grip of fascism from the perspectives of substantially different "gray-zoned" subject positions—namely, semimandatory fascist youth, onlooker, antifascist, and Jewish victim. For Levi, the "exaltation of violence" opened the way to the fascist ideological attack against reason. Levi who conceived Nazism as the "German version of fascism," saw the former as a radical version of fascist ideology. The camps were the model for the fascist "New Order."[94]

Levi reflected on the sacrificial aspects of fascist violence. Fascist violence had the ultimate aim of destroying the humanity of the self. Levi traced the continuum of fascist violence from the Italian fascist squads of 1922 to the world of Auschwitz: "The Blackshirts had not just killed Turin's trade unionists, Communists and Socialists. First they made them drink half a kilo of castor oil. In this way a man is reduced to tatters, is no longer human ... There's a direct connection between the Turin massacres [of 1922] and the entry ceremony in the Nazi camps, where they stripped, destroyed your personal photographs, shaved your head, tattooed you on the arm." He concluded, "This was the demolition of man; this is Fascism."[95]

Fascists around the globe shared this view of their actions as a total attack against their enemies, albeit not its critical ethico-political implications. For the fascists the victimization of the enemy was another example of the centrality and desirability of violence in fascist ideology. Mussolini and the Argentine, Japanese, Brazilian, Colombian, Peruvian, and Romanian fascists considered the enemy to be a defining character of their own notion of the self.[96] In short, Jews and other enemies defined what the fascists were not and, by opposition, what they actually were. Not all fascist ideologies were as radical as Nazism in terms of their victimization of the invented enemy of the people. Similarly, other forms of fascism were not as extreme in terms of their desire, their "will," to put their fantasies about violence and demonization in practice. For most "sources" living during the time of fascism (1919–45), Nazism was a peculiarly radical version of it. In other words, Nazism was German fascism. This appreciation was shared by most fascists and antifascists. After the war and the Holocaust, this experiential conceptualization of fascist ideology was displaced by newer forms of historical meaning-making and selective postwar memory processes. Whereas before 1945, global fascism served the purpose of illuminating the global ideological implications of Nazi processes of victimization, after 1945, fascism as an explanatory device often obscured central dimensions of the Shoah experience, especially the experiences of its Jewish victims. In this context, the different experiences of all victims of the Nazis were homogenized, obscuring the ideological hierarchies and victimizing imperatives present in German fascist ideology.

After the war, and until recently, fascism and Nazism were generally conflated in public memories. This conflation buttressed a form of collective silence about the identities of the victims of the Holocaust, and hence the ideological peculiarities of Nazi persecution. This was the case when these notions of fascism were embraced either in Western or in Eastern Europe.

In the East and the West, the inclusion of Nazism within global fascism, or global totalitarianism, served the purpose of downplaying the main features of Nazi victimization.

This situation obliterated the history and memory of victims. It also downplayed the particularities of transnational fascism, as it was understood at the time of the Shoah. In turn, many historians of fascism and the Holocaust presented an uncritical take on this transnational peculiarity of fascism. In fact, they often ended up mutually excluding their respective fields of knowledge. Especially generic historians of fascism replaced a mutually inclusive living field of ideological experiences and genocidal practices in the past with definitions, glossaries, and "high theory" from the present.[97]

Concurrently with this exclusion, historians of the Holocaust have concluded that fascism has no connection whatsoever with Nazism. For example, Saul Friedländer, a major historian of the Holocaust, stresses the singularity of what he aptly calls Nazi redemptive anti-Semitism. Friedländer emphasizes the pseudoreligious dimension of the Holocaust, that is, the extermination was a "sacred end and not a means to other ends."[98] He concludes that no similar trait can be found in other countries.[99] In Friedländer's master works *Nazi Germany and the Jews* and *The Years of Extermination,* the global history of Nazi endeavors is explained through the enactment and reception of Nazi policies, both nationally and internationally. To be sure, Friedländer states that the Holocaust "is an integral part of 'the age of ideology,'" but he also clearly differentiates between global fascism "in Italy and elsewhere" and Nazism in Germany. In other words, for him fascism can be a transnational ideology but not in Germany. Friedländer's work is especially innovative in its emphasis on the experience of the victims. In this regard, the lack of references to fascism as experienced and interpreted by the victims is surprising. The transnational history of global interpretations of fascism could provide another angle for thinking about the Nazi transnational project of conquest and destruction, especially in terms of how it was interpreted by its victims.

Developing transnational and comparative approaches outside the framework of the Nazi empire is often anathema in Holocaust historiography. However, the adoption of a global historical approach to Nazism may not necessarily mean a general downplaying of the Holocaust as an extreme event within an extreme history.[100] Eurocentrism, which is also a trademark of many studies of fascism, plays an important role in current pleas for uniqueness in Holocaust historiography. Whereas Africans, and also Arabs, experienced an equally unique brand of Italian racism in the forms of mustard gases and other chemical weapons, summary executions, and killings of civilians, the Nazis effected one of the most severe events in history. In short, it was a radical departure, a turning point in history. But empire, fascism, and racism link the Holocaust with the world outside Europe. More recently many historians of Nazism have focused on German and European imperialisms as central precursors of the Nazi genocide in the East.[101] All in all, as Hannah Arendt suggested many years ago in her *Origins of Totalitarianism,* global ideologies and imperialism were central elements of the history and prehistory of fascism and the Holocaust.[102] They also continued to play a role in its aftermath.

In their radical display of raw, unmediated physical violence, Nazis pushed the fascist experience to the extreme. In a sense, Nazism became fully different from other forms of fascism. However, fascism exercised its genocidal potential by engaging in genocidal practices in Italian fascist Africa and Civil War

Spain. Transnational fascists (from France to the Ukraine) also collaborated in the Nazi Final Solution by providing logistical and ideological support and, last but not least, killers. However, Nazism presents a radical departure from other fascist formations. Nazism is not a generic "ideal type" of fascism but the culmination of its most radical possibility.

Fascism as a movement and as a regime rose and fell promoting civil war. This was at last the Italian legacy of Mussolini's fascism: a country divided and a near apocalyptic fight that required radically violent means, including fascist collaboration, in sending Italian Jews to Auschwitz.[103] But perhaps more importantly, the legacy of fascism goes beyond Italy and Mussolini. Not only did Italian fascism send Jews to Auschwitz after 1943 but links existed from the far-distant Argentine fascists, who justified the extermination of the Jews; to the French and Dutch collaborators who corralled them; and to the Baltic and Ukrainian fascists who killed them. Transnational fascism was the global ideology that made that crime possible.

Nazism in its radical spiral of integral "sacred" terror against the Jews left the fascist pack behind. It was in the Nazi empire in the East that the Nazis decided to literalize in the concentration camps the most circular notion of Nazi fascism, the notion of the abject. In Auschwitz, a closed and controlled laboratory of fascism, the Nazi idea of the abject as the existential enemy of the people, the most detached and psychotic aspect of Hitler's ideology, became a reality.[104]

THE FASCIST HISTORY OF VIOLENCE

Fascism was an ideology of violence. It took violence so seriously that it not only devoted thousands of pages of books and speeches to it but also made violence a political imperative. Violence defined fascist practice. In other words, there is no fascism without political violence. There is no real fascism without a total, existential enemy of the people and its consequent political persecution.

The logic of violence in fascism is central for thinking through its ideological and aesthetic dimensions. Violence defined fascism's conceptual representations, especially with respect to fascist genocidal notions of the abject and sacrifice. Violence constituted fascism and the fascists. Violence was ascribed a sacred status and made fascism an extreme political theology. It was a primary idea of the world as rooted and ruled by violence in apocalyptic times of emergency. As the Chinese Blueshirts stated, this was why fascism "is the only tool of self-salvation of nations on the brink of destruction. It saved Italy and Germany.... Therefore, there is no other road than imitating the fascist spirit of violent struggle as in Italy and Germany."[105] Like the Blueshirts in China, the Portuguese Blueshirts also identified the apology for violence with international fascism. Violence was the aim of fascism but also the starting point of politics: "Violence is the essential and intelligent start of all good politics because without violence and in adversity, conquest is impossible."[106]

There was no place for other ideas, insofar as in fascist minds alternative politics represented a rejection of the idea of fascism as the only possibility for politics. Those with other ideas were necessarily positioned against the national community of leader and people. They had no legitimate place in fascist politics or society. For fascists, it was theoretically logical that the enemy fully deserved to be met with violence. The logic of violence was equated with power. To put it simply, the logic of violence constituted a core element of fascist ideology. A practical outcome of this ideology was the victimization of those deemed to be different. This form of political victimization was entirely modern in the fascist sense precisely because, although it claimed to be rooted in old myths from the past, it was actually a violence legitimized by and through a modern political myth of the leader, the nation, and the people.

In fascism, belief was connected to an act of faith in the conductor. Fascism presented its leaders as living myths. While in Germany the *Führerprinzip* presented Hitler as the ultimate sacred source of truth and authority, in Brazil, Argentina, Spain, and beyond, fascists identified the politics of the leaders with a transcendental mythical truth. In Argentina, Leopoldo Lugones, the country's most famous fascist, related truth to power and the divine. For fascists truth was a matter of almost divine intuition and detached from practical corroboration. Like Lugones, Spanish fascist writer Ramiro de Maeztu posited the existence of an "eternal truth." It was in the search for right and truth "as transcendental essences" that reality emerged. Similarly, Gustavo Barroso argued that Brazilian fascism was the best political formation on earth because it represented "eternal truths." These truths of Brazilian fascism promised an extraordinary change, the "new times," when the "unity" of the spirit, the cross, and the nation would rule. Like Lugones and de Maeztu, Barroso identified the rise of a new era with the aesthetic and political primacy of an absolute truth.[107]

Fascism connected the reality of the movement and its leaders with a mythical past of heroism, violence, and subordination. In fascist ideology, the leaders personified an epochal continuum establishing a direct link, a unitary front with the people and the nation. In turn, the leader was the ultimate source of popular sovereignty, responsible only to himself. Fascists were obsessed with the infallibility of their leaders because, for them, their assumed lack of error reflected the core divine truths of the ideology. Unlike liberalism or socialism, which they believed had nontranscendental roots, fascists longed for a return of the mythical warring heroes, and that is what they expected from their leaders.[108] Fascism was a political religion. Its modernity especially lay in the fact that it repositioned the place of the sacred in politics.

It is important to stress the particular modernity of fascism with respect to the sacred and the unconscious. As historian Angelo Ventrone argues, the fascist critique of modernity was apocalyptic, but it also proposed an alternative modernity at the service of conquest and domination. Fascists wanted to replace what they saw as mechanistic, repetitive, and involuntary modernity with a "qualified" modernity in which the fascist could tame matter and the economy. Fascists saw their modernity as the "domination of the spirit and the political." They placed an "ethics of war" and a violent sense of masculinity and community at the center of these concerns.[109] For this reason, for fascists violence was the ultimate form of politicization.

Violence, and the lawless use of violence, is a defining aspect of both fascist practice and fascist theory. Violence, as Primo Levi cogently put it, became an end in itself.[110] Fascism brandished power and violence as ideological aims rather than means. In fascist ideology, violence is not only instrumental, it is mainly a form of intuition, of creation. It is not only a mobilizing myth but also a dark negative sublime. Namely, violence is elevated to the greatest form of politics.[111] For Mussolini, violence was power without restraints. It was a nonrational state that provided the nation and the individual with the security of being protected from the menacing outer world. For thinkers like Max

Weber and Karl Marx, or even in part for Georges Sorel (who nonetheless exalted violence in regenerative and redemptive terms), violence has a primary role in politics but needs to be restrained one it has achieved a useful end. These authors clearly differ from the fascist theorists of violence.

In the fascist ideal, violence loses its instrumentality and becomes a direct source of knowledge.[112] Violence defines fascist identity. It is a key dimension of the inner self. Violence becomes a transcendent experience that renders politics an almost sacred field of action. In Mussolini's case, violence was an ethical force that helped fascism achieve a radical break from ordinary concerns. Here the notion of sacrifice is once again central. Over time, Mussolini best expressed this idea in the famous fascist catchphrase, "I don't care" (or I don't give a damn), which was inscribed in the showrooms of the permanent fascist revolution in 1942. For Mussolini this action of not caring was related to the acceptance of death and "purifying blood" as redemptive forces.[113] Even as late as 1942, when considering the future of the Italian nation, he could not (or did not want to) conceal the fascist embrace of violence that the Nazi war of destruction promised him.[114] As was the case for Hitler, or for the Argentine fascist *nacionalistas,* violence and war were for Mussolini sources of political orientation and personal and collective redemption.[115] Spanish fascists talked of the "sacred violence of action," which for them was equally rooted in justice and right. Similarly fusing politics and holy violence, Eugenia Silveyra de Oyuela, one of the most extreme Argentine fascist intellectuals, asserted that violence was legitimate as a result of God's war against the internal enemies. For her, this was the situation in Argentina: where "red hordes" had invaded the country, "we have the invaders in our midst, and we are, in fact, in a state of defensive war. This is a licit war for the Argentine who needs 'to defend the rights of the threatened homeland.'" The motto of the Egyptian Blueshirts was "Obedience and Struggle" (*al-tcah wa al-jihad*), and this idea of struggle was also reflected in their oath, "I swear by almighty God, by my honour and by the fatherland that I will be a faithful and obedient soldier, fighting for the sake of Egypt, and that I will abstain from whatever would pervert my principles or be harmful to my organization." A world away from the Middle East, the Chinese Blueshirts asserted that violence had to be directed toward all political rivals: "There must be a determination to shed blood—that is, there must be a kind of unprecedented violence to eliminate all enemies of the people."[116] If Chinese fascists considered violence the way to achieve the true politics of the people, the Colombian fascists, the Leopards, asserted, "Violence, as illuminated by the myth of a beautiful and heroic fatherland, is the only thing that can create for us a favorably alternative in the great fights of the future." The myth of fascism as rooted in the notion that the inner self and collective unconscious forces could lead only to violence and death was the preeminent form of conceiving politics as essentially divine.

Fascists connected violence and death, in and though politics, to a radical renewal of the self. For example, the Romanian fascists linked the sacred nature of violence to the idea of regeneration and salvation of their warriors through death as sacrifice. For them, as "God wanted" it, "the germ of a renewal can grow only out of death, of suffering." Romanian fascists did "love death." Death was for them, "our dearest wedding among weddings."[117] A feeling of imminent danger embedded in violence was part of the fascist way of life, and death was an outcome of the fascist response to the political enemy, and eventually the self. As Mussolini declared, "Living dangerously, should mean always being ready for everything—whatever the sacrifice, whatever the danger, whatever the action, when the defense of the fatherland and fascism are concerned."[118]

Violence was, for fascism, essentially expressed in the totalitarian fascist state and its "spiritual" and "ethical" imperialism. As Mussolini stated,

> The Fascist State expresses the will to exercise power and to command. Here the Roman tradition is embodied in a conception of strength. Imperial power, as understood by the Fascist doctrine, is not only territorial, or military, or commercial; it is also spiritual and ethical. An imperial nation, that is to say a nation which directly or indirectly is a leader of others, can exist without the need to conquer a single square mile of territory.[119]

Imperialism is for fascism a state of becoming rather than a state of being. To be sure, fascism does not differ in this sense from other imperialist formations.[120] However, it diverges in that it is presumably a "proletarian imperialism" when it is viewed as the ultimate expression of Mussolini's nationalist displacement of class struggles onto national struggle. Paradoxically, for Mussolini, fascist imperialism was the ultimate form of anticolonialism. Imperialism was the political antithesis of decadence. In other words, an active, new fascist form of imperialism eliminated the possibility of "becoming a colony."[121] Fascist imperialism proffered itself as heir to Roman imperial traditions. But the importance of Romaness notwithstanding, Italian fascism, in contrast to the ancient Romans, promoted the idea of a war without end.[122] In other words, Mussolini conceived of war as preemptive action to strengthen Italian leadership in the Latin world—indeed, as an imperialist move against "plutocratic empires—"a war of civilization and liberation. It is the war of the people. The Italian people feel it is its own war. It is the war of the poor, the disinherited, and the war of the proletarians."[123] When projected onto a global stage, fascist imperialism was the ultimate form of people's violence and power: "Fascism sees in the imperialistic spirit—i.e. in the tendency of nations to expand— a manifestation of their vitality. In the opposite tendency, which would limit their interests to the home country, it sees a symptom of decadence. Peoples who rise or rise again are imperialistic; renunciation is characteristic of dying peoples."[124] For fascists, imperialism was at the center of the fascist matrix. It provided them with a sense of moving from theory to practice, through war and violence, in the name of the people. In short, it represented a tangible expression of fascist action situated beyond ritual and theory. The different failed attempts to create a formal fascist international have to be understood within the larger framework of fascist spiritual imperialism.[125]

Spiritual imperialism also included the conception of the Nazi genocidal empire. Whereas the Nazi radical version of fascism stressed the perceived enemy as the defining aspect of its ideology, most fascisms ascribed to it a less fixed placed in fascist ideology. These key differences notwithstanding, fascism was a global phenomenon that included Nazism. There is no such thing as a fascist platonic type. Italian fascism was the first fascist movement in Europe, and it was the original point of reference for other fascist movements. It was not, however, a form of fascism from which all other fascisms were derived. Understanding the Italian case is central to the global understanding of fascism, but *fascism* as a term and a reality refers to a transnational network of shared opinions and feelings. Fascists in Europe and across the world were identified with the "idea." Above all, fascism was, and is, an idea about the world, the people's national community, and the leader that occluded other readings of reality. Fascism confuses reality with truth. Hannah Arendt defines ideology as providing a circular vision of the world that occludes perception and empirical experience. Fascism represented the ultimate ideological gaze in this Arendtian sense.[126] Among political ideologies, fascism represented an ideological lens through which to see and read the world. But it was more than that. It paradoxically implied a denial of reality, an ideological detachment from it that changed it, and even created a new reality and a new definition of the possible in ideological politics. Yet this fascist contribution to the dark side of modernity was not only a singular and tragic historical experience but also part of the broader history of challenges to democracy. In fact, this history includes fascism's most distinctive descendant, modern populism.

FASCIST POPULISM?

Fascism is not populism, but it is clear to historians that both share important affinities regarding the people, the nation, the leaders, and their enemies. They are different chapters of the same history. The *longue durée* intellectual trajectory of fascism and populism is essentially global. It has a long history as part of the itinerary of ideas of democracy (and dictatorship) across the globe and a shorter one as part of the transcontextual history that turned fascism to populist postfascism in power after the end of World War II.

To put it playfully, if democracy starts in Athens, modern democratic populism begins in Buenos Aires. The other stops in this long, schematic genealogy of ideas and regimes of power are manifold, but we could tentatively mention the following: 1) preimperial Rome and its grappling with the concept of the people, as well as the role of tribunes and plebeians in this earlier political context; 2) the Paris of the French Revolution and its creation of a modern notion of popular sovereignty; and 3) Rome again, along with many places like Berlin, Lima, Aleppo, or Tokyo, with their respective fascist counter-revolutions against the democratic legacies of the enlightened revolutions.[127]

While classical Athenian democracy emerged from the collapse of tyrants and monarchs, and modern democracy emerged in the French Revolution as the product of a rejection of absolute monarchy, fascism came out of democracy.[128] It was an unexpected, negatively dialectical offspring of popular sovereignty. As a movement, fascism was at times involved in political persecution, street fighting, and the assassination of the preconceived enemy, and it combined this extreme violence with a militarization of politics and the adoption of varied electoral strategies. Fascists often participated in the democratic game, but they were not democratic in any way. In fact they explicitly wanted to destroy democracy. As a regime, fascism became at all times a dictatorial formation, emerging from the democratic crisis of representation that came out of the ruins of World War I. However, it was also rooted in the modern principles of the people and the idea that the leader represents and conveys the desires of the national popular community.

Similarly rooted in this triad of people, leader, and nation, the modern populism that emerged as a regime after 1945 was not a static or an obvious outcome of fascism. Populism was not fascism. Populism had existed in incomplete forms as a set of ideas and movements before the rise of fascism. In turn fascism incorporated some elements of early forms of populism and at times converged with it. At the time of fascism, and in countries as different as Austria, the United States, France, Argentina, or Mexico, many early populists (whom in this book, in part to differentiate between substantially different contexts, I call either prepopulists or protopopulists) became fascists or fellow travelers of fascism, while others clearly rejected fascism. But after the demise of fascism, all populists clearly rejected the violence that had defined fascism as an ideology and a practice of power. Fascism, to be sure, featured traits that we might call populist, but fascism should not be conflated with the postfascist, modern populism that emerged out of its defeat.

From the perspective of the theory of populism, one might argue that fascism was an incomplete populism, a populism without democracy. But historically, fascism was substantially new and thereby different from early populism, as well as from the postwar modern populist regimes, in that fascism fully rejected democracy. Fascists were also keen to present a multiclass authoritarian front that would later be typical of populist regimes, but they did so by establishing a single-party dictatorship with no legal role for the political opposition. Nonetheless fascists and populists both translated this idea of the unrepresented whole into a homogenizing idea of the nation as the social community of the people. As Peter Fritzsche explains, in the case of Germany, "The aim of Nazism was the realization of a racially purified 'people's community' or 'Volksgemeinschaft,' which relied on violence and exclusion even as it promised to overcome the deep divisions among Germans. The idea of the 'people' was both the rhetorical ground on which the National Socialists operated and the horizon for which they reached." Geoff Eley also argues that "Combining together widely disparate and heterogeneous interests and demands, the ideal of the *Volksgemeinschaft* promised to make a damaged and corrupted Germany once again whole." For other European cases such as Spain or Italy historians have similarly presented fascism as being endowed with an extreme form of antidemocratic populism. As António Costa Pinto argues, fascism stood against reactionary principles precisely because it had the aim of destroying liberalism without restoring the old order. They wanted to create a new man and a new civilization. This was the context of fascist mass plebiscitarian politics and its calls for social reform. For the Portuguese Blueshirts, as was the case for many other fascist movements, corporatism first appeared as a combination of these concerns about the masses and a nondemocratic way that established a new form of populist consensus.[129]

This antiliberal and anticommunist version of corporatism was a key element of the global circulation of fascism and its politics of the people. Stressing this contextual situation provides a more complex view of the social nationalism of global fascism and its close interactions with other interwar dictatorships similarly opposed to "demoliberalism." As Costa Pinto observes, "Powerful processes of institutional transfers were a hallmark of interwar dictatorships ... corporatism was at the forefront of this process, both as a new form of organised interest representation and as an authoritarian alternative to parliamentary democracy. The diffusion of political and social corporatism, which with the single-party is a hallmark of the institutional transfers among European dictatorships, challenges some rigid dichotomous interpretations of interwar fascism."[130]

All in all, fascism emerged as a reaction against the legacy of the Enlightenment. It rejected liberal democracy and replaced it with dictatorship. This replacement was theoretical as well as practical. While historians have important doubts regarding the real application of corporative practices, few disagree with respect to the centrality of corporative ideas within fascist ideological circles and fascist regimes.[131]

Starting in the 1920s, corporatism increasingly became a synonym for antiliberal and anticommunist dictatorial forms of government. During this period, Mussolini included corporatism as a central element of fascism. It was part of a "new synthesis" that "overcomes socialism and liberalism."[132] Mussolini was not alone. His corporatist "third way" between liberalism and socialism became a global vehicle for the diffusion and reformulation of fascist ideas. Corporatism became one of the arguments put forward by transatlantic fascists as well by the representatives of the "hybrid dictatorships," the authoritarian fellow travelers of the fascists, who thrived during this period.[133] For these regimes, corporatism represented a form of sovereign legitimacy that established a system of representation without downplaying in any significant way the authority of the dictator. If more generally, dictatorship was rooted in a trinitarian notion of popular sovereignty, according to which the leader personally embodied the nation and the people—or as the fascists put it, one man, one people, one nation—corporatism provided a theory for regulating conflict in capitalism and under the supreme arbitration of the leader.

While in nondictatorial forms of representation, corporatism presented the state as the arbiter of interest groups (as would be the case later on for early postwar populist regimes in Latin America), under totalitarian corporatism, there was in general no difference between leader and state with regard to corporatist organization. In theory, corporatism worked as an ideological means for the legitimation of the dictator. Nevertheless, was corporatism only a theoretical bluff or had the fascists meant what they said? To paraphrase the Italian historian Matteo Passetti, it was neither a bluff nor a true revolutionary change in the fascist organization of the state. Similarly, Alessio Gagliardi, called our attention to the need to understand this failed project as a successful form of popular legitimation.[134] This legitimating power of the corporatist dictatorship was created to last. In fact, as Costa Pinto cogently argues, it was a deep-seated element of the dictatorial European response to liberalism: "Corporatism put an indelible mark on the first decades of the 20th century, both as a set of institutions created by the forced integration of organized interests (mainly independent unions) in the state, and as an organic-statist alternative to liberal democracy."[135]

In this context, the fascist critique of capitalism was not against capitalism per se, but rather against forms of capitalism that according to fascists had ignored the needs of the people. For example, the program of the Spanish fascist Falange stated that they repudiated the capitalist system that disengaged itself from popular needs and dehumanized private property. For them, fascism was on the side of the working people. As José Antonio Primo de Rivera expressed it, "We have in common with socialism the aim of advancing the fate of the proletariat." But as Italian fascists also argued, fascism was opposed to socialism—they wanted all of the people to be united with the fatherland. Fascists worldwide wanted "social justice" for the people and the nation. Mixing nation and people, fascism was thus conceived of as "authentically popular" because, as Italian fascist Carlo Costamagna argued, under fascism the people ceased to be an "amorphous mass." Fascism differed from liberalism in maintaining a nationalist notion of the people as needing to be led by the leader and the state. Fascism took from liberalism the concept of the general will of the people, but as Costamagna maintained, "For fascism the general will it is not a will expressed by each citizen." A common understanding among fascists was that only the leader of the state incarnated this tradition and made decisions in its name. The fascist notion of the people collapsed the distinction between the past and the present and created a fascist myth of the people: "For fascism, the people is the infinite number of generations that follow each other as the flow of a river and for this reason these past generations are revived in the most remote of descendants." This idea of the people made fascism stand against liberalism and socialism: "Fascism is as anti-liberal as it is anti-socialist, and in this place between liberalism and socialism fascism finds its originality. In this way it shows its revolutionary character."[136]

The fascist politics of the people were supposed to create a harmonic relationship among capital, people, and nation. As the Argentine fascists affirmed in murals displayed in the streets of Buenos Aires, fascism was going to defend the "superior interest of production." "The time has come to harmonize capital and labor in order to save the nation from the voracity of professional politicians. You are with us or against us." As would later be the case for populism, for fascism, corporatist solutions could only be headed up by the leader, who in turn would be advised by technocrats and experts rather than professional politicians. Fascism was not opposed to technocracy, but technocracy had a secondary role with respect to the leaders of the people. In this regard, it was no different from populism.

Across the globe, fascists opposed the dictatorship of the proletariat with their own idea of a people's fully organized national community. They defended the people and the nation against international forms of capitalism. As the Brazilian fascist Gustavo Barroso explained, fascism, which combined the defense of God, family, and property with social justice, was against international capitalism and communism. If for the Brazilian Green Shirts, *capitalism* was not a pejorative term in itself, but became a problem only when it was not national and social, for the Argentine fascists it was clear that incorporating the people, and especially the working classes, into mass politics was a key dimension for the success of their movement.[137]

For the Argentine fascist Leopoldo Lugones this relationship between the nation and the people was the starting point of any modern theory of the state. For him, corporatism belonged almost exclusively to the politics of global fascism, but he also proposed an Argentine national version of it. Lugones saw the fascist politics of the people as being essentially antipolitical. He argued that, as a needed historical process of political reform, modern dictatorship was not the expression of conservatism, or more generally a return to the past, but a "revolutionary" attempt to radically modify the organization of the state in "authoritarian reactionary" and prepopulist fashion. By reactionary authoritarianism, Lugones meant the national and popular reaction against the "universal crisis of liberalism."[138]

The national and social reorganization of the administration that Lugones advocated included the reestablishment of domestic loans; the extirpation of "foreign agitators"; the imposition of national defense in economic and military terms; and, more important, the reform of the electoral system in terms of corporative structures of government, or what Lugones, with self-proclaimed "impersonal objectivity," called "functional representation." Lugones argued that functional representation, with a universal but qualified vote and organized in corporations and vocational groups, was the form of nationalism that was more adapted to the needs of Argentina. The Argentine people, and not the "amorphous masses," would be the electors of this political system. Lugones identified ordinary politics with liberal democracy. In contrast, he saw the corporatist system as part of the global fascist reaction against electoral representation, but he also diverged from Italian fascism in the sense that he wanted one corporation (the military), even beyond the dictator, to reign supreme. Lugones advocated for the "imposition of the military technique at the governmental plane." He insisted on the need for an "Authoritarian reorganization" (*reorganización autoritaria*) of the state that would be solidly rooted in a new popular form of legitimacy.[139]

From Sweden to Egypt, and from Portugal to Syria, fascists believed in the socially popular nature of their politics. All fascists wanted to represent the working people, whose authentic national habitus they opposed to the antinational laziness of the elites. Fascist ideologues claimed to adopt an alternative position that genuinely transformed traditional politics into people's politics. As Mussolini saw it, from the start fascism wanted to bring politics back to the people. He had "faith" in the "inalterable" fascists program of "going to the people." But this search for the people was far away from notions of democratic electoral representation or what he dismissed as "electorialism." As the Colombian fascist Silvio Villegas reminded his followers, the people's role was to obey the Duce. Hitler had said that he "never felt as the dictator of my people but rather as its conductor." The German dictator claimed to be "indissolubly united with my people as a man and as a conductor." Mussolini in turn, affirmed that the people "delegated" its sovereignty and power in the persona of the leader. Villegas concluded that "Hitler and Mussolini rule with the people and for the people."[140] The Egyptian Green Shirt Ahmad Husayn put forward a strikingly similar interpretation of the fascists politics of the people: "By working night and day for the interest of the people as a whole," Mussolini and Hitler had overcome social divisions. They exemplified, "the genuine rule of the people for the sake of the people."[141] Similar José Vasconcelos, the most famous Mexican fascist, talked about "the liberating totalitarianisms of Hitler and Mussolini." These leaders fought for the people and against the "international banking democracy." Vasconcelos presented Hitler as the incarnation of the idea of his nation. For him, Hitler and Mussolini were giving a "productive lesson to all the Hispanic peoples of America." If they learned this lesson, Latin Americans could "incarnate the collective will and convert it to a creative element and suddenly decide to change the paths of history."[142]

For fascist followers around the world, there was no fascism without the people. Mussolini had named his newspaper *The People of Italy*, and distinguished between the "true people" and those who did not belong in that group. As Matteo Pasetti observes, this theory of the people and the antipeople first legitimized political violence and then acted against parliamentary democracy. With the affirmation of the fascist dictatorship, and the defeat of its internal enemies, the homogenization of the people was combined with racism, imperialism, and the creation of new external enemies. In global terms, these fascist notions of the people were not conceived as democratic concepts, but their existence established significant continuities between fascism and populism in history. As Roger Griffin also argues in his famous generic definition of fascism as a palingenetic form of *populist* ultranationalism, fascism was a "peculiarly undemocratic mode of populism." Thus Griffin stresses, perhaps more than other scholars, that fascism was a fascist populism.[143]

Calling fascism a fascist populism often leads to the confusion of ideas and contexts. Fascism was not merely a subset of populism. If these ideas of fascism as populism help us to identify important links between fascism and populist strategies and conceptions, their historical distinctions are also important. This is especially clear once we leave behind Eurocentric views, and the focus shifts to a more global perspective. For example, most historians of Latin American fascisms stress the distinctions between fascism and populism. In countries like Chile, Colombia, Peru, Bolivia, Argentina, and Brazil, fascist groups presented totalitarian ideas of the people that proved influential in the subsequent history of modern populism but this does not mean fascists and populists were the same. This was especially the case after the fall of fascists regimes, once postwar Latin American populist regimes inaugurated a new modern form of populism as the preeminent authoritarian road to power. Similarly, in India, ideas of the people's community held important continuities with the later developments of Indian nationalism in a very different postwar, democratic context. In the Middle East, a right-wing political radicalism that often resembled, but was also significantly different from, European fascisms "prepared the ground for long-term authoritarian trends in the postwar Arab states." In Japan, fascism offered a combination of populist-sounding themes and appeal, mixed with the idea of *kokutai* (national polity), thus establishing continuities with the politics of the past and the present.[144]

Across the globe, fascist ideas of the nation, the mythical leader, and the people unleashed mutually connected processes of consensus building and dictatorial repression, inclusion, and exclusion. As Michael Wildt explains, in Nazism, the idea of the community of the people meant some people were included and many others were excluded. Similarly, Dan Stone argues that the Nazi people's community implied "an endless process of 'becoming the Volk.' The more the process was realized, the more alternative conceptions of ways of living became marginalized."

This processes was a key element of the ideology of fascism, as Aristotle Kallis cogently put it, and "fascist ideologies offered the opportunity to enact a future without 'others', dominated by the regenerated and cleansed national community in a powerful, complete and homogenous state."[145] Yet for tactical and ideological reasons, fascism needed a constant supply of enemies. In Nazism, this led to a dynamics of radicalization that increasingly moved from the invention of the enemy as antipeople to its persecution and extermination. In other forms of fascism, this move from the rhetorical enemy of the people to its actual personification in the bodies of its victims was never as radical, but it was nonetheless central.

Modern populism also embraces this intolerant creation of the people as dependent on the exclusion of others. In fascism and populism, the presence of the people-antipeople binary defines political relations, and historically both political ideologies have held to a homogenizing idea of the people. This process led to increasing political marginalization of dissenters while it also generated, for some periods, wide consensus and participation. As Dylan Riley argues, fascism pooled together claims of democratic legitimacy with authoritarian means: "Fascists combined the claim to represent the people with a rejection of politics as the institutionalized struggle of groups over control of the state. Fascists held that elections, parliaments, and discussion about public affairs—in short, the stuff of politics—were incapable of constituting and representing a 'general will.'" The fascists wanted to replace institutional representation and political struggles with "a form of nonpolitical interest representation."[146] In fascism, the total homogenization of the people happens only once electoral democracy is destroyed along with the imagined enemies of the people.

Like fascists, modern postwar populists like Juan Domingo Perón wanted to take away political representation from professional politicians. As we will see in the next chapters, populist leaders claimed that only they could speak for the people and protect them against their enemies—namely, the antipeople. However, Perón did not want to replace electoral representation altogether, nor did he want to eliminate the multiparty system. In contrast with fascism's, the populist processes of homogenizing the people are generally restricted to the rhetorical creation of its people, and they refrain from the extreme practices of violence that define the progression of fascism from the theory of the people and its enemies to the persecution and even elimination of the latter. In other words, unlike fascism, populism does not fully marginalize the "enemies of the people" from the political process. Rather, its leaders and followers want to defeat their candidates with formal democratic procedures. Elections and not elimination are key sources of legitimacy in populism. Even if one were to argue fascism has populist tendencies, and even though it defines itself politically against the enemy of the people, it does not require its victims to play an active role in politics after the destruction of democracy has been accomplished.

The fascist notion of the people produces consensus through political violence. It turns enemies of the people into enemies of the state. In doing so, it consolidates totalitarian dictatorships. The populist homogenizing idea of the people promotes intolerance within democracy. It embattles democracy without destroying it. Populism creates, and depends on, minorities to vote and lose in open elections. These minorities are not eliminated or even substantially persecuted. Their role is to vote for those who have been designated the antipeople. Only after winning democratic elections can populist leaders claim their legitimacy as the only true expression of the true community of the people.

Fascism was against electoral representation, while populism channeled elections in authoritarian terms. The historical continuities and distinctions between fascism and populism—namely, how forms of the inclusion and participation of the many in fascism and populism were coupled with marginalization and exclusion—are generally lost in theory. While, some theorists reduce fascism to being just another type of populism, others simply ignore their historical connections. The most productive example of the failure to acknowledge the historical context is the key work of the preeminent Argentine theorist of populism Ernesto Laclau.

Laclau is the author of arguably the most significant current theory of populism. He is also attentive to the global dimensions of populism, and this attention is generally lost on his many anti-populist critics. If fascism is generally absent in his famous work *Populist Reason*, it is overwhelmingly present in his earlier work from the 1970s. He argued then that, rather than being reactionary, fascism became one of the "possible ways of articulating the popular democratic interpellations into political discourse." Fascism used mass politics and the idea of a unified people to guarantee that socialism would not be a popular alternative. "Fascism has been the extreme form in which popular interpellations, in their most radicalized form—jacobinism—could be transformed into the political discourse of the dominant fraction of the bourgeoisie." Debating those who attempted to ground populism in a specific period and context, Laclau argued that populism appeared at different times and places. In this context, he suggested that fascism was just one populist experience among many others. In short, for Laclau, Fascism is populism.

In his treatment of fascism and populism as forms of democratic interpellation, Laclau collapses important boundaries between the two. While fascism did first appear within a democratic context, it also used democratic interpellations to destroy democracy. In this sense, fascism presented populist forms when it was part of the opposition but not when it was the regime. This important dimension in the work of Laclau was relegated to insignificance in his most recent and influential work on populism. Without sufficiently noting this change, Slavoj Žižek, another prominent theorist of fascism and populism whose work lacks historical perspective, blamed Laclau for ignoring the perils behind the link between fascism and populism. Populism, even when it was on the left, preserved the capitalist edifice, leaving it untouched, and could not be emancipatory insofar as it presented a notion of the enemy that was deeply rooted in protofascist tendencies. Radical popular politics were replaced with the desire to destroy the enemies of the unified people. He stated, "fascism definitely is a kind of populism." In making fascism a subspecies of populism, Žižek showed how fascism had populist undercurrents and why populism displayed fascist tendencies. However, important historical distinctions between fascist and populist enemy-making theories and practices were lost in his analysis.[147]

Fascists and populists shared a notion of the people as threatened by the ultimate enemies, which led to alarmist ideas of the onset of apocalyptical times and crisis that only their leaders could resolve. In fascism, this notion of the people was radically exclusionary, and eventually racist, in most if not all cases, while most populist notions of the people, even when they were xenophobic and racist, tended to be more indeterminate and rhetorical. The fascist notion of the people moved theory toward practice in radically violent ways that were absent from modern postfascist populism. Dictatorship was the form of governance under which this radical violence took place. Populism, on the other hand, represented an unstable mix where electoral democracy could be squared in practice with authoritarianism.[148]

Fascism often used democratic means to eliminate democracy while constantly and paradoxically claiming that its dictatorial totalitarianism was the best means of popular democratic representation. Leaders like Mussolini in Italy or Uriburu in Argentina claimed that fascism and dictatorship represented higher stages of democracy.[149] As is well known, these fascist understandings of democracy led to the destruction of democratic forms of representation and the rule of law. Extreme fascist violence led to war, genocidal imperialism, and the Holocaust. After 1945, the result of this extreme interpretation of the supposed desires of the "majority" led to a sort of crisis of fascist thinking on representation that paralleled its lack of power and legitimacy in the emergent Cold War era. This was the context in which the Peronist third way emerged as a reformulated fascism, one more rooted in democratic forms of representation. Other Latin American populist regimes soon followed in countries like Brazil, Bolivia and Venezuela. These classical populist regimes were not imitations of Peronism but rather converging symptoms of a new political epoch in which populism would take center stage and achieve and keep power. This is what I call a new complete form of populism that differed from fascism. Emerging from the ruins of fascism, this new modern populism was very different from its ancestors. After fascism, it implied a transnational rethinking of the need to leave totalitarian dictatorship and extreme violence behind while keeping authoritarianism. The result was a political ideology radically different from the original. This new modern postwar populism in power was a new genus not a political subspecies.[150] As had happened before with fascism, only after the epochal turning point of ideas and movements had reached power for the first time did populism become more complete as a formidable challenger of liberalism and socialism.

Modern populism arose from the defeat of fascism as a novel postfascist attempt to return the fascist experience to the democratic path, thus creating an authoritarian regime form of democracy that would stress social participation combined with intolerance and rejection of plurality. In populism, political rights were highly strained but never eradicated, as they had been under fascism. Modern populism pushed democracy to its limits but generally did not break it. Early Cold War Latin America was the first context in which such a postfascist attempt to redefine democratic theory and practice took place. It was there and then that modern populism first emerged as a regime.[151] Thus, after 1945 fascism became populism, which is the subject of the next chapter.

TWO

What Is Populism in History?

Populism is an authoritarian form of democracy that emerged originally as a postwar reformulation of fascism. Before the demise of fascism, some early ideologies and prepopulist movements had existed in countries as different as France, Russia, and the United States but in an entirely different context. It was after fascism left the world stage that populism became for the first time a regime. This was a turning point in history like the rise of Mussolini's and Hitler's regimes. Before its first regime forms, fascism was also a mere protest movement rather than a successful road to power. Once it first reached power in Italy, fascism became a truly global political paradigm. Then transnational fascists substantially changed their perspective. It was now a successful path to power and no longer a political style for opposition to liberalism and socialism. In this sense, Mussolini's revolution had groundbreaking and global effects similar to those of the Russian and French revolutions. If these revolutions and the fascist regimes first consolidated in Europe, populist regimes first emerged in Latin America after 1945. The populist regimes, such as those of Juan Perón in Argentina and Getulio Vargas in Brazil, were not true revolutions but rather revolutionary symptoms of the creation of a new political, early Cold War paradigm for ruling the nation.

Before fascism, populism had also been an authoritarian political style for opposition movements. After fascism, the political field was clear and populism become complete. It became a fully fledged authoritarian political paradigm—namely, an influential way of dominating the state in the absence of fascist powers. Like fascism, populism was not a surrogate for other politics. Populists were not simple messengers of the people but actors in their own right. As the fascist ones had done before them, populist regimes acted and decided in the name of the people, but now through democratic means. In other words, populism was not a mere parenthesis in history. More than a mere democratic form of fascism, populism was a new political phenomenon for a new era in history. Modern populism was anchored in the Cold War and was originally a response to the crisis of political representation that had first created fascism and then contributed to its demise. For this reason, explanations of populism and its politics need to be situated in populism's historical contexts.

While fascism's aim is dictatorship, and it seeks to abolish the separation of powers and the rule of law, populism has, at least in modern history, almost never destroyed democracy. Nonetheless, populists serially undermined the rule of law and the separation of powers without fully abolishing them. For fascists, elections had no significance, but populists considered them meaningful. To be sure, populist democracy was nationalistic and was less cosmopolitan and emancipatory than other democratic forms. At the same time, because populists increased electoral participation, populism could be seen as an enhancement of democracy.

The historical complexity of populism, therefore, has stymied recent attempts to provide simplistic definitions by either inflating or reducing the term to a static formula. Indeed, the more simplistic the definition, the more detached we are from what populism distinctively represents in the history of politics.

Understandably, historians have reacted against reducing history to a curio cabinet of artifacts for theorists to select as needed. Such a reductive approach represents a radical form of contextualization that is more antiquarian than historiographical. While antiquarians are collectors of relicts from the past, professional historians analyze and interpret past contexts with respect to their variations and continuities in the present. If some theorists display this antique, and antiquarian, view of history, others stress the long history of the term *populism* without sufficiently addressing the different contexts of its political history and theory. As Pierre Rosanvallon cogently points out, populism has a long history that includes actors as varied as the sycophants of ancient Greece, the radical journalist of the French Revolution Jean-Paul Marat, and the Russian and American "populists" of the nineteenth century.[1] But Rosanvallon, like many other theorists, does not sufficiently engage with the modern authoritarian, postwar history of populism, a symptom of a general tendency in the political theory of populism to exclude fascism from the picture.

And yet fascism and totalitarianism are key parts of populism's long history, and the ways in which populism has been and continues to be used are not limited to its origins. Nonetheless, it is important to acknowledge these first populist moments and then assess its subsequent bifurcations and repercussions with respect to their various historical phases: the early populist trends in nineteenth-century Russian and American politics,

the prepopulist formations on the right (e.g., Boulangism in
France, Lueger's movement in Vienna, and the South American
patriotic leagues), and the interwar protopopulist precedents in
Latin America (e.g., Cardenism in Mexico, Yrigoyenismo in
Argentina, and the first Varguism in Brazil). The post-1945
phases of what can be considered modern populism, which
emerged after early populism and the prepopulisms of the right
that preceded the Great War, include the following:

1) Classical populism. Argentine Peronism was at the
   forefront, but this term also encompasses the second stage
   of Varguismo in Brazil (1951–54), Gaitanismo in Colombia
   (late 1940s), and the José María Velasco Ibarra era in
   Ecuador (1930s to the 1970s), as well as postwar populist
   experiences in countries like Venezuela, Peru, and
   Bolivia.

2) Neoliberal populism. Carlos Menem in Argentina (1989–
   99), Fernando Collor de Melo in Brazil (1990–92), Abdalá
   Bucaram in Ecuador (1996–97), Alberto Fujimori in Peru
   (1990–2000), and Silvio Berlusconi in Italy (1994–95,
   2001–6, 2008–11).

3) Neoclassical populism of the left. The Kirchner administrations in Argentina (2003–15), Hugo Chávez (1999–2013)
   and Nicolás Maduro (2013–) in Venezuela, Rafael Correa
   in Ecuador (2007–17), and Evo Morales in Bolivia (2006–),
   as well as the leftist neoclassical populist parties in
   Europe, such as Podemos in Spain and Syriza in Greece.

4) Neoclassical populism of the right and extreme right. The
   Peronist extreme right of the 1970s, to the predominance of
   current right-wing movements and leaders that are generally in the European opposition but can also be in power in

countries like the United States, the Philippines, and Guatemala, as well as in power coalitions like those in Austria, Italy, and Finland. These forms of neoclassical populism also include the regimes of Recep Tayyip Erdogan in Turkey and Viktor Orbán in Hungary. Opposition forms of neoclassical populisms of the right and extreme right include UKIP in England, the National Front in France, the extreme right in Greece, and the movements led by the xenophobe Pauline Hanson in Australia and Avigdor Lieberman in Israel, among many others.

Modern populism begins with the early Cold War, postfascist contestation of democracy in Latin America, which points to the centrality of Peronism to any study of the history of populism. What's striking about the case of Argentina is not only that it became the first populist regime in history after Perón was elected to power in 1946 but that its form of populism has morphed into all of its possible varieties. In other words, Peronism, created in opposition to the American-led, postwar liberal-democratic consensus, both represents the first modern power form of populism and exemplifies all of the different phases of populism—from the authoritarian populism of the first governments of Perón (1946–55), to the leftist Montoneros guerrilla and the neofascist right wing Triple A in the 1960s and 1970s, to the neoliberalism of Carlos Menem of the 1990s and the neoclassical populism of the Kirchner administrations in the new century.

The need to put populism in its modern context is even more pressing in light of the current inflation of analyses of populist politics as a political malaise that has no specific point of origin. Returning the populist phenomenon to its global histories forces us to rethink negative stereotypes about populism as a concept and to reconnect it to the contexts of its emergence. What I want to insist on here is the need to bring history, and historiography, back to the theoretical debates about populism.

Populism presented a variety of historical possibilities that included extremely different experiences swinging from the left to the right extremes of the political spectrum. Nonetheless, and to recapitulate, this ideological pendulum always combined several common features:

1) An attachment to an authoritarian, electoral, antiliberal democracy that practically rejects dictatorship

2) An extreme form of political religion

3) An apocalyptic vision of politics that presents electoral successes, and the transformations those transitory electoral victories enable, as revolutionary moments in the foundation or refoundation of society

4) A political theology founded by a messianic and charismatic leader of the people

5) A consideration of political antagonists as the antipeople— namely, as enemies of the people and traitors to the nation

6) A weak understanding of the rule of law and the separation of powers

7) A radical nationalism

8) A notion of the leader as the personification of the people

9) An identification of movement and leaders with the people as a whole

10) The claim of antipolitics, which in practice means transcending politics as usual

11) The act of speaking in the name of the people and against the ruling elites

12) A self-presentation of its standing for true democracy and against imagined or real forms of dictatorship and tyranny (the European Union, the parallel or deep state, empire, cosmopolitanism, globalization, military coups, etc.)

13) The homogenizing idea of the people as a single entity that, when populism becomes a regime, is then equated with its electoral majorities

14) A deep antagonism, and even aversion, to independent journalism

15) A dislike for pluralism and political tolerance

16) A stress on popular culture and even, in many cases, on the world of entertainment as embodiments of national traditions.[2]

GLOBAL POPULISM IN THE PRESENT: EUROPE, LATIN AMERICA, AND BEYOND

Populism has returned to Europe and the United States with a vengeance. However, rather than being a new creation, populism has reappeared as a dynamic reformulation of previous populist cases both outside and inside Europe and the United States. Most critics agree that Euro-populists are united in their desire to undo the European Union's transnational premises. In Europe, this new populism represents a return to the nation, a vertical idea of democracy, and the outing of long-standing, and supposedly past, xenophobic continental traditions. In fact, they were not gone but had only been ignored and repressed in the memories of a continent that, after 1945, was refounded on the antifascist rejection of those ideas. Converging developments in the United States are apparent in the Tea Party's attack on institutions (notably, the 2013 government shutdown) and in other recent populist attacks on more dialogical traditions, as well as in the resurgence of a nativist, and sometimes racist, stance toward Hispanics, Muslims, and other minorities, especially as exemplified in the success of Donald Trump, the Republican candidate for president in 2015–16.

For many Latin American observers, the return of populism to the center signals the global dimensions of a political experience long associated with Latin American history. Latin America's embodiment of the populist tradition in politics is not simply a stereotype. From General Juan Domingo Perón to the late comandante Hugo Chávez, populism has often defined the politics of the region. But the strength of European and American engagements with populist politics (in England, France, the Netherlands, Germany, Austria, Italy, Hungary, Greece, Trump's America, and elsewhere) has forced Latin Americans to also rethink the apparent historical peculiarities of their histories in a broader global sense.[3]

Is Latin American populism a template for Europe and the United States? Does its history reflect the pathos of the tumultuous European and American present? In Europe and Latin America, but also in Asia, Australia, and Africa, populism is witnessing a global rise.[4] Populists worldwide invoke the name of the people to stress a form of highly hierarchical leadership, to downplay political dialogue, and to solve a perceived crisis of representation, increasingly by attacking institutional checks and balances. They do so to assert a direct link between the people and the leader, relying on a form of leadership that might best be described as religious (in the sense of its strong tendency to deify its causes and leaders). Finally, populists conflate temporal electoral majorities with the people of the nation as a whole. Populism buttresses social and political polarization. Fewer spaces are left for the expression of political minorities. Their political rights are not eliminated, but their democratic legitimacy is undermined. Populism, in short, is an authoritarian form of democracy.

If current Latin American experiences with populism veer toward a tense combination of a limited expansion of social and political rights with authoritarian trends, Europe and the United States are witnessing the overpowering presence of a populist right that engages in the latter while neglecting the former. In this sense, Europe and the United States resemble the Latin American past more than its present. It would be difficult to understand current populism separately from its past formulations, and this history is a transnational one. Modern populism has a lot to do with the Global South, especially Latin America, specifically with the way populism was originally engendered in that part of the world as an electoral regime form of postfascism.

I propose a preliminary historical framework for understanding populism's bewildering shift back and forth between left and right movements and regimes and across the oceans. After situating my approach to populism historically as a reformulation of fascism, I briefly critique the functionalist, regionalizing, and transcendental theories of populism. I also provide a transatlantic genealogy of its contextual reformulations, from postfascism to neoliberalism, and from neoclassical Latin American leftist forms to the nationalistic rightist ones so prevalent in Europe and the United States. In short, I am taking part in a larger interdisciplinary dialogue. This very ambitious task cannot, of course, be fulfilled in a single book. Nonetheless, I believe that my approach can help bridge some significant gaps between history and theory that have been occasioned by the absence of many historians from these theoretical discussions, as well as by theorists' similar lack of engagement with historiography.[5]

ORIGINS OF MODERN POPULISM AS POSTFASCISM

Because modern populism is a reformulation of fascism in the context of postwar democracies, I distinguish between it and early populisms, in which democracy was severely limited. For example, in the first half of the nineteenth century, populist forms sometimes coexisted with slavery and later with the racist suppression of voting rights and other forms of exploitation that, especially after 1945, were increasingly becoming antithetical to modern conceptions of democracy. Thus, as a nineteenth-century European and American phenomenon, especially in autocratic regimes such as tsarist Russia's, and in the context of the elitist politics of representation in the United States, *populism* was a term for a popular and at the same time national means to fight the state that envisioned a nationalist and more participatory role for the masses. In these contexts, democracy was extremely curtailed in the modern sense of extended universal political and social rights, or did not exist at all. The Russian Narodniki or the American People's Party both stressed the need for social and political equality at the same time that they tended to present a unitary and mythical idea of the people as essentially right and virtuous.[6] Hypothetically, one could argue that once democracy had been more or less established the term *populism* no longer applied in the same way that it had before. Authors like Isaiah Berlin in Europe and Gino Germani and Torcuato Di Tella in Latin America maintained that populism could exist in societies "standing at the edge of modernization."[7] This so-called modernization thesis is historically problematic precisely because populism never ceased to exist after these processes of democratic consolidation. It constantly reappeared well beyond the standard points of modernization across the Atlantic and beyond.

Isaiah Berlin stressed that populism lacked a clear program, but it was intimately linked to a totalizing view of society. It fused nationalism with the regenerative notion of the unified people posed against the minority-controlled state. It particularly emphasized the existence of enemies who threatened the life of the "spontaneous integral group and the sense of brotherhood which unites them." It was potentially or practically against minorities and institutions, but it also stressed equality for the national group. Was this early populism, then, an inner contestation of democratic representation at the time of oligarchic liberal regimes? What was its connection to newer authoritarian trends? Berlin notes that populism is incompatible with fascism and other forms of totalitarianism, the latter of which he calls "pseudo-populisms."[8] Rather than being merely opposites, populism and fascism belong to a converging political and intellectual history. Even considering that the core of populism is democratic but not liberal, the history of fascism is meaningfully related to the history of populism. In fact, democracy was born with its dialectical other, the contemporary and reactionary counter-Enlightenment that at different times contested it from within or without.

Especially before World War I, and in contrast to early American and Russian populist movements, various prepopulist authoritarian movements of the right (in Austria under Karl Lueger; in France under General Georges Boulanger; in Argentina, Brazil, and Chile with nationalist patriotic leagues, among others) were vehicles for incorporating the masses. At the same time that they played the democratic game, they also attempted to limit democracy from within. In the name of the people, pre-populists were xenophobic and racist and practiced extreme forms of nationalism.[9] While not all forms of right-wing prepopulism turned into fascism, all fascisms had prepopulist roots. Thus, in transatlantic contexts like Germany and Italy, or Chile, Argentina, and Brazil, prepopulism was radically reformulated as transnational fascism, especially after the practical and symbolic devastations of World War I.

The interwar crisis of representation led to totalitarianism in many European countries. In short, it led to the elimination of democracy and its replacement with fascist totalitarian forms of dictatorship. If these forms of prepopulism often ended with the destruction of limited forms of democracy, it was only after the fall of fascism that populism re-emerged as a vertical, and often intolerant, form of democracy. Such experiments in political ideology radically changed populism, which originated as a regime outside Europe. In fact, historical analysis shows that these modern Latin American populist experiences complicate the notion that populism was a simple pathology of democracy. From Peronism to the Bolivian, Brazilian, and Venezuelan cases, Latin American populisms pose significant challenges to the most negative dimensions of the definition of populism as anti-Enlightenment. Their expansion of social rights can also be seen as lasting enhancements of democracy.

THE EMERGENCE OF MODERN
POPULISM IN LATIN AMERICA

After the fall of European fascisms in 1945, a modern populist regime first emerged in Latin America. Peronism was not only the first modern populist regime in history, but it is one that has also had spectacular bifurcations throughout its history. These forking paths started with its stunning emergence as a Cold War reformulation of fascism—that is, a revolutionary rejection of fascist violence that emerged out of a military dictatorship, led by Juan Perón, but created in 1946 the first postwar case of populist democracy. Peronism continued with the left-wing Peronist guerrillas and the right-wing Peronists of the 1960s and 1970s; with the neoliberal stage of the Peronism of Carlos Menem, when Peronists joined the so-called Washington consensus in the 1990s; and finally with the left populism of the Kirchners (2003–15). Throughout its long history, a central facet of Peronism's populist ideology has been its refusal to produce a clear programmatic position. Peronism (as a movement, as a regime, and even more so as an ideological way of doing and understanding politics) has the flexibility to be in a state of constant reformulation. Even when some politicians leave the political game, Peronism, with its continuous refurbishing of the electoral machinery, perks, and clientelistic relations with the electorate, remains. This Peronist metamorphosis represents the fluctuating nature of populism as it constantly searches for absolute majorities, demands total allegiance to authoritarian forms of leaderships, and last but not least challenges not only liberalism but also popular forms of radical democracy.

Peronism is not fascism, but fascism represents a key dimension of its origins.[10] Fascist leaders wanted a dictatorship whose leader would deny the legitimacy of electoral means to power. Such was the case of Mussolini in Italy; Hitler in Germany; and the fascist leaders in Argentina, China, and many other places. All of them participated in the experience of transnational fascism. But after 1945, the Argentine military officer Juan Perón, in a contextual search for legitimacy, inverted the terms of the issue and, in fact, created the first form of modern populism. Unlike fascism, Peronism embraced electoral democracy. As a practical leader of a dictatorship that starting in 1943 had ruled the country, Perón won the presidential elections to become a bona fide democratic leader. Peronism destroyed (or even caused the self-destruction of) the military dictatorship, which had Perón as its de facto leader, and built a new, postwar way of understanding democracy.

Peronism emerged in the context of the decline of liberal and secular Argentine traditions in the interwar years. After the conservative restoration started in the 1930s, the military steered Argentina closer to other authoritarian fascist dictatorships of the period, such as those in Portugal and Spain. However, unlike in those countries, in Argentina, the military junta eventually embraced democratic electoral procedures and ceased to be a dictatorship. The dictatorship of 1943 constituted a full frontal attack on Argentine secularism. The coup of 1943 "nationalized" Catholic education (making it mandatory in public schools), erased the autonomy of national universities, and legally banned political parties. As signaled by the anti-Semitic writer, and the dictatorship's minister of education, Gustavo Martínez Zuviría (Hugo Wast), the agenda was intended to "Christianize the country," decrease immigration, increase the national birth rate, and eradicate secular doctrines.[11] More importantly from the Peronist point of view, after 1945, the democratically elected president Perón maintained, and sometimes deepened, the social reforms (e.g., improving working conditions, enforcing labor laws, giving more rights to farm and urban workers, fully funding state retirement, significantly expanding the power of unions, restricting the conditions under which workers could be fired, enacting paid holidays and vacations) applied during his term as the secretary of labor of the military dictatorship.[12] Perón also maintained an active racist immigration policy that discriminated against Jewish immigrants and encouraged white, Catholic immigration from Italy and Spain.[13] In political and ideological terms, the coup of 1943 announced the power of the military, which was inspired by an ideology that was nationalist, neutral (that is, pro-Nazi and pro-German in an anti-Nazi hemispheric context), authoritarian, anti-imperialist, and clerico-fascist. The history of the military dictatorship is, in large part, the odyssey of Perón to appropriate their commands and reshape it as an elected democratic government. These changes were realized in the context of what scholars call a "revolution within a revolution," in which young officers led by Perón used the coup to reframe the institutional bases of the country in populist terms.[14] During the period from 1943 to 1955, ideology was constantly reformulated to adapt to the multivaried demands of different social and political "Peronist" actors, from the fascists within and outside of the military to the left-leaning unions and the working class at large. Polarization was a foundational element of the new Peronist order. As the prominent historian Raanan Rein observes, Peronism divided Argentine society into two absolutely opposing factions: "To members of the working class, Peronism represented a real improvement in their living conditions." Peronism also gave them a sense of participation and pride. In contrast, for most members of the middle and upper classes, and for most Argentine intellectuals, "The Peronist decade was a traumatic experience." Now displaced from the official world of politics, "They were shocked to realize that they had lost not only control of the political and social processes in the country, but also their understanding of those processes."[15]

Argentine Peronism was the first attempt to "democratize" the antiliberal legacies of fascism for the Cold War context.

Peronism ruled in a context of basically no unemployment and represented a substantial increase in state support for public health care and education. In the same context of economic expansion and new legitimacy for the expansive role of the state after 1945, other movements, including the second phase of Varguism in Brazil, the Bolivian revolution, Gaitanismo in Colombia, and the postwar presidencies of José María Velasco Ibarra in Ecuador, soon followed it. After 1945, protopopulist movements like Aprismo in Peru and Betancourism in Venezuela became modern populist formations of the Cold War that increasingly combined anticommunist stances, extreme polarization, and negative views of opponents as enemies with a critique of liberalism and strong doses of egalitarianism. Overall, these new democratic populist regimes and movements challenged the liberal understandings of democracy.

These were not the first such attempts in Latin American history. To be sure, there were important interwar precedents such as Cardenism in Mexico (1934–40), Yrigoyenismo in Argentina (1916–22 and 1928–30), and the first era of Varguism in Brazil (1930–45). Another important precedent was the Peruvian APRA party led by Víctor Raúl Haya de la Torre from the 1920s onward. But all these experiments were greatly shaped by the different national, regional, and global contexts before and during World War II. These protopopulist regimes and movements were very different from the prepopulist, right-wing movements that had been more typical of the European, American, and Latin American cases before the Great War. If early and prepopulist movements were incomplete forms of populism with no regime form in their sight, protopopulist ones were regimes without enough populism. Protopopulisms were first marked by the realities of revolution and counter-revolution, including the Mexican and

Soviet revolutions, which were central; by the then recent legacies of oligarchic republics; and, subsequently, by anticolonialist struggles and the global war between fascism and antifascism.[16]

These forms of protopopulism were all quite different, but none of them considered that liberalism was their main enemy as would later be the case with modern populism. They focused instead on transcending the untouched legacies of the oligarchic states that had preceded them. These protopopulist regimes presented themselves as nationally inspired "correctives" to the old forms of Latin American liberal democracy, but while they wanted to correct the liberal past, they never fully broke with it. Rather, they were keen to stress the limits of those democratic models for young nations in search of autonomy.

Argentina's protopopulist Yrigoyenismo was linked more to the conservative past than to its Mexican and Brazilian protopopulist counterparts. In Argentina, radical protopopulism led to the expansion of political rights but only for men and only in the context of a system that combined charismatic leadership, a strong executive, and the expansion of the army's role in handling social unrest with sporadic, but significantly high levels of, antileftist repression in Patagonia, Buenos Aires, and other places. In Mexico, protopopulism presented an authoritarian system, in which elections did play a role in particular local contexts, especially in terms of intraparty competition. At the same time, Mexican protopopulism incorporated significant parts of the population (urban sectors, peasants, and the working class), especially through the party and the corporate structure of the state.[17] There were similar developments in Brazil under Vargas, but Vargas situated himself clearly to the right of the political spectrum, creating a corporatist dictatorship from 1937 to 1945. Cardenism and Varguism saw themselves as revolutionary actors from above. They were born in power. Unlike modern democratic populism (from Peronism to Trumpism and Lepenism), these protopopulisms witnessed, and at times produced, high levels of political violence. Both Cardenism and the first Varguism eventually opposed global fascism and locally repressed the fascists and the extreme right. In Brazil, the first Varguist phase was for the most part a dictatorship that actually destroyed the elitist formal democracy that had preceded it. In Mexico, the Cardenista period led to the institutionalization of one-party rule, a strong but temporally limited executive, and the practical minimization of electoral democracy. The Mexican and Brazilian protopopulist regimes cannot be considered to be as fully democratic as modern democratic populism would be after 1945. And yet, much more so than Argentina's Yrigoyenismo, movements in Mexico and Brazil established important antecedents for the populist future, including new forms of economic nationalism and the consequent incorporation of the urban working classes into the authoritarian pact. The protopopulism that was even closer to what modern populism would be after the war was Aprismo in Peru.

The APRA (American Popular Revolutionary Alliance) movement was very active, not only in Peru but also, to a minor extent, in other parts of Latin America, as an urban party and an alliance of workers, students, and middle-class intellectuals—a coalition that the leader called "the union of the arm and the brains." The nexus between them was increasingly the mythical leadership of Haya de la Torre. During these years, Haya de la Torre put forward a Latin American, anticommunist, and antifascist front for "national defense" and the "affirmation of sovereignty" against "omnipotent enemies." Central to this model was, as Haya stated, that "There is no such thing as good or bad peoples or masses, there are good and bad leaders." The Peruvian leader presented APRA, and his own leadership, as the means to defeat the enemies from within and from without. APRA became an actual party in the early 1930s, and it often switched from democratic procedures, in democratic times, to armed insurrection in dictatorial ones. In these early years, as Carlos de la Torre explains, it is possible to note a "moralism, religiosity, and intransigence that characterize populist discourses." Aprismo also featured the "myway-or-the highway" logic of populist contestation that even included racist criticism of its opponents (as would later be the case with Gaitanismo in Colombia). Starting in 1931, and most definitely after 1945 with the emergence of the Cold War, it was singularly clear that Aprismo was a Peruvian nationalist protopopulist organization despite its Latin Americanist rhetoric. It put forward a postwar anti-imperialist front against both communism and liberalism under the vertical leadership of Haya, who was officially defined as the "Jefe Máximo," the chief interpreter of the "vague and imprecise desires of the multitude."[18] Even though some historians have dubbed it the first Latin American populism, before the postwar era, Aprismo was attached to a more traditional model of multiclass paternalism and had a more diffuse idea of populist popular sovereignty, a more traditional link between the leader and the people, and a much less nationalist perspective. All in all, these protopopulisms (Cardenism, the first Varguism, Yrigoyenism, and early Aprismo) constituted significant and clear precedents for the modern populisms, especially Peronism, that emerged after 1945.

The histories of protopopulisms in Mexico, Argentina, Peru, and Brazil show they were deeply influential, and after 1945, in countries like Argentina, they were combined with more proper prepopulist and fascist legacies. This does not mean that fascism was as pervasive in the rest of Latin America as it had been in Argentina. In most of Latin America the long-term history of liberalism in power, which was more protracted than in other places where fascism emerged as a regime (e.g., Germany, Italy, and Spain), shows it was peculiar to most Latin American cases of populism: even in places like Colombia that had the most violent outcomes, the liberal rules of the political game were too entrenched to be completely eliminated. Argentina was a different matter. The country witnessed an attack against the liberal tradition that was unequaled in other Latin American countries.

In the new context in which liberal democracy had reemerged as the most legitimate form of government in the West, fascists worldwide, first and especially in Argentina, went back to fascism's right-wing, prepopulist roots, organically reframing them for the postwar context. As a dictatorial outcome of modern democracy, fascism was rooted in the previous experiences of authoritarian prepopulist reactions to democracy, from nineteenth-century Bonapartism and Boulangism in France, to the social, Christian anti-Semitism of Karl Lueger in fin-de-siècle Vienna.[19] But once it came into power, in Italy in 1922 and in 1933 in Germany, fascism destroyed democracy from within. Fascists worldwide put forward similar proposals. After their global defeat in 1945, many fascists, and global right anticommunists, realized that to gain legitimacy fascism could no longer be rooted in dictatorship. This signaled the emergence of modern populism as we know it today. The genealogy of modern populism is rooted in this radical attempt to reinscribe the fascist tradition, and, more generally, to move away from extremist dictatorial nationalism.

For the fascists who had survived the demise of the fascist regimes, the Cold War presented a new dichotomy between the liberal-democratic forms of capitalism and Soviet-style communism. They wanted to escape the newly established bipolar world. Modern populism was first proposed as a third position aimed at overcoming the Cold War dilemma of choosing between communism and liberalism. In its first historical instantiation (that is, in the first historical experience in which this "democratic" rethinking of fascism became a power regime), populism was called Peronism. Rather than adopting a preformatted version of Cold War neofascism, Peronism in Argentina was the first movement that attempted to adapt the legacy of fascism to a novel democratic framework. It was also the first example of a modern populist regime.

For many of its adversaries, Peronism was a new fascism adapted to democratic times. This was also the case for other examples of 1940s populism in Latin America. Latin American countries experienced deep changes after World War II. The Brazilian Getúlio Vargas, Ecuadorian José María Velasco Ibarra, and Colombian leader Jorge Eliécer Gaitán were all accused of being fascist and Peronists. But, in fact, they constituted a national populist response to the limitations of democracy in their countries. This involved denunciations of existing limits to social rights and an authoritarian way of identifying the people and the nation with their own personas and agendas.

Like Perón, Vargas had ruled an anticommunist dictatorial regime (in his case the Estado Novo, 1937–45), but he later reconverted to democratic procedures and won the presidential elections in 1951. This "new Vargas era" was essentially populist. Vargas had defined his previous dictatorial approach as the single alternative to the interwar threat of civil war. But the times were changing. Now Vargas was a democratic politician. He reformulated the terms of his dictatorial Estado Novo for a new democratic context. Like Perón, Vargas rejected political and economic liberalism. Also like Perón, he was an anticommunist. His policies reflected equally a manipulation of the working classes and a perceptive reading and means of expressing and acting on their concerns. In other words, Varguismo combined authoritarianism with social democratization. As were many of his Latin American peers, Vargas was accused of being the "Brazilian Perón," but he stressed a Brazilian response to that country's crisis of hegemony that, as expected, was related more to Brazilian developments than to Argentine ones. Peronist Argentina was not the platonic form of modern populism. It was rather the first populist regime among the many to emerge in postwar Latin America.[20]

Thus, similar developments happened in Colombia, where the surge of populism was the unexpected consequence of a widely extended Latin American tradition of excluding popular sectors from political decision making. As in other parts of the region, postwar populism in Colombia was a result of a lack of popular political representation, the existence of a big divide between the elites and most citizens, and social inequality. Jorge Eliecer Gaitán, like Perón, was influenced by fascism when he visited fascist Italy. Gaitán read his graduate thesis in front of Mussolini's entire cabinet, but, like Perón, he moved to the left, combining a fascist style with unitary ideas of the people and a push for social rights to address a majority of citizens who were disenfranchised. Gaitán felt an affinity with the Peronist third position between capitalism and communism. He also stressed the need for a "defensive nationalism" against imperialism. This populist reformulation was misunderstood, by conservatives as a "fascism of the left" and by liberals and the left as the fascism of Hitler and Mussolini. Thus, like Perón, Gaitán was often accused of being a fascist and was also charged with being a Peronist. But as in the case of the Argentine leader, Gaitán was not a fascist but was actually one of the key politicians, who especially after 1945 adapted older ideas for the new democratic realities. As Enrique Peruzzotti argues, populists saw in electoral procedures one of the constitutive elements of their political legitimacy. In this, they sharply differed from the fascists, who did not ascribe any true legitimacy to elections and who stressed the absolute need for dictatorship. Gaitán does not fit this latter fascist pattern. His assassination in 1948 halted a formidable political career and, more importantly for the immediate future, populism in Colombia, resulting in a gruesome civil war and, eventually, the country's only and brief modern military dictatorship.[21]

In Ecuador, a fascist party that was influenced by the Falange supported Velasco Ibarra in his third presidency (1952–56). Similar political movements had supported Perón's rise to power. Initially, workers and Catholic sectors that were fiercely anticommunist supported Velasco. But as with Peronism, Ecuadorian populism mixed left- and right-wing ideas and followers. Velasco's return to power in 1944 was eventually backed by leftists and rightists, who claimed to be supporters of the Allies in the Second World War. As the leading scholar of populism Carlos De la Torre notes, Velasco Ibarra's political thinking, which was influenced by Simón Bolívar's pessimism about democracy, idealized strong executives and even temporary dictatorship. These views were also reinforced by his longstanding but not mimetic admiration for Peronism. Velasco Ibarra was exiled in Buenos Aires during some of the years of classical Peronism (1943–55).

Leaders like Perón, Gaitán, and Velasco Ibarra transformed political arguments into all or nothing fights for a new moral order. This is what De la Torre, calls the "transmutation of politics into ethics or even into eschatological redemption." Acting and speaking in the name of the people, classical populisms emerged at a time when democratic procedures were weak. They provided a voice to those who felt unrepresented, but did so at the expense of the legitimate right to dissent and by morphing the voice of the leader into the "source of all virtue."[22] Similar developments happened in Peru, Bolivia, and Venezuela. In fact, if leaders like Víctor Raúl Haya de la Torre in Peru and Rómulo Betancourt in Venezuela had been initially close to communism, they had clearly switched to the populist mix of vertical antiliberal leadership and political demands for social change, especially after 1945. Like Gaitán, Haya never reached power, but unlike the Colombian leader, who was assassinated in 1948, Haya went into exile and remained a key actor in Peruvian politics. Banned in Peru, he demanded the return of electoral participation for himself and his followers. His postwar populism was characterized by decreasing calls for social reform, an ever-increasing commitment to the myth of the charismatic leader, sincere unconditional support for the United States in its Cold War against communism, and an alliance with Peru's previous oligarchic enemies.[23]

Populism in Bolivia, as was already the case in Argentina, and would be the case in Venezuela, first reached power by participating in a military dictatorship. Major Gualberto Villarroel, the dictator and leader of the junta, and Víctor Paz Estenssoro, the leader of the Revolutionary Nationalist Movement (MNR) had close links with the Argentine military junta of the GOU (Grupo de Oficiales *Unidos*) led by Colonel Juan Perón in Buenos Aires. As it had done with Perón, the United States equated the Bolivian junta with the coming of fascism to Latin America. To be sure, Argentines probably had some role in the Bolivian coup.

But the most important features of the Bolivian coup were not fascist but protopopulist. Transnational connections were indeed important, but the Bolivian events had specific national roots that pointed in the direction of a national version of Bolivian populism. As it had with Peronism, Bolivian populism's support for dictatorship would later morph into authoritarian electoral democracy. Historian of Bolivia Laura Gotkowitz explains that the MNR first supported dictatorship but also put forward a socially inclusive vision of a "mestizo nation." This was a nationalist, and at times xenophobic, model for social inclusion that at the same time stressed national unity and ascribed legitimacy to the country's majority of Indians and mestizos. It also sought to control this majority "that … was pressing its demands on the state." The Villarroel-MNR dictatorship severely limited political rights, and even expanded some national fascist tendencies, resorting to political assassinations and imprisoning members of the left-wing opposition. But also at this time MNR leader Victor Paz Estenssoro explained they wanted to turn the "government of Villaroel as the point of departure for the creation of a new legality, a revolutionary legality at the service of the people." The MNR aimed at a new regime form—in fact, it sought a legitimacy rooted in the people. Eventually the dictator was killed by a mob, and the MNR leadership was exiled after 1946. Just some five years later, the MNR had renounced its fascism, and adopted a third-way position that moved it clearly to the left of the Bolivian political landscape. Paz Estenssoro was now the leader of a worker-supported nationalist revolutionary party. Against it were the military and the Bolivian right under the banner of the Bolivian Falange. It was in this early postwar moment (1952) that the MNR came to power on its own, but once again not through open electoral procedures. In fact, the

MNR won elections in 1951 through a limited-democracy process that restricted the votes to only a minority of alphabetized individuals. In any case, a dictatorial junta blocked its access to power. In 1952, the MNR led a revolution in the name of the people and their votes. By that time, it had left behind its previous fascist influences and incorporated a new working-class base with Marxist and Trotskyist roots. The MNR revolution had extensive urban and rural roots, and it led to a radical increase in the Bolivians' opportunities to participate in the politics of their country, including universal suffrage, nationalization of the tin mines, and agrarian reform. Although it presented its actions as a "blow" to the oligarchy, for Gotkowitz the MNR did not link citizens' rights with "broader ideas of liberty and equality, nor did it link them with the history of participatory struggles to free the nation from colonial bonds." The agrarian reform itself was "reformist" in nature, giving preference to private rather than communal possession of the land (before the reform, 6 percent of landowners possessed 92 percent of developed lands). Still, it significantly changed land distribution (after the reform, 20 percent of the lands were redistributed) in one of Latin America's most unequal countries. After the revolution, the MNR rooted its legitimacy in expanded electoral procedures, unitary nationalism, and a homogenizing notion of popular sovereignty. As Gotkowitz argues, the defining feature of its revolution was its democratizing impact, an expansion of democracy that was marked by the "tension between support and restraint of indigenous political participation." Bolivian classical populism increased polarization and downplayed political, social, and ethnic plurality while significantly expanding democratic representation. The MNR combined a unitary notion of the people versus the oligarchy with relatively low levels of personalism.

In this moderate populist sense, it resembled the Venezuelan case, in which populists also initially had an alliance with the military, which soon implied a move to the left of the political spectrum. In its classical form, the MNR was initially a much more radical populist movement than Peronism, Velasquismo, Aprismo, Gaitanism, and Varguism. This had as much to do with its postwar rejection of fascist violence (transnational and national) as with the particularities of its revolutionary rise to power. But eventually, and in populist *transformista* fashion, Paz Estenssoro broke in the 1960s with the left of the party and clearly realigned himself with the American-led Cold War and the Bolivian military.[24]

In Venezuela, Acción Democrática adopted slogans such as "Venezuela first" and "to divide is to identify" while it was engaged in the coup of 1945. It then won presidential elections two years later, obtaining 74 percent of the votes. Like Peronism, Varguism and the Bolivian MNR, it also switched from participating in a dictatorship to becoming a populist democracy. Like Peronism and Varguism, Acción Democrática engaged in a wide program of social reform that rearticulated social relations, defined new political identities, and enhanced popular representation and participation.[25] All in all, the Peronist way of adapting fascism to the Cold War democratic realities was also adopted in other Latin American countries. Even if the origins of other Latin American populisms were not, like Peronism's, fascist, populism had elements such as political theology, the mythical idea of history, and the ritual nature of political spectacle and political religion that were related to fascism.

Rather than being the form that shaped all others, Argentine populism was the first actualization in a regime of a global need

shared by global anticommunist thinkers and militants, including fascists, to overcome liberal democracy and "real socialism."
Located far from the experiments of European fascists, and not
excessively touched by their resounding defeat, Argentina
became a viable space in which transnational fascism, and more
generally anticommunism, could rethink itself in a very different
context.[26] However, Argentina was clearly not the reason for the
predominance of populism in Latin American politics as a whole.
Brazilian or Bolivian populisms were not less influential than
Peronism and both regimes were outcomes of global and regional
postfascist realities. In other words, Latin America overall was
the site of the first consecration of populism in power, and the
ripple effects of this historical foundation were of the utmost global significance.

I want to stress the relevance of populism's transcontextual
connections, and more specifically of Latin American history,
for thinking about the universal implications of past and present
forms of populism. In many ways, I believe the center can be
seen more clearly from the margins.[27] Thus, in its emphasis on
the fascist genealogies of populism, and how it was created and
changed over time, my historical framework moves away from
standard dichotomies between the Global North and Global
South. In this sense, Donald Trump, Hugo Chávez, Marine Le
Pen in France, and Recep Tayyip Erdogan in Turkey are practically, especially in their styles, and theoretically connected with
Hitler and Mussolini, at the same time that they represent a
radical break from classical fascist politics. They are not fascists,
but their politics share a fascist historical background. This historical relationship between fascism and populism is generally
lost in its translation to theory.

POPULISM BETWEEN HISTORY AND THEORY

For some political theorists populism constitutes a democratizing response to a widespread crisis of representation, while for others it poses undemocratic limitations on the present and future of democracy. Thus in mainstream approaches, populism is regionally presented or functionally reduced to a symbol, a symptom, or even a pathology of democracy. At best, theorists generally portray populism as part of the historical opposition to liberal democratic representation. According to this framework, populism exemplifies a historical concept, and history itself plays only a minor role in illustrating a theory. At worst, populism is a concept without history.

Theorists of populism often treat history as if it were a passive receptacle of long-term structural change, the particular temporal space where the quasi-transcendental conditions needed for the creation of populism take place. According to these theories, dynamic historical processes are often replaced with more static transhistorical ones such as "modernization," "caudillismo," and so forth. Populism is, then, a temporal marker for the failure, "late coming," or success of such structural changes or continuities. Some scholars, therefore, especially in Latin America, view populism as fixed in the past (or in different pasts) and separated from the present. Others generally equate historical contexts with a more generic view of a cyclic or systemic crisis of democracy. As historian Alan Knight has pointed out, circularity prevails when crisis and populism are equated, the result being that the former is explained in terms of the latter.[28] For Knight, populism needs to be studied historically from the point of view of the style of leadership: "Defining populism in terms of style has the virtue of flexibility and—perhaps most important—historical fidelity. That is, it seems to correspond to the historical record in a way that other—often more precise theories/models—fail to do. And it is surely preferable to have a rough rule-of-thumb which works than a highfalutin theory which defies reality."[29] Knight's criticism of theorists who reduce history to an illustration, often ignoring historical reality, is salient, especially his argument that theories "gain in precision and sophistication, but fail on the crucial criterion of historical fidelity. They are neat but wrong. Or, to put it more accurately, the neater they are the wronger they are. Thus, while they do not entirely lack insight or explanatory power, they cannot form the basis of a generic model."[30]

Knight, however, also tends to dismiss the analytical perspectives opened by critical theory. He rather typically confuses theory with generic models and conflates theory as a whole with specific theories of populism, including the so-called modernization thesis. The root of the problem for many theorists is that their specific theories of the populist phenomenon are stuck in a centuries-old understanding of history as a positivistic discipline. Historians, on the other hand, have changed their approaches in radical ways over the last two centuries, rethinking their discipline's own historicity, addressing the limits of representation, reframing national and transnational histories, and critically combining contextualization with historical interpretation.

Political scientists, sociologists, and critical theorists, but not so much historians, are the ones who tend to work on populism as a concept. In addition, most theorists outside Latin America stress the need to understand the multimillennial concept of the people over populism's long history without dealing with Latin American, and other Global South histories of populism.[31]

One can find this Eurocentric, North Atlantic focus on populism in functionalist works that replace the theory and history of populism with a more quantitative, descriptive, and self-proclaimed pragmatic approach. This approach does not explain the diverse historical meanings of populism but rather takes them for granted, or assigns the broadest definition to populism as a movement defending popular sovereignty and placing the people in opposition to the elites.

Many decades ago, Isaiah Berlin argued against enforcing inelastic definitions. He was writing at a different time, before the social sciences returned to forms of neopositivism that downplay the connections between history and theory. He playfully presented a field of populist studies that had a pathological condition. A Cinderella complex of populism affected the field,

> by which I mean the following: that there exists a shoe—the word "populism"—for which somewhere there must exist a foot. There are all kinds of feet which it *nearly* fits, but we must not be trapped by these nearly-fitting feet. The prince is always wandering about with the shoe; and somewhere, we feel sure, there awaits it a limb called pure populism. This is the nucleus of populism, its essence. All other populisms are derivations of it, deviations from it and variants of it, but somewhere there lurks true, perfect populism, which may have lasted only six months, or [occurred] in only one place. That is the idea of Platonic populism, all the others being dilutions of it or perversions of it.[32]

Eurocentric views are not the exclusive realm of neopositivistic Platonic thinkers but are also present in some of the most innovative and synthetic theoretical approaches to the topic. There is no denying that Europe has been at the center of these histories and their theorization, but the old continent has always been engaged in fluid conversations and transfers with the Global South. In practice, Europe has always been the province of a larger context, which is why simply separating Europe from other regions is a problem. Studies of transnational exchanges and reformulations provide the context in which comparisons can be made, but the field of populist studies has produced many comparisons and little transnational research. The latter address, for instance, how different transatlantic examples think and act in terms of their synchronic and diachronic convergences, their affinities with and opposition to other populist experiences. This is exactly what a transnationally focused political and intellectual history can provide to theory. But so far, few theories have seriously considered history as a critical interlocutor rather than as an object to be used for the illustration of theory. This is clearly the case in seminal works, such as Margaret Canovan's groundbreaking analysis of the trajectory from the Roman and medieval reformulations of the concept of the people to the modern constitution of populism as a key dimension of democracy, and in Pierre Rosanvallon's suggestive research on the first appearance of populist themes, which resulted from the ambivalent and intrinsic duality of democracy as it emerged in the French Revolution. Both authors claim that the attempt to represent the will of ideal majorities without institutional mediations has been a constitutive dimension of the inner tensions of democracy throughout its long history.[33] However, while for Canovan populism is a legitimate member of the democracy club, Rosanvallon maintains that populism is "an inverse perversion of the ideals and procedures of democracy."[34]

Both Canovan and Rosanvallon have made stereotypical references to classical Peronism and Latin America, venturing outside Europe in a way that undermines their influential theories of democracy. Oddly, when Canovan writes of populism outside Europe, she conflates it with dictatorship. Yet she does not explain how a constitutive form of democracy such as Peronism is presented in her account as a dictatorial formation.[35]

For Rosanvallon, populism is a specific pathology posed against democracy. It degrades democracy to a circus full of apocalyptic connotations. His functional analysis considers populism a "form of political expression in which the democratic project allows itself to be absorbed and to be fully vampirized by counterdemocracy." By placing populism outside the democratic project, Rosanvallon concludes, "Populism is the extreme of anti-politics." Populism is for him a "political pathology" that belongs to an era "marked by the growth of counter democratic forms."[36]

Many others share Rosanvallon's functional idea of populism as a symptom, and portray populism's trajectory as a coda to something else. Its complexity is confused with its indetermination as a "thin ideology." Scholars of populism like Cas Mudde and Cristóbal Rovira Kaltwasser offer a minimalist definition of populism as an ideology that divides society into two morally opposed groups, the people and the elite, and has regional subtypes. For them, populism is less relevant than other concepts or ideologies. By identifying populism as a structural, if transient, answer to certain political conditions, the authors construct their own version of populism as a phenomenon that has no conceptual history of its own. In contrast, other minimalists, who explore the trajectory of the concept while claiming that the term has only recently acquired importance in Europe, offer only a cursory examination of non-European cases and interpretations in order to locate the European populist experience relative to others.[37]

In many theories of populism, Latin American, African, or Asian cases represent the symptomatic Other. Especially for Europe, these stereotypical views use a jargon of authenticity about the European liberal self that betrays how populist tendencies were also present in Europe's history from early on. According to these theories, populism is somehow placed outside history because it recurrently works as a corrective to illiberal, moralistic, totalitarian, or otherwise undemocratic tendencies in democracy. Principally, Latin America is considered part of the populist equation but remains within the framework of the traditional Europe/non-Europe dichotomy. Center and periphery are accepted as defining absolute features in these approaches. In other cases, the focus on Europe means few connections are made outside the continent other than small analogies or examples. For example, an influential scholar and public intellectual like Rosanvallon, who stresses the modern European illiberal dimensions of the phenomenon, fails to extensively address the key Latin American points on the trajectory of populism as a concept and as a regime model for the development of democratic, antiliberal politics after 1945.

POPULISM AGAINST PLURALISM?

Many scholars of populism stress its authoritarian and even totalitarian tendencies. One of the most influential theorists of populism, Carlos de la Torre, argues, "Populist disrespect of pluralism is explained by their view of the people as a subject with a unitary will and consciousness, and of rivals as enemies of the virtuous people."[38] But De La Torre also notes that "Despite their totalitarian intentions to penetrate the private sphere to create new political subjects, populist leaders did not establish a one-party rule, preserving some limited spaces of pluralism and contestation." He observes that notwithstanding their goals to control social life and create "new subjects," populists "did not fully colonize the public sphere and civil society. Populists' source of legitimacy was not based on uniformity of opinions staged in mass rallies and elections with just one ticket. Their legitimacy was grounded in winning elections that in theory could be lost."[39] De la Torre stresses, "Rather than arguing that the logic of populism is inherently antidemocratic, it is more fruitful to analyze its uncertain relationship with liberal democratization." Populism has a double legitimacy rooted in elections but also located in the streets, "in inside and outside" institutions and procedures: "Classical populism expanded the franchise. Contemporary radical populists embarked on permanent political campaigns." For De la Torre, a populist case like Evo Morales's in Bolivia shows how populism can enhance political participation while demonizing members of the opposition.[40] In Bolivia, and particularly for most of the country's indigenous people, who had lived for many decades under a combination of racism, authoritarianism, and neoliberalism, populism's combination of democratic and undemocratic features clearly expanded their political and social participation.[41]

Populism and participation are key elements in current discussions among theorists of populism. Political theorist Jan-Werner Müller points out that populism is an undemocratic response to the undemocratic tendencies of technocracy, and that it more generally betrays a distrust of the foundations of the European postwar order.[42] For Müller, as for Paul Taggard and Benjamin Arditi, populism is a symptom of, and a problematic response to, the lack of true citizen participation.[43] Müller cogently notes the antifascist foundations of this European order, returning our attention to how populism is adapted as a recurring temporal response to the predominance of elites. Müller presents the view of populism as "an exclusionary form of identity politics" that "always" poses "a danger to democracy." To be sure, his analysis is also attentive to populism's symbolic dimensions and its moralistic imagination, but it also undermines the ambivalent times where populism has not only restricted but also enhanced participation in democracy, from early Peronism to Colombian Gaitanismo to the early American populists of the end of the nineteenth century. Müller insists, "Populism is not a path to more participation in politics,"[44] But this approach relies on downplaying the complex, and seemingly contradictory, history of populism or on excluding from its theory some of its most important historical experiences across the Atlantic and beyond. In this context, history can help theorists complicate the theories of populism by grounding them in the ambivalent and thorny nature of populism in history.

Populism emerged as an authoritarian form that nonetheless rejected dictatorship. Theories of populism, therefore, need to address both its participatory and its exclusionary dimensions in terms of different historical processes, in which they are usually combined. In fact, after 1945, populism was more dangerous to dictatorship than to democracy. Especially in Latin America after the end of the Second World War, populism combined an increase in popular political participation with important anti-democratic features. This tension within populism connects its history to our efforts at conceptualization. Context always stands in the way of high theory. Binaries such as the ones presented in generic theories of populism are never helpful for framing a critical democratic theory that is attentive to history. The challenge for history and theory is to escape from their opposition to each other. In contrast with the generic insistence on opposing historical experience to transhistorical definitions, I propose situating populism historically in terms of its genealogical, contextual, and often antithetical, relation to fascism. If the European and global postwar liberal-democratic order was cemented in anti-fascist foundations, highlighting the fascist and postfascist origins of its current populist contestation is important.

Some current observers fear that populism may again transform into fascism, and if that happens, a theoretically inflected historiographical approach would show that, while many of the prepopulist forces eventually became fascist in the interwar years and even after 1945, some of the fascists switched back to democracy.[45] Leading political theorists such as Nadia Urbinati, Carlos de la Torre, and Andrew Arato have put forward a historically framed notion of populism that historians of populism need to consider when analyzing the phenomenon. Moving from their theoretical insights to historiography, I emphasize how these connections emerged historically, especially after the populist reformulation of the fascist totalitarian legacy.

Framing populism historically clarifies why its return to Europe and North America has actualized these regions' past xenophobic and antidemocratic traditions. Populism is not a simple external response to elites and bureaucracies but is rather a criticism of democracy from within. Populists have historically regarded their critique of the status quo as a radicalization of democracy by way of returning the power to the people. What this radicalization might entail has differed from left to right. The emergence of populist responses from the left to social inequality often signals that the dubious quality of the coupling of democracy and neoliberal austerity measures is not insignificant in the so-called European periphery, especially in countries like Greece and Spain. These responses cannot be conflated with the Euro-right populism without losing sight of significant ethico-political and analytical distinctions. Even when, in typical populist fashion, leftist populist movements like Syriza and Podemos mixed a critique of income inequality with the binary of the elite versus the people and nationalism, connecting them generically to right-wing populism is misleading.[46] Like their contemporary Latin American counterparts, left-wing European populists of the twenty-first century criticized neoliberal exclusions, technocratic solutions, and citizen disfranchisement by traditional parties. Even when they insisted on transcending the left-right divide, these parties were clearly located on the left of the political spectrum. In fact, they occupied spaces traditionally reserved for the nonpopulist left. Podemos especially reformulated the logic of Spanish politics as a discussion on income inequality and austerity measures. This was owing to its stress on the "caste," and the self-reflexive inspiration it found in the work of Argentine political theorist Ernesto Laclau and in the examples of Latin American neoclassical, left-wing populisms. Podemos, formed in 2013, was a response to the economic crisis and the perceived mimetic nature of the traditional Socialist and Conservative parties and their mutual embrace of neoclassical economic paradigms. Podemos' founding group included Laclausian scholars, who were deeply interested in the Latin American forms of populism, especially Bolivia's but also Venezuela and Argentina. Podemos stressed opposing those who were "above" while representing those who were "below." One of its leaders, Iñigo Errejón, in fact, followed Laclau in countering the binary of a right-wing populism in Europe and a leftist one in Latin America, maintaining that a populism of the left was possible in Europe. Podemos' leaders explained Spanish politics through another key binary, that of "democracy versus caste" (*democracia versus casta*). They clearly identified themselves and the people with the former, while asserting that traditional parties represented the latter. The populist axiom of the people versus the elite was at the center of the "hegemonic" struggle. Pablo Iglesias, the leader of Podemos, asserted that politics was about the imposition of one's own narrative over that of the enemies of the people. As he explained, "In Spain … there is a people that they wanted to humiliate but this people has a very clear idea of who are its enemies: the political and economic elites that have robbed the people and have enriched themselves at the expense of the people." Change, in other words, would come only when the establishment was removed from power, and power was placed in the hands of the people. The people and the fatherland were intrinsically good, but they had been the victims of a scam.

As critics from the left observed at the time, Podemos might have argued in theory that "the people are the [only] ones that need to decide," or that existing democracy was curtailed by the "economic powers and the caste." But in practice, the party was increasingly leaving its commitment to assembly-like, collective decision making behind, in favor of entrusting political decisions to the leaders, especially Pablo Iglesias but also Iñigo Errejón and Juan Carlos Monedero.[47] In a sense, the closer Podemos was to reaching power, the more vertical and populist it became. This populist transformation from collective decision making to popular delegation was even more acute in Greece.

More than Podemos, and owing to its accession to power in 2015, Syriza, which was formed as a coalition of left-wing parties of the parliamentary and extraparliamentary left in 2004, represented an even more challenging historical experience to generic definitions regarding the nature of populism in Europe. Originally stressing a pluralist rather than a homogenizing idea of the popular collective, Syriza eventually turned in a more classical populist direction. Once in power, Syriza formed a coalition with a minority partner, the small, xenophobic right-wing party ANEL. Eventually, Syriza also acquiesced to the austerity demands of the European Union and of necessity veered to the center. In practice, it shifted from critiquing austerity measures to managing them as they were imposed on Greece by the European troika. Like other populist movements that transformed themselves after reaching power, Syriza became less pluralistic and less horizontal. As Giorgos Katsambekis explains, Syriza became "much more vertical" and leader-centric, downplaying its calls to the social movements, which now often mobilize against the Syriza-ANEL government; undermining internal democracy and polyphony; and engaging in a more pragmatic technical discourse focused on implementing the new austerity program in an allegedly "fairer way."[48] When in power, populism often adopts a novel form of transformism that constitutes a new elite while increasing its popular support and social polarization, once again distancing citizens from meaningful participation in political decisions. As Antonio Gramsci observed many decades ago, this type of transformation converts popular demands into vertical politics, blocking more emancipatory politics.[49]

In this context, left-wing European populists were close to transformative Latin American movements like the Peronist Kirchnerismo, which governed Argentina between 2003 and 2015. Kirchnerismo originally proposed horizontal strategies aimed at transcending the politics of Peronism, but once affirmed in power, it had in typical fashion combined left- and right-wing ideological motifs while claiming to be the people's only option against neoliberalism. Highly idiosyncratic, Kirchnerismo clearly reformulated classical Peronist's third way, extending it beyond the socialist left and liberalism. Europe also exhibited peculiar examples of this phenomenon. Europe has populisms such as the Italian Five Star Movement, led by the comedian Beppe Grillo, that mix right and left proposals. An amalgam of right and left, the Five Star Movement has confronted traditional parties and also populist movements of the right.[50]

All in all, to argue that populism in Europe and the United States is mostly a right-wing phenomenon, or that Latin America is characterized by a uniform left-wing brand of populism, or, for that matter, that populism is absent in the rest of the world, would be problematic. The antipopulist idea of a nonpopulist left that is supposedly more European and a Latin American one that is overwhelmingly populist is simply historically wrong. The same goes for the equally stereotypical propopulist idea that what Europe needs is a left-wing "latinoamericanization."[51] The distinctive but sometimes converging historical experiences of countries like Argentina, Ecuador, Brazil, Bolivia, Venezuela, Italy, Greece, Spain, France, Germany, Turkey, South Africa (with Jacob Zuma), and Thailand (with the Thaksin movement) contradict these stereotypes that crisscross the Atlantic and beyond.

Europe is not automatically on the right nor is Latin America simply on the left. For example, in the 1990s Latin American populism was generally on the side of neoliberalism, whereas in the following decade, the populist Latin American left prevailed in the region. Nonetheless, in the second decade of the twenty-first century, Europe and the United States have undeniably become world forces of xenophobic populism, from the National Front in France to the Dutch populism of Geert Wilders and from the Tea Party to President Trump. This dominant right-wing mode is present not only in clear-cut, right-wing populist parties but also in more conservative forms that eagerly adopt key features of the anti-immigrant and nationalist populist program of intolerance for pragmatic or ideological reasons. At the time of Trump's inauguration in 2017, Theresa May in England and Mauricio Macri in Argentina represented this mimetic conservatism, a sort of populism light.[52] Populism often shows "the porous frontier" between the moderate right and the extreme right.[53] The European right, in its journey from fascism to postfascism, has internalized democracy to the extent that it now contests democracy on its own terms. But this contestation rather than furthering democracy confines it to ethnic and nationalistic connotations. Only some inhabitants of the nation are acceptable as citizens. As Nadia Urbinati, one of the foremost theorists of populism argues, populism "disfigures" democracy and potentially challenges its future. Urbinati stresses that, while populism is a democratic form of government, its republican preoccupations tend to displace more properly democratic ones.[54]

Urbinati's historical and theoretical critique of populism is rooted in a contextual understanding of democracy attentive to the larger domain where populism interacts with other notions of democracy that equally limit its historical possibilities. In this sense, populism might be read as pushing itself outside the political realm, rather than as being or becoming the political as such. Urbinati's approach forces us to rethink canonical assumptions about the links among populism, unpolitical forms of deliberation (such as those of technocrats, "experts," and other nonpolitical authorities), and plebiscitary forms of democracy. She explains that "Populism is the most devastating corruption of democracy because it radically overturns representative institutions (notably elections and party pluralism) and transforms the negative power of judgment or opinion from one that controls and monitors politically elected leaders to one that rejects their electoral legitimacy in the name of a deeper unity between the leaders and the people; it opposes ideological legitimacy against the constitutional and procedural one."[55]

Drawing on Urbinati's key theoretical framing of populism as an idealization of democracy that leads to specific disfigurements, I would stress how modern populism emerged from a Cold War defacement of fascism. The fascist model was extremely influential, inspiring leaders who ranged widely across the political spectrum in the interwar years.[56] But after 1945, Latin American populism proposed reformulating democracy in a more vertical way that simultaneously expanded and constrained democracy.

There are important distinctions between the histories and present realities of Europe, the United States, and Latin America. European and North American populisms are presently closer to fascist xenophobia and nationalism than the Latin American ones. All in all, the new dynamic of transnational right-wing populism promises more limitations to democratic life in Europe and the United States than the social and authoritarian effects of Latin American populism.[57] In any case, returning populism to its postwar history allows us to situate and analyze these convergences and distinctions.

EXPLAINING POPULISM AND ANTIPOPULISM

Going back to the issue of populism and theory, not all theorists exclude populism's transatlantic, and global, dimensions, but even here pinning down populism often leads to idealized versions of it as either the purest manifestation of democracy or as its ultimate antithesis. In Ernesto Laclau's famous and seminal work, the provincial European view of populism is transcended. Laclau, in fact, sometimes tends to overcome all national and historical boundaries. Ultimately, he presents populism as politics "as such." For Laclau, populism is a form of power founded on the basis of dividing society through antagonistic social demands. These unarticulated demands follow a "logic of equivalence" in order to dichotomize social space. For Laclau, the "populist rupture" establishes an internal frontier, a deep polarization of society, namely, the division of society into two camps: "power and the underdog." In populism, demands are made by popular subjects, which are then articulated by leaders who defend them in the name of the people and against the powerful, or the elites. Above all, Laclau maintains populism has a "political logic."[58] This perceptive, but also transcendental and sometimes circular, explanation is often positioned outside history. Recently critical theorists Andrew Arato and Nadia Urbinati have placed Laclau's approach in the sphere of the political theology that defines populism and of the democratic disfigurations that it engenders. In short, they have highlighted the antidemocratic dimensions of Laclau's interpretation.[59]

These criticisms are significant, especially because Laclau is the founder of a school of thought that understands populism as the ultimate agent of democratization. Laclau and his school generally focus on the populist left, which he tends to view as the true form of populism.[60] For these scholars, populism is a structurally defining element of systemic calls for equality and against domination, that is, populism leads to political emancipation. For Yannis Stavrakakis, "It seems very difficult to imagine democratic politics without populism, that is, without forms of political discourse that call upon and designate the people—and not, for example, the rating agencies or the *aristoi*—as their nodal point, as a privileged political subject, as a legitimizing basis and symbolic lever to further egalitarian demands."[61]

Stavrakakis shows that the highly problematic tendency to demonize populism conflates popular demands with populism, often betraying untroubled assumptions about the normative dimensions of liberal democracy.

In turn, Jacques Rancière notes the ritual denunciations of populism are part of an elitist attempt to downplay popular democratic expression. By stressing a one-sided version of Latin American populism (from Perón to Vargas to Chávez), Rancière explains that in Europe, the term populism is used to talk about "another thing."[62]

For Rancière, the term *populism* is reserved for those identified with the hatred of democracy. Rancière places life in a democracy in opposition to the status quo, which downplays citizen's participation—a situation he identifies with "states of oligarchic law ... where the power of the oligarchy is limited by a dual recognition of popular sovereignty and individual liberties." In such limited democratic spaces, the term *populism* is used to mask neoliberal attempts to rule without the people. Rancière recognizes that extreme right parties are a consequence of, and a reaction against, the "oligarchic consensus" of technocrats and experts, but he hesitates to call them populists. He stresses how populism is used to conflate democratic responses to neoliberalism with racial and religious fanaticism. Populism, then, is a term of attack but not of analysis.[63]

In contrast, following Laclau, scholars like Stavrakakis, Jean Comaroff, and Étienne Balibar defend using the concept of populism for analytic and normative purposes. Comaroff observes that populism is always used more as a way of "marking difference than denoting content, and its meaning [is] ... largely relative to the standpoint from which it is deployed." She explains, "Despite (or perhaps because of) its paradoxes, populism is more than ever a concept to be conjured with across a wide spectrum of public debate in our present world. This is perhaps most dramatically evident in postcolonial, post-totalitarian contexts, where the memory of collective oppression remains vivid: in Latin America, Russia, and Zimbabwe, for example, but also arguably in the Italy of Berlusconi, the France of Sarkozy, the Netherlands of Wilders." She also includes countries like South Africa and the United States among those where it's necessary to consider populism as an existing form that disputes neoliberalism: "Populism in some form is a necessary condition of all antiestablishment movements, past and present, progressive or conservative ... [and] "is in itself never enough to fuel sustained, politically constructive mobilizations"[64] For his part, Balibar argues, "I do not reject the term as such, especially because I am reminded of its long and ambivalent history as a political category inside and outside Europe, which it is especially worth studying in this moment." Balibar equates the current criticism of political and social inequalities with a democratizing form of populism, a "becoming political of the people."[65]

Taken together, these important critiques of antipopulism question normative assumptions about liberal democracy and its technocratic tendencies, and show how the government of experts limits democratic interactions. However, the responses to antipopulism also often engage in an idealized version of populism, especially Latin American populism, conflating the different uses of populism by the left (especially in the United States, where before the rise of Trumpism populism often meant simply being concerned about or catering to popular demands) with its manifold historical meanings across the Atlantic and beyond. Thus, democratic responses to inequality are more or less mechanically identified with populist discourse and practice.

While authors who adhere to the model of liberal democracy usually diagnose populism as a pathology, scholars who sympathize with the notion of radical democracy tend to think of populism as a healthy, even at times an emancipating, force that strengthens political representation. Is it possible to bridge this gap? Cristóbal Rovira Kaltwasser, a Chilean scholar of populism, notes the need for transatlantic research and also for considering how

> analyzing the relationship between populism and democracy depends to a great extent on normative assumptions and preconceptions of how democracy should function. Thus, the impact of populism on democracy has tended to be less an empirical question and more a theoretical issue, which is answered mostly by speculations deriving from an ideal standpoint of how democracy should be. How to overcome this normative bias? I maintain that the most promising way is to follow those authors that develop a minimal approach to studying populism vis-à-vis democracy.[66]

Rovira Kaltwasser's own proposal undermines the problem of one's own subject position in relation to the object of research. His presentation of a putatively neutral, "less normative" definition of populism is itself not without normative conditions. He endorses a "minimal" definition of populism that replicates Laclau's own notion of populism as everything that is related to the political. Rovira even puts forward an idea of populism as part of every individual's inner self. This sort of populist unconscious can, according to him, be confirmed by "empirical investigations" like the ones Mudde performed. This view of populism as a pathology of the self is necessarily transhistorical. Rovira argues, "Empirical investigation reveals that the majority of individuals have populist attitudes that are in a state of latency. They are in a sleeping mode, and they are activated when faced with certain contextual situations. In other words, most of us have a 'little Hugo Chávez' within us, but it is located in a hidden place, and thus it does not define our political preferences."[67]

Ironically, Rovira Kaltwasser criticizes Laclau's notion of populism as being politics as such, but he himself offers an idealized, one might add romantic, take on "empirical investigation" as both replacing critical theories of populism and neutralizing normative, or ethico-political, subject positions in research. The result is a sort of thinly layered theory filled with bouts of data about the functioning of political parties and other putatively more graspable units. This high theory of populism, like the more antipopulist ones, waters down history and theory while enforcing the ideal of the neutral scientific researcher.[68] As we saw in the previous chapter with respect to theories of fascism, all generic schools displace historical interpretation in favor of definition. Definition aims to close off discussion on the subject, thereby establishing a new consensus that overcomes previous perspectives and allows supposedly more neutral researchers to empirically test the generic definition. In both cases, minimal definitions are formed on the basis of self-referentiality, and often enforce a thinly disguised, refurbished form of positivism. Such minimalist theories often downplay the role of radical violence in fascism and excuse the authoritarianism of populist forms. For instance, when confronted with historical phenomena that go against the theory, these scholars simply silence these inconvenient histories. Thus, just as the Holocaust has not been given its proper and challenging place in the history of transnational fascism, the inconvenient emergence of Trumpism, which certainly deserves a significant place in the history of populism, has simply been excluded from the field of populist studies. Cas Mudde, for example, does not include racism and xenophobia in his definition of populism because they are forms of nativism and thus conflict with his minimalist definition. According to Mudde, Trump's case was very different from the European populist right because, in his view, Trump "singled out illegal immigration" but did not attack "the status of the U.S. as a multicultural immigration country." Moreover, although Mudde noted that Trump has spoken about "'the Muslim problem' at least since 2011, he is much more nuanced in his views of Islam and Muslims than people like Marine Le Pen and, certainly, Geert Wilders." The populist version of Trump does not fit Mudde's definition. Mudde argued, "Where populist leaders claim to be the *vox populi*, the voice of the people, Trump is the voice of Trump." But radical narcissism, charismatic messianism, and mythical thinking often appear in the history of populism as essentially attached to racism, nativism, and xenophobia. And, of course, Trump eventually, and within the populist nature of his candidacy logically, claimed at the Republican National Convention that he was "the voice of the people."[69] Stressing generic definitions minimizes the outer democratic edges of populism in history. As a reformulation of fascism for democratic times, populism, especially on the right, always has the potential to go back to its origins, as some European and American populists have recently demonstrated.

When homogenized with the left-wing variants, right-wing radical populism is released from its most dictatorial and authoritarian dimensions. In history, the populism of the left and the right were and are often antithetical, but under the generic positivist banner, they tend to be conflated. Historical distinctions are silenced by high theory.

The ideal of the detached researcher who uses definitions to analyze data replaces the need to think through the political from a critical theoretical perspective. What historian Dominick LaCapra has aptly defined as "born-again positivism" plays along extremely well with "Up above the world so high" theory.[70] Critical theory, on the other hand, points to potential problems with the unreflective use of data to confirm theoretical axioms. In fact, this is also an especially strong dimension of the critical work of Laclau. In his important works, Laclau provides pathbreaking examinations of populism, but his perceptive diagnosis must be distinguished from his prognosis. Populism for Laclau is a normative model to be endorsed, especially in Latin America. He contrasts parliamentarism, open discussion, and plurality of positions with the principle of dual embodiment (by the people and the leader) and the need for vertical leaderships in the context of friend–enemy relations. Contemporary, mythologized examples of Latin American populism, especially of leaders in countries such as Venezuela and Argentina, ground Laclau's argument. His ideas reflect the often-uncited and unacknowledged influence of thinkers like Sorel and the fascist-leaning Carl Schmitt of the *Crisis of Parliamentary Democracy.*[71]

Laclau's penchant for a normative model of populism leads him not only to focus on Latin America much more than his theoretical peers but also to embrace the normative idealization of the region. Latin American scholars do not find it surprising that Laclau's conceptual antagonist is Italo-Argentine scholar Gino Germani, since Germani is precisely who early on connected the dots between fascism and the Latin American populist experiment of Peronism.

Gino Germani was an Italian antifascist intellectual, who crossed the Atlantic to escape fascism and also helped to remedy a provincial European understanding of the modern political experience of populism. Surprisingly, Germani has been and continues to be much ignored, or he is relegated to a perfunctory footnote in the European and North American interpretations of populism. His work needs to be readdressed by those interested in the history and theory of populism.[72] Germani's own interest in the relationship between Peronism and fascism is informed by personal experience.[73] This sociologist was a child when fascism came to power, and an adolescent when the totalitarian state was established in his native Italy: "In my early youth I experienced the total ideological climate involving the everyday life of the common citizen, and more strongly so, the younger generations. Later, in Argentina, where I went as a political refugee, I met another variety of authoritarianism."[74] This reference to the Peronist phenomenon as another form of authoritarian rule illuminates his comparison between Argentina and Italy. Germani stressed that, from a comparative perspective, Peronist Argentina seemed to lag behind in relation to the Italian historical process. Despite the notable divergences in their social structure and political history, the two countries had similarities that gave way to two different forms of authoritarianism. For him, Peronism (as populism at large) was the result of contextual demographic and class structure changes, and Germani drew on this for his sociological explanation of populism as a vehicle for class mobilization in underdeveloped societies. Unlike many theorists, Germani differentiated between the contextually situated class formations that constituted the core of the movement. But he also tended to ignore the agency of working-class actors who followed Peronism and the many attempts by the populist regime, and by Perón himself, to expand the multiclass dimensions of his movement.

Germani often restricted his theory to the modern form of populism that Peronism represented. However, thanks to his groundbreaking comparative works, along with those of Argentine historian Tulio Halperín Donghi, populism studies started to grasp the revolutionary character of Peronist populism and its complicated genealogical relationship with fascism. As Halperín Donghi notes, the Peronist revolution was confirmed by electoral procedures, giving life to a novel regime of "plebiscitary democracy." For him, Peronism elevated the principle of the ruling party to the status of a national doctrine.[75] As Halperín has also noted in a famous 1958 article, the relationship between fascism and Peronism was ambiguous, but this was not a reason for fleeing from historical and comparative analyses.[76]

Fascists and Peronists came to power when liberal-democratic regimes that were thought to be solid or well established failed. Both used totalitarian politics in the sense of the organicism and absolute integralism that Mussolini and the Argentine fascist *nacionalistas* had attributed to the term before 1945. Both regimes gave a totalitarian answer to the crisis that modernity had provoked in the public's perception of laws, the economy, and the legitimacy of the state. Both regimes were clearly antiliberal, anticommunist, and antisocialist, and yet they treated their enemies in very different ways. Lastly, both regimes mobilized their populations from the top down, using propaganda and various actions, promoting mass politics, and convincing majorities that the leader represented them and the nation as a whole. But while fascism mobilized the middle class, Peronism rallied the working class. While fascism gave war, imperialism, and racism to Europe and the world, Peronism never provoked war at all. Peronism, like other Latin American classical forms of populism, was a specific postfascist response to fascism that radically reformulated it.[77]

FASCISM BECOMES POPULISM: FROM
PERONISM TO TRUMPISM AND BEYOND

A new way of understanding democracy, Peronism embraced popular sovereignty through winning elections and adopting democratic forms of representation, but also radically enhanced the figure of the leader, who was promoted as the best interpreter of the people's will. Its followers were asked to place their faith in the leaders' intuitions and in constant policy changes. They were, and still are, asked to trust that what the leader wills both encompasses and surpasses their political understanding. In populism, the legitimacy of the leader resides not only in the former's ability to represent the electorate but also in the belief that the leader's will goes far beyond the mandate of political representation. This is because populists maintain that the leader innately knows better than the people what they really want. In populism, populist leaders are the object of representation and the subject of popular delegation within the context of formal democratic procedures.[78] The elected leaders personify popular sovereignty, and possess a great degree of autonomy relative to the majorities that elected them.

As a political ideology, populism, like fascism, liberalism, and communism, amplifies short-term political participation, while at the same time minimizing it in the long run. In populism, as in other current manifestations of democracy, such as neoliberalism, meaningful political participation by citizens does not translate well from rhetoric to practice. In short, populism is a modern understanding of the political that features a hybrid combination of unstable ideas about popular sovereignty, leadership, and how a capitalist society should be organized and ruled. Rooted in a postwar rethinking of fascism and a clear

rejection of its extreme violence, populism embraces the democratic principle of electoral representation fused with authoritarian leadership. Modern populism in its classical Peronist
form actively encourages social reform, creating forms of state
capitalism attached to a new elite through its links with the
leader and movement that partly lessens income inequality.

Classical populism represented the fascist combination of
extreme nationalism and a non-Marxist reading of the socialist
tradition that fascists like Benito Mussolini understood so well.
But the populism of General Juan Perón was born into a complex ideological cradle that combined the legacies of fascism
with those of its enemies: Perón maintained that "We are not
sectarian.... If there is something in communism that we can
take, we take it, names don't scare us. If fascism, anarchism, or
communism have something good, we take it."[79] Borrowing
from the left and the right, Perón took the accusation of eclecticism as a compliment. This "eclecticism," which Perón shared
with Mussolini, distanced him from the Italian dictator in practical, and later in theoretical, terms. Fascism's sustaining features were its idealization of violence and war as the sublime
values of nationality and the leader's persona. In military terms,
it mobilized the masses, but it tended to demobilize them in
social terms. Peronism inverted the terms of the fascist equation, distancing itself from the fascist models, and became a sui
generis political ideology. That Peronism reformulated fascism
and became an elected populist regime was a matter of foundational significance in the broader history of modern populism.[80]

For everyone, including its creator, Peronism was the unexpected result of an attempted fascist reform of Argentine political
life. Fascism was always Perón's model, but Peronism was not
merely a new form of fascism. As historian Tulio Halperín Donghi

has suggested, "If the example of fascism couldn't give concrete orientation to the Peronist movement, instead it contributed very effectively by disorienting it."[81] The fascist model tended to focus on objectives that did not coincide either with the realities of Argentina and the global postwar Cold War or with the vertical and horizontal contradictions of the leadership and bases of the Peronist movement. While Argentina appeared to be ripe for fascism, the world showed itself to be too ripe for it.[82]

Over the course of the journey traveled by Peronist ideology and practice, from the messianic idea of fascist leadership to the profound transformations of unionized Peronism, and from Perón's inspiration in fascism to the worker's movement, a dynamic interaction between leader and followers developed that inhibited the autonomy of the former and mobilized and transformed the latter. Converging arguments can be made using other examples of classical Latin American populism, especially the Varguista and Gaitanista movements. A similar logic would later be applied to the neoclassical populist movements in the context of crises between political factions that opened the way for leaders of other groups to turn to populism. For example, in Turkey and Thailand, populism appeared belatedly and was clearly a political choice by leaders who had not been populists before. In these countries, leaders like Erdogan or Thaksin Shinawatra (2001–06) moved to populist policies after a relative absence of populist rhetoric at the beginning of their governments. As Ertug Tombus explains, in the case of Turkey, Erdogan's AKP party understood itself to be the sole democratizing agent, which paradoxically led to an increase in authoritarianism. Erdogan came to power in 2002, but he fully embraced a populist style and vision only much later, in 2007. Thus, in Turkey, and during a moment when secular groups seriously contested Erdogan's politics, populism emerged as a later choice for understanding the political and for doing politics. As Tombus argues, by that time "Erdoğan showed that for him democracy is only a stage of plebiscitary acclamation; that democratic procedures and principles are worth respecting only as long as they lead to the consolidation of Erdoğan's power. Constitutional limitations and the rule of law are nothing but obstacles before the will of the people, which is, for them, embodied by Erdoğan and the AKP."[83] This logic of authoritarian consolidation in the name of the people, and in defense of democracy, was pushed further after the failed antipopulist coup of the Turkish summer of 2016. The enemy was now everybody perceived to be opposed to the leader.

In Thailand, Thaksin Shinawatra, a media magnate, adopted the role of voice of the people and even popular ways of speaking and dressing. He harassed critical media and presented his politics as a "soft authoritarianism," while claiming in 2006, "I am the major force in government and everyone is just my helper." As political theorist Benjamin Moffit notes, the Thai leader argued that intellectuals, NGOs, and civil society groups were "enemies of the nation." At one point, the party slogan was "Populism for a happy life."[84]

With populism, the enemy was the opposite of the people and the leader. The centrality of the people and the enemy in the rhetoric of the demagogic populist leader led to the dual emphasis on the needs and desires of both leaders and followers and to the increasing exclusion of others symbolically and, occasionally, practically. The result was a downgrading or even the elimination of democracy, either through the leader's increasing recourse to authoritarianism (Turkey) or through the appearance of an antipopulist dictatorship (Thailand) that toppled populism. In the case of classical Peronism, both trends were present. From his 1946 election onward, Perón increased his authoritarianism until he was eventually toppled in 1955 by even more authoritarian and violent antipopulist dictators.

Populism surged as an authoritarian alternative to the fascist violence of the past, a response that included retuning fascism in a democratic key, as well as a new focus on those citizens who remained unrepresented politically. This is why Eric Hobsbawm, one of the most influential historians of the last century, believes fascism had such an effect in Latin American history.

For Hobsbawm the ideological impact of fascism was "undeniable" in the Americas. Nonetheless, he noted that this impact was not the result of a mimetic engagement with Europe but of a democratic transformation. At the same time that Hobsbawm failed to see the national particularities of fascism in Latin American, he recognized its populist outcomes acutely: "It was in Latin America that European fascist influence was to be open and acknowledged, both on individual politicians, like Colombia's Jorge Eliecer Gaitán (1898–1948) and Argentina 's Juan Domingo Perón 1895–1974), and on regimes, like Getúlio Vargas' Estado novo."

Without sufficiently analyzing the significance of the postwar context in Latin America, Hobsbawm stressed fascism's substantial transformation when it crossed the Atlantic. He underlined the originality of its transformation into populism, which he attributed to nationalist structural factors: "What Latin American leaders took from European fascism was its deification of populist leaders with a reputation for action. But the masses they wanted to mobilize, and found themselves mobilizing, were not those who feared what they might lose, but those who had nothing to lose." These structural factors explained why, in addition to the idea that "oligarchy" was the enemy, populism rather than fascism took hold in Latin America. Even when these populist leaders were on the right, and even if they had been sympathetic to fascism, their followers eventually steered them to the left. In contrast, Hobsbawm saw American populists, such as Huey Long and his "conquest" of Louisiana in the interwar years, as rooted more in a radical and left-wing tradition "that cut down democracy in the name of democracy." For Hobsbawm, American populism belonged to the left because of its appeal to "the egalitarianism of the poor." For him, this was "the most successful and possibly dangerous demagogic populism of the decade."[85]

Because populism could be rooted more in the right, or originate from the traditions of the left, it was always more inclusive than fascism. Interestingly Hobsbawm inscribed fascism and populism in the context of the "fall of liberalism." But I would argue that after 1945 a new context emerged that separated the experiences of fascism and populism.

Populism's global history also includes the United States, where populism could be either left or right wing. American historians have long discussed these issues, especially since the appearance of the pathbreaking works of Richard Hofstadter in the 1950s. Before Hofstadter, American historiography regarded populism as solely a left-wing phenomenon in the tradition of the late nineteenth century, but he insisted that American populism had important authoritarian features. Influenced by the works of the Frankfurt school, Hofstadter stressed the authoritarian, irrational, pastoral, antiurban, and even anti-Semitic and anti-intellectual nature of early American populists. After Hofstadter, many scholars still identified populism with the left, but others emphasized the dual possibilities of populism as either progressive or reactionary. From Jacksonian democracy to

McCarthyism, and from the rabble-rousing anti-Semitic and profascist speeches of Father Charles Coughlin and the prepopulist right-wing nativism of Charles Lindberg before 1945, to the candidacies of George Wallace in 1968 and Ross Perot in 1996, American historians have debated whether populism was a response to modernity or a rejection of it. But historically, and I would add also transnationally, populism's political and social leanings depend on the contexts.

In the United States, as everywhere else, postwar populism was a modern response to actual or perceived crises of liberalism and the new early Cold War experience of a world without fascism. American historians generally do not explore the transnational implications of postwar modern populism and the fact that it was exactly at this time that classical populism emerged in Latin America. Focusing on national traditions, these historians note that, particularly just after World War II, owing especially to an invigorated anticommunist movement and, soon after, to a fierce reaction against the civil rights movement, populism definitely turned from being a phenomenon of the progressive left to one of the reactionary right. Most historians of American history do not address the fact that populism's turn from progressive to reactionary, that is, to a more clearly predominant right-wing form, coincided with other global trends, especially, but not exclusively, anticommunism and antiliberal Peronism, among other third-way movements that crystalized after the resurrection of liberalism, which took place after the war. The United States was similar to the rest. The distinction between pre-1945 American progressive populism and right-wing anticommunist populism that solidified against the New Deal corresponds chronologically with my own distinction between prepopulism and protopopulism and classical populism in Latin America. The new American populism that became dominant in the 1940s with the aim of defending a unified people from the liberal elites shared many impulses with other national and transnational cases.[86]

Many American history scholars agree that populism turned toward the right in the postwar period, but as historian Ronald Formisano stresses, there were important exceptions to this tendency. In some cases American populism put forward an amalgamation of progressive and reactionary motifs, both of which were reflected by, for example, the supporters of Ross Perot's third-party presidential run in 1992.[87] Nonetheless, Formisano notes that in the 1990s, the religious right "had moved firmly into the Republican camp." These moves, and the increasing colonization of the GOP by nativist, and ever-more xenophobic populist themes, explain the many grassroots "tea parties" that emerged after the election of Barack Obama in 2008: "While the Tea Party burst onto the scene in 2009 protesting government spending, high taxes, and bailouts, its passions have been animated as much by the cultural preoccupations of the religious right and allied groups focused on the rights and place in society of women and undocumented immigrants." Anti-immigrant xenophobia was especially central to Tea Party ideology. Also important was racism and neoliberal fears about President Obama's very moderate response to the economic crisis. In their analysis of Tea Party gatherings in Massachusetts, Vanessa Williamson, Theda Skocpol, and John Coggin noted, "At public gatherings, Tea Party rhetoric seems to take a page from Hofstadter's 'paranoid style of American politics,' decrying the president as a threat to American democracy, in ways that seem far out of proportion to any actual political or policy happenings."[88] The Tea Party led many Republicans toward polarization and the demonization of the sitting president, with Donald Trump one of the most famous advocates for the so-called birther movement. The fantasy behind the lie that President Obama was not born in his own country was typical of the populist drive to strip political legitimacy from those they judged to be of the elites and against the people and the nation. When Trump became the name of America's populist right, and became the president of the country the circle was complete. American populism had found its leader, making whole an until then incomplete form of populism.

In the early decades of the twenty-first century, the Tea Party and President Donald Trump have continued these national but also transnational populist traditions. For *Breitbart*, a white supremacist website that played a notable role in Trump's path to the presidency, and whose CEO was the chief strategist of Trump's campaign, Trump provided a leading example for "populist, nationalist candidates" across the Atlantic. *Breitbart* stated, "Globalism has suffered a series of powerful blows, especially with the continuing rise of populist parties in France, Germany, Austria, Italy, Great Britain, Hungary and elsewhere. As in the case of the Brexit referendum, the establishment—including its sounding box, the mainstream media—stand in defiant denial of the facts and then rend their garments when their predictions prove illusory." If *Breitbart* argued that Trump's populism was going to save America, Italian populist Beppe Grillo argued that Trump's victory was a turning point in world history: "This is a wide-ranging fuck off. Trump has pulled off an incredible V-Day." In turn, Marine Le Pen, maintained that Trump's triumph represented a "global revolution," the victory of the will of the people over the elites. For Le Pen, "Clearly Trump's victory is an additional stone in the building of a new world destined to replace the old one." Le Pen had adopted the slogan *"Au nom du people"* for her own presidential campaign, arguing, "We are at a crossroad.... This election is a choice of civilization." Like Trump, Le Pen identified her own position with that of the true patriot: "the division is no longer right-left (but) patriot-globalist."[89]

These transnational shared affinities and contextual similarities announced the new cataclysmic victory of populism in the world's most paradigmatic and famous democracy. This fact silenced the conventional American calls for exceptionalism in politics and in the longstanding tendency in American historiography to ignore parallel transnational histories. As the expert on fascism and authoritarianism Antonio Costa Pinto argued, with the birth of Trumpism, it became clear how problematic it was to argue that American democracy was not part of a wider right-wing populist trend.[90] The United States is a province of global history, albeit a central one that singularly affects all others. Indeed, there are some symptomatic peculiarities to American populism in history. Founded in the country where liberalism came to reign supreme, American populism necessarily had to go back and address the country's liberal beginnings as a republic. In fact, the United States was, as Andreas Kalyvas and Ira Katznelson argue, the "world's first liberal regime." Founders of the American republic like Thomas Paine and James Madison reshaped political virtue as political representation. They defined modern democracy as the representative of the people.[91] Their solution was a novel combination of popular sovereignty and political representation. For them, power was not absolute and authority ultimately derived from the people. Electoral procedures were the expression of that. Representatives governed for a time in the name of the people, but absolute power resided only in the people. The latter, and not their temporary representatives, were the granters of political legitimacy. In practice, and from the beginnings of the republic, this ideal has not always been achieved. In electing representatives, the people exchanged direct for indirect rule, which placed limits on expanding democracy. In addition, those whom the people delegated to act in their names were enabled to enact political processes that often enforced forms of domination. For example, for Hannah Arendt, the uses of popular sovereignty were easily driven to unequal and authoritarian outcomes. As Kalyvas explains, Arendt "warned against the homogenizing drive of sovereignty that destroys the constitutive multiplicity, the very plurality, of the public space by violently imposing the dangerous fiction of a unitary macro-subject, the People-as-One."[92]

To be sure, notions of popular sovereignty in history had equally presented egalitarian and authoritarian outcomes. As in other cases, the United States was not an exception in being ambivalent about the notion of sovereignty: promoting and limiting democratic outcomes. As political theorist Jason Frank reminds us, the history of that country is constituted by these invocations of the people as "the only legitimate fountain of power": "The people have been used to justify popular revolution against colonial authorities and to found a constitutional order premised on 'excluding the people in their collective capacity'; to embolden the states and to empower the union; to authorize vigilantism and to affirm the rule of law; to create a broad populist front against Gilded Age economic exploitation and to perpetuate some of the nation's worst racial atrocities; to increase the power of the presidency and to return power to the grassroots."[93]

Across the globe, candidates and other political leaders often invoked the popularity of their ideas to insulate them from criticism from the press or the academy. The result was a teleological tendency to regard any analysis of populism as elitist or out of sync with the needs and wishes of the supposed national majority. This situation exposed critics to accusations of symbolic aggression against whatever reality had been assigned to the term *popular.*[94] Especially in the United States, the popular and populism have often been used as if they were synonymous, the result being that both have been identified with legitimate, especially progressive, causes that recuperate the needs of the people.

In fact, the term *people* is a neutral one that has been appropriated equally by different national actors representing political movements from liberalism to fascism. Fascists have spoken in the name of the *popolo* or the *volk,* real socialists have also linked a people with the nation, and liberals have referred to "we the people" as a foundational expression for the modern era.[95] But in populism, all these traditions became connected. In this context, populism conflated political representation with full delegation and linked both with a mythical idea of the past, when democracy really worked. Thus, populism presented itself as a return to the past but also as a future when tolerance and diversity would cease to have a prominent political role. More than in other places, American populism has always been able to go back to its democratic origins, but as everywhere else these origins often were watered down, restricted to the majority, and mythically conceived as a source of redemption from plurality.

As was the case for the rest of the world, the end of the Second World War significantly transformed the United States. The postwar economic order and the new hegemonic status of liberalism minimized the populist potential of the left, allowing the populism of the right to be the predominant strain north of the Panama Canal. Nonetheless, for the rest of the century populism was co-opted, and restrained, by more conservative elements inside and outside of the Republican Party. This situation increasingly changed, especially after the related cycles of neoliberalism, technocracy, and economic crisis of our new century. Finally, in 2017, American extreme-right populism reached power.

At the level of a movement, the Tea Party, and later Trumpism in the United States presented similar authoritarian interactions to those who have historically defined populism across the globe. The logic of populist radicalization exalted the opposition between the people and the Other—namely, the imagined enemies of the people. This extreme antagonism was precisely what many followers wanted from their leaders. As Pablo Piccato and I argued in 2016 with respect to Trumpism, "Some observers believe—or, perhaps, hope—that Trump's followers misunderstand or don't believe in what he represents. They're wrong." These observers included President Barack Obama, who suggested that Trump's followers were misguided. However, several studies observed a correlation between resentment against African Americans and immigrants and support for Trump. We argue that "His supporters like Trump not despite his anti-democratic qualities, but precisely because of them."[96] Populism cannot be reduced simply to its charismatic leaders nor can their impact be explained simply by whether they are true or false messengers of the people. Leaders and followers respond to each other's expectations and shape the reality of the movement. In fact, this was how modern populism was born as a regime, leading to the democratization of Argentina's dictatorial system. But the opposite can also happen, for example, a leader voted in by a big minority or a tiny majority (as was the case in Maduro's Venezuela) might decide to move further away from democracy, eliminating the need for electoral legitimacy that is constitutive of populism in history.

As the modern history of populism shows, this first became evident in the case of Peronism. Under Perón, Argentina experienced a significant redistribution of income, and the rights of urban and rural workers improved, with wages rising and jobs increasing. Initially, the structural reforms of the social base accomplished by Perón and the dictatorship of 1943–46 were not accompanied by democratic procedures. Thus, the followers could not formally express their support for the dictatorial regime and its leading figure. This could not have been done without delegitimizing the dictatorship. Perón resolved this contradiction by calling for elections to legitimize his leadership, which up until then was a dictatorship. Moreover, when he was removed from his dictatorial posts in 1945, and during the famous popular demonstrations in his favor, Perón was able to position himself as the leader of a popular coup against the dictatorship. He then won the presidential election in February 1946. The result was a democracy that combined expanding social rights, increasing the electoral participation of his supporters, and limiting the political rights of the opposition.

FROM PAST TO PRESENT

This novel form of postwar politics later became the classic case of Latin American populism. As an authoritarian version of electoral democracy, populism represents itself as being outside ordinary politics. It makes nonelectoral claims for democracy. Fewer spaces are left for political minorities to express themselves, and they are accused as traitors to the "real" will of the nation or, worse, as mere puppets of foreign powers plotting against the country. Finally, populism conflates state and movement, enforcing forms of clientelism that feature the leader as the incarnation of the people. Indeed, Perón saw his leadership as the eternal link between the people of the nation as a whole and the security apparatus of the state. As he argued in an early third-person reference to himself in the famous speech of October 17, 1945, "In this historical hour for the Republic, let Colonel Perón be the link of union that would make indestructible the brotherhood between the people, the army and the police. Let this union be eternal and infinite so this people will grow in that spiritual unity of the true and authentic forces of nationality and order." Perón positioned himself as a law-and-order leader. He could bring together a divided public but would do so by eliminating all distinction among the people. In doing so, the Argentine military man elevated the police and the armed forces against imagined enemies of the people, both inside and outside Argentina, who compromised not only the country's national security but also its identity. As we argued with Pablo Piccato and Dirk Moses, Trump, too, had mixed us-versus-them alarmism, jingoistic statements, and the idea of law and order with the fiction that he is the "messenger" of the people. In his "American carnage" inauguration speech, Trump said the American people had defeated a minority of politicians: "For too long, a small group in our nation's capital has reaped the rewards of government, while the people have borne the cost." Trump has also claimed that the country was beset by crime, stating falsely on the campaign trail that the "murder rate" was the highest it's been in almost half a century and that the police "are the most mistreated people" in America.[97]

As a good pupil of classical populism, Trump was actualizing Perón's brand of populism, which depended on a view of secular constitutional democracy as the source of national decline. By representing themselves as the personification of their nations and peoples, these leaders wanted to turn their countries upside down under the mantle of an electoral mandate. In Trumpism, this fiction was made even notwithstanding the reality that Trump had lost the popular vote. In Peronism, this authoritarian view of democracy actualized the need to use the popular vote to legitimize the interwar synthesis of nationalism and non-Marxist nationalist socialism. In his memoirs, Perón clearly identified Italian fascism and Nazism with this "socialism with a national character." Referring to his visit to fascist Italy, he stated, "I chose to do my military assignment in Italy because it was where a new national socialism was being tested. Until then, socialism had been Marxist. In contrast, in Italy, socialism was sui generis, Italian: fascism."[98] Perón radically rearranged fascism in a newly democratic, antiliberal key. But populism is not Argentine, Latin American, North American, Asian, or European. Instead, it is a global phenomenon with distinctive European, Asian, American, and Latin American histories. It is, and was, the outcome of the interconnections and transfers of political ideas and historical experiences throughout the Atlantic and beyond.

Populism first emerged as an antileftist democratic solution and an attempt to overcome the Cold War dichotomy between liberalism and communism. By way of "democratizing" the nondemocratic experiences of fascism, Peronism morphed into the first postwar example of a populist regime. Other regimes soon followed in Brazil and Bolivia and among other Latin American countries.

After its modern emergence as a reformulation of fascism, populism has had various and contrasting histories. As Hans Vorländer argues, populism can act as "the good, the bad and the ugly." It can have diverse and even contradictory effects on democracy. It can stimulate it, narrow it, or even destroy it.[99]

In Latin America, classical populist regimes have generally combined authoritarian plebiscitary presidential leadership, the electoral support of large popular majorities, and an expansion of social rights. More recently, the European populism of the right, on the other hand, generally has targeted immigrants and emphasized European disintegration. In its most recent historical formations, populism represents a nonpluralistic response to the global economic downturn and a widely perceived crisis of representation fueled by the continued presence of an elite of technocrats that switches from government to government and is seen as indifferent to growing social gaps.[100]

These responses to neoliberalism come from the right and the left and sometimes, as in the case of the Five Star Movement in Italy or the Kirchnerista Movement in Argentina, they are amalgamated. This amalgamation disputes the traditional demarcations between left and right, but it does not eliminate important, even substantive, distinctions between, for example, the leftist populism of Evo Morales's movement in Bolivia and the xenophobic populism of the True Finns in Finland.[101] Their extremely different responses to neoliberalism explain why left and right cannot ultimately be collapsed under the guise of non-historical generic definitions. Yet populism constantly reshapes existing standard ideological boundaries.

Populism on both the left and the right has become a political force in Europe. On the left, Greece and Spain are the most relevant cases. In England, Italy, France, Slovakia, Bulgaria, Denmark, Finland, the Netherlands, Germany, and Austria, populist right-wing politicians stress the need to return power to the "people" and take it away from "oligarchic elites." Although they are often considered not to be part of Europe, both Turkey and Russia constitute clear forms of populist leadership, in which the opposition is presented as contrary to the will of the people. Golden Dawn and the Jobbik Party in Hungary, which have promoted a more extreme form of populism than many movements, can be seen as followers of a new fascism, or more simply forms of neo-Nazism.

These moves back and forth between fascism and populism ultimately represent the possibility of unmaking democratic-authoritarian versions of populism and simply returning populism to fascism. On the "moderate" side, UKIP's activities in England successfully contributed to the Brexit of 2016, and, more generally, to European disintegration. They proposed a return to the nation and an antipolitical rejection of institutions.

When they are in the opposition, populist formations are incomplete and limited to the function of protest parties within the system. Not being in power, their influence is related to how they affect the political agenda. They assume a function that works in the direction of intolerant nationalism and against cross-national bonds for citizens. The success of this populist right, a success epitomized by, but certainly not restricted to, a series of events ranging from the multiple anti-European referendums to Brexit, shows its particular strengths in finding ways to oppose the status quo—antiplurality; expressions of outrage; generic discontent, more specifically criticism of immigrants and the press; and above all, the return of jingoistic nationalism.[102] In most cases, this populist right presents the paradox of a "people" standing against the potentials of democratic life and pluralism, but this is coupled with another paradox:—antidemocratic values speaking in the name of democracy against tyranny, fascism, or dictatorship. As Rancière observes, oligarchic forms of sovereignty are linked to politics as kinship or race. Both represent antidemocratic forms acting against a more equal democracy.[103] If populism, as we will see in the next chapter, poses limits to the notion of popular sovereignty by way of combining it with Trinitarian ideas of leaders and peoples, neoliberalism also presents a dual notion of sovereignty. After many decades of support for dictators in the Global South, neoliberalism now combines faith in the agency of the market with the legitimacy of electoral procedures on a global scale. As Wolfgang Streeck contends, neoliberalism represents a form of sovereignty that does not meaningfully rely on democratic participation because it also relies on the imperatives of the market. Thus, by displacing the participation of the citizens in politics, neoliberalism also puts forward its own challenge to democracy and even combines popular sovereignty with the sovereignty of the market. One dimension of this conciliation between capitalist and social life is that the logic of the market tends to be naturalized and then presented as a moral or ethical imperative that is before or above politics. For Streeck, "Neoliberal capitalism and electoral democracy can live together peacefully provided democracy is deprived of its capacity for egalitarian political intervention in the 'free play of market forces.'" The result of this deprivation is the "authoritarian enforcement of a capitalist monoculture."[104]

Both neoliberalism and populism desire to rule in the name and interests of the people but without considering the legitimacy of alternative visions of society. This is especially the case in Europe, but even when they want the destruction of the European Union, most of these new European populist movements of the right do not attempt to destroy democracy. They only attempt to limit its reach and curtail its emancipatory potential. However, the return of fascism to Europe appears in the form of the radicalization, in some countries, of the most authoritarian genealogies of populism. This is not the case of most Euro-populisms; but in Greece, the Golden Dawn is deeply rooted in the fascist past. The country's financial crisis, and the insistence by Germany and the European Union on enacting harsh neoliberal austerity measures, has generated populist responses that evoke the phantoms of interwar European fascism. The neofascist Golden Dawn Party openly uses a logo resembling a swastika. Its supporters have perpetrated violent physical attacks (including murder) against immigrants and political opponents, and its party line includes anti-Semitism and Holocaust denial. Similar sentiments are on the rise in Hungary, where the nationalistic, anti-immigration, anti-Semitic Jobbik Party is one of the most important political formations in the country.[105]

On the other side of the Atlantic, the successful presidential campaign of Donald Trump repositioned the United States as a world center of right-wing populism. With his insistence on ethnic and religious discrimination, Trump embraced racism in explicit ways that surpassed the more strategic repackaging of the National Front in France and the Austrian Freedom Party.

As a response to liberalism, but also to the left, Europe and the United States are witnessing a return of a right-wing form of populism that brings it back to the classical authoritarian version of Latin American populism. But this is happening without reproducing the latter's socially inclusive emphasis. Right-wing Euro-populists and American populists have replaced the Latin American populist critique of social inequality with a jingoistic push to exclude ethnic, religious, and immigrant minorities from the nation. In a context of increasing social inequality, European and American populist leaders of the right stress the need to disentangle the citizens from traditional forms of democratic representation. For them, the leaders represent an incarnation of the "real" people, as opposed to the whole of the inhabitants of the country. In Europe, for example, in countries like England, the Netherlands, France, and Italy, these antiminority views transcend the view of the populist movements and are increasingly accepted by conservative and even social democratic politicians. In Latin America, populisms of the right and the left generally stressed regional integration. This is not the case of right-wing populism in Europe and the United States. Although populism emerged in the 1940s as an anticommunist response to the left that combined social redistribution and state capitalism, in the 1990s, it morphed into a new antileftist attempt to combine vertical leaderships with free market economics. These austerity programs were often presented as responses to increasing economic dysfunction and recession. In reality, these programs failed in their attempts to solve both these issues and contributed to a minimization of the state's ability to bridge the social gaps in Latin America. The recent Latin American populisms associated with the left in Bolivia, Venezuela, and Ecuador are clearly outcomes of this right-left populist cycle. As a response to the populism of the right, they now conflate state and movement, enforcing forms of clientelism that promote the leader as the effective provider for the people. Even when social gaps are bridged, political polarization prevails.[106] In contrast, the recent European and American populist experiences resemble the earlier forms of classical populism, although in a much less inclusive form than Peronism or Varguism in Brazil. Not long ago, scholars of populism assured us that a country like Germany (a leading power in the West) was somehow immune to populism, as if they were a paradigm to emulate.[107] In fact, Germany is also a leading example of a more extended Euro-American form of xenophobic populism.

The new populism of the European right—in its radical form (Greece, Hungary) or in relatively smaller doses (France, Italy,

Austria, Germany and The Netherlands)—is surprisingly open to its predemocratic foundations. The same logic drives the twenty-first-century adventures of American populism. At best, this populism is still ambivalent about democratic institutions. At worst, it wants to destroy them. Especially in Europe, the possibility of populism's return to its undemocratic genealogy raises the following question: Would Euro-rightist populism refashion itself, downplay its recently acquired democratic credentials, and reactualize the repressed fascist past? Taking up racist, neofascist positions against democratic pluralism and minority rights, Greece's right-wing populists and their Hungarian counterparts— along with many other anti–European Union parties—offer up the European brands of populism as actually willing to return populism to fascism. Going back to the dictatorial fascism would mean the dissolution of what populism has been since 1945, in short, a democratic authoritarianism.

Classical populism rejected not only dictatorial fascist forms but also high levels of political violence, racism, and anti-Semitism, together with war and militarism. To be sure, Perón welcomed many Nazis and other fascists, and Vargas also persecuted minorities in Brazil. But Perón also allowed Argentine Jews to be full members of the nation as long as they declared themselves Peronist Jews. Vargas's campaigns against minorities resembled the contemporary illiberal trends of American democracy (for example, Franklin Delano Roosevelt's actions against Japanese Americans), rather than Nazi-style fascism's racist laws. Populism implied a rejection of fascist ways. While the past was characterized by violence, the future was going to be different. As Perón said in 1945 before he was elected, "One does not win with violence. One wins with smartness and organization ... the future belongs to us." Similarly, Eva Perón said that she made a clear explicit distinction between the Peronist regime and the Franco dictatorship during her visit to the latter, when she explained to Carmen Polo, the Spanish dictator's wife, the essential difference between the will of the people that Peronism expressed and the imposition of violence that Franco represented: " I put up with it a couple of times until I couldn't stand it anymore and I told her that her husband was not a ruler by the votes of the people but because of the imposition of a victory. The fat woman did not like it a bit."[108]

Peronism and other Latin American populisms polarized their societies, but they did not engage in high levels of repression and political violence.

Similar authoritarian developments in democracy have pervaded the last two decades of Latin American populism; populism married vertical forms of democracy with vertical forms of leadership. For example, the case of Venezuela under Chávez and Nicolás Maduro often complicates ideal-typical pictures. Their populist regimes strengthened the army and popular militarism, occasionally engaging in anti-Semitism. Although Comandante Chávez first participated in a coup (as Perón had done in 1930 and 1943), he was later fully committed to democratic elections, even though he limited other democratic procedures. Thus, generally Latin American populism left fascism behind and actually embraced the authoritarian forms of democracy that defined it so well. It is unclear whether European or American forms of neoclassical right-wing populism are equally committed to formal democracy, as has generally been the case throughout most histories of left- and right-wing Latin American populism. Fascism is always looming above the past and present history of populism, especially in Europe. In sharp contrast with most Latin American versions of populism, which are firmly rooted in formal democracy, Euro-populism runs the risk of returning the populist phenomenon to its prepopulist or even fascist origins. Unmaking the postfascist reformulation of fascism, the most extreme European populisms have been increasingly turning into neofascism.

Populism is the opposite of diversity, tolerance and plurality in politics. It talks in the name of an imagined majority and dismisses the views of all whom it considers part of the minority. Especially on the right, its enemies often include religious and ethnic minorities and always include the independent press. Perón spoke in the name of the people and imagined himself to be the opposite of the elites. Like Le Pen, Wilders, Trump, and many other contemporary leaders, the Argentine general set his own persona against politics as usual. He represented antipolitics, and conceived of his own role in messianic terms. He was tasked with radically changing Argentina, giving it a new historical foundation at a time of terminal crisis.

If Perón was the epitome of twentieth-century populism, the new right-wing strain represents populism's new wave for the new century. This time, however, populism returns to some fascist themes that Perón and classical populism had rejected. The American populist right—and its European counterparts such as France's Marine Le Pen, the Italian Northern League, or Germany's AFD and Pegida—has returned to xenophobia in a way that the Latin American conductor would never have imagined.

If the rejection of racism was one of the key elements in Perón's version of an authoritarian democracy that distanced itself from the fascist and xenophobic views of the past, today racism seems again to be at the center of politics. Shaped in the context of the early Cold War, populism represents a third way between the traditional left and the traditional right. It disputes the logic and the idea of democracy from within. From fascism to Peronism and from Le Penism to Trumpism and back, populism remains a powerful response, and a significant challenger, to both conventional and more radical emancipatory forms of politics. It represents an equally daunting challenge to any critical, historically informed theory of democracy.

THREE

Populism between Democracy and Dictatorship

Dictatorship is one of the foundations of modern populism, and yet populism is not dictatorship. In the context of the early Cold War period, this paradox played out in modern populism's renunciation of dictatorial rule, which in turn created a new, authoritarian regime form of democracy. The fascist dictatorial experience was a key factor in the emergence of populist regimes, and populism was is in part defined in terms of its opposition to dictatorship. "Fascist dictatorship," a specific historical type of mass modern dictatorship, then, is central to the genealogy of populism. Some approaches to populism emphasize the more recent oppositional links and continuities between populism and Cold War dictatorships, and in these pages, I am in conversation with those perspectives. In contrast to them, I stress the need to understand the ambivalent, oppositional nature of populism in terms of its firm rejection of pre–Cold War fascism's version of dictatorial rule.[1] Populism was a form of antiliberal, authoritarian democracy well before the emergence of the now classic Cold War dictatorships in Brazil, Pakistan, El Salvador, and many other places, and it was and continues to be defined by its contextual rejection of dictatorship. At the same time, populism still shares some dictatorial elements, carried forward especially from the remnants of the fascist global experience of mass dictatorship that ended after the end of World War II.

Can populism as an ideology, a movement, and a regime be democratic *and* highly anti-institutional? Can an anti-institutional style of politics that shares many dimensions with dictatorship become its opposite? Or, rather, can pondering populism's incongruities take us only so far if, as I argue, both are true and have always been part of the experience of modern populism. Answering these questions, therefore, requires understanding how and why these apparent contradictions became part of populism when it was finally constituted as a regime form after 1945. Moreover, the answers are embedded in the complex and varying connections between populism and dictatorship that have existed in different contexts, which is to say that the theoretical question posed by the affinities between populism and dictatorship needs to be framed historically. Surprisingly, many scholars of populism, especially those who provide the more simplistic definitions, or the ones that only study populism as a movement in opposition, do not address the key issue of what was happening when populism reached power. Yet this is key for understanding the history and theory of populism. To put it bluntly, it is not possible to have a complete picture of populism without analyzing how and why it ruled.

Anti-institutionalism is a central facet of fascist dictatorships and modern populism in power. To be sure, both attempted to overcome a perceived sense that liberalism was in crisis, which they characterized as a crisis of democratic representation. For example, fascist dictators and populist leaders rejected the mediating role of institutions and aimed to establish a direct organic link between the leader and the people. But what are the differences between populism and dictatorship? The main one lies in their contrary stances toward political violence, or even political persecution and political death. While populist democracies are closer in practice to endorsing the necessity of violence to solidify power when it is monopolized by the state and not executed by it, dictatorships, especially the fascist ones, tend not only to monopolize violence but also to exert it widely on its citizens, many times outside the rule of law. This anti-institutional dimension of dictatorial rule, which is central to the unleashing of political violence, stands in sharp contrast to populism's stance toward violence.

DICTATORSHIPS AND INSTITUTIONS

What is modern dictatorship? How is it different from tyranny and despotism (namely, the categories used to refer to illegitimate forms of rule through repression and violence in contexts before the emergence and consolidation of modern democracy) and why is this distinction in the history of concepts so central to the historical understanding of populism? To put it simply, modern dictatorship is a form of ruling the nation that combines violence and popular consent with a dictator who rules in the name of the people, but in practice his dictum is above laws and institutional procedures. In modern dictatorships, some legal procedures are maintained, but they are superseded at any moment by the will of the dictators.

As Andrew Arato suggests, dictatorship stands as the opposite of modern democracy. Unlike classical tyrannies, modern dictatorships are ideological systems with absolute promises of "transition" to a new order. In other words, they represent a clear alternative to constitutional democracy. Roman dictatorship was itself temporary in nature as an institution of the republic, whereas modern constitutions do not consider the possibility of a more or less permanent dictatorship. As Arato indicates, there is an immense gulf between the ancient and modern meanings of the term *dictatorship*. If the ancient tradition often involved the legal establishment of an extralegal magistrate, this happened as a parenthesis from normal politics. In contrast, the modern dictator subverts the constitutional democratic order and combines illegal or extralegal activity with claims of popular sovereignty (i.e., dictators argue that the people want them, as opposed to elected leaders, to stay in power more or less forever). An advocate of dictatorial rule, the authoritarian thinker Carl Schmitt argued, before he became himself a Nazi, that dictatorship was the best form of identification between the executive and the people in the age of modern democracy. In opposition to older forms, the new dictatorships resolved the conflict between representation and delegation, legitimacy and legality, procedures and directly ruling the nation in the name of the people. Modern dictatorship combined the old notions with the new ones, incarnating popular sovereignty in the persona of the dictator and no longer distributing power among the three branches of government. Thus, the modern term *dictatorship* emerged out of the need to conceptualize the new reality of authoritarian rule and the emergence of "extraordinary governments" that changed the order of things. They eliminated democracy and combined a disregard for the rule of law; high levels of repression; elimination or subjugation of the press; and the rejection of free, contested elections with mass consensus and, more generally, the transgression of institutions such as the separation of powers and free speech.[2]

All modern dictatorships are capable of engaging in highly ideological, "anti-institutional politics" and embracing forms of radical revolutionary violence that are opposed "to existing forms of normalcy (defined by legality, procedural democracy or bureaucracy)."Thus, some modern dictatorships, which Hannah Arendt mistakenly believed were excluded from nontotalitarian forms of dictatorship, use language and actual violence to dehumanize and render the Other abject. In other words, nontotalitarian dictatorships can participate in radical anti-institutional violence without resembling fascist, totalitarian forms of dictatorship. At the same time, fascist dictatorships are also for a period of time capable of supporting institutional politics but only to a limited extent because the state's unleashing of violence, and not its Weberian restriction of it, is a key dimension of fascist ideology. The corollary of this violence defines fascist dictatorship's anti-institutionalism. Especially in modern dictatorships of the fascist type, one can observe an inversion of the object of analysis of the penal norms of the state. The state cannot be considered primarily as legislator but as the subject that violates the law. Arato points out that fascist and nonfascist dictatorships can be equally anti-institutional.[3]

Mass dictatorship can be simultaneously nontotalitarian and extremely violent and highly ideological. The case of Argentina's Dirty War dictatorship (1976–83) perfectly illustrates this point. The Dirty War was not a real war but an illegal militarization of state repression. Its extreme violence was not unique to Cold War Argentina but also appeared in Chile, Guatemala, Indonesia, and many other dictatorial formations. They all rejected democratic procedures, and all engaged in widespread repression and killings. In the Argentine dictatorship of the 1970s, ideology drove the bureaucracy of repression and violence.

No government technocrats disputed the radical methods that were driven by ideology. Like the concentrations camps of the Nazi regimes, Argentina's were organized by the administrative power of the state specifically as sites of ritualized violence. In the Argentine clandestine detention centers, no limits were placed on dictatorial violence. Within these camps, the dictatorship was fully shielded from public view, and it imposed "total domination." The camps had a fascist ethos and constituted a politically created universe where violence reigned supreme. They were a world beyond the law, built to fulfill and to reconfigure the ideological demands of fascist theory and its anti-institutional drive to victimize the government's supposed enemies of the Argentine people.[4]

Like Argentina's, most Cold War dictatorial forms of dictatorship differed from contemporary populism's with respect to the latter's peculiar understanding of the political. But could modern populism be equally anti-institutional? Populist anti-institutionalism clearly rejected the dictatorial stress on violence and repression, and this rejection constituted a sine qua non condition for the legitimacy and sustainability of the populist regimes. Even so-called moderate dictatorships like General Juan Velasco Alvarado's in Peru (1968–75) and the *dictablanda* of General Marcos Pérez Jiménez (1952–58) in Venezuela or the more violent but still relatively restrained ones like the late Franco regime in Spain (1960s) and the military dictatorship in Brazil (1964–85) did not use the state monopoly on violence, and the consequential limitation of its use, only as a political metaphor.[5] They also used these strategies to install the global and local memories of recent repression, torture, and state violence in the minds of the people. In contrast, modern populism is not theoretically rooted in violence but rather in electoral decisions made by a majority of citizens. Even when General Juan Domingo Perón or, later on, Commander Hugo Chávez and many others had attempted coups in their earlier histories as populist leaders, they more or less rejected the violence that is more typical of mass dictatorships. Perón himself was originally the leader of a military dictatorship, but he eventually relied on elections and other democratic procedures to ratify his rule, and this shift made a difference with respect to the use of extensive state violence against the opposition. Most histories of populism show that, especially when in power, it combined, and still combines, a high degree of anti-institutional politics (and even displays some totalitarian patterns) with a low degree of anti-institutional violence.

Populism's anti-institutional dimensions were a result but also a negation of the fascist past. Classical populism was connected to fascist theory, but it also explicitly proposed its demise and the creation of a nonliberal "third way," anticommunist democracy. Populism is more connected to fascism than to other Cold War forms of dictatorship, which were often explicitly antipopulist. Yet populism is not fascism at all, which is to say it is not dictatorial in the fascist anti-institutional sense. Despite recent historiographical attempts to downplay the latter, historians of fascism like Paul Corner have stressed the centrality of the dictatorial repressive dimensions of fascism. And this centrality of repressive violence marks a key boundary, an epistemic wall, between populism and fascism.[6]

While fascism clearly rejected democratic procedures, post-1945 populist versions of democracy like Peronism in Argentina or Varguismo in Brazil not only rejected fascist anti-institutional politics (and its consequential politics of violence) but they also embraced free elections and, more generally, electoral representation as it was regularly conceived of in liberal democracies. In this formal sense, and from its modern inception, populism cannot be considered a form of dictatorship. But populism proposed a rejection of "demo-liberalism" that often conflated legality with legitimacy, ignoring some political freedoms while stressing or even expanding social and political rights, which sometimes included the voters' participation in the electoral process.

Can we talk about a populist form of totalitarianism? To be sure, postwar antifascist observers often thought the populist rejection of liberal democracy resembled the totalitarian dimensions of fascist dictatorship. This was, for example, true of antifascists like the Italian sociologist Gino Germani and the Argentine writer Jorge Luis Borges.[7] This is also the view of many current European or American observers, who conflate the past and present experiences of fascism and populism. Contextually, how these interpreters react to statements by Peronists, Le Penists, or Trumpists, which uncannily resemble dictatorial forms of fascist leadership, is understandable. This is especially the case for past and present populist statements that fuse the leader with the sacred will of the people and the totality of the nation.

The leader appears dually as a godlike figure and the national hero of the people. For example, Eva Perón, the wife of the general, elevated him to a totality that encompassed the nation and the people: "I haven't done anything; everything is Perón. Perón is the Homeland, Perón is everything, and all of us are at an astronomical distance from the Leader of the nationality. The Homeland is saved, because it is in the hands of general Perón."[8]

Elements of the fascist theory of a dictatorial form of leadership are very clear in this example of populist self-understanding of politics as direct rule, from the "astronomical distance" between the leader and his subjects to the notion of the messianic leader as a transcendental savior of the people and the nation. The leader is the recipient, but also the savior and the announcer, of a future of national redemption. This applies to most populists, from Perón to Trump and from Chávez to Le Pen. And yet populist leaders have been elected and re-elected, and populist regimes have almost never abolished free elections.

To recapitulate some of my key arguments, populist forms are significantly authoritarian. But in contrast to classical fascism, which uses and abuses democracy to generate dictatorship, populism does not destroy democratic representation nor fully present itself as above the rule of law. In the past and in the present, many antifascist and antipopulist observers have failed to see the dual nature of the postfascist, populist idea of representation and the equally dual nature of the interaction between the leader and his or her followers. Populism also argues for a "dual state," in which the leader's position has an extraordinary place. But in contrast to fascism, the populist leader is not entirely above formal procedures and institutions.

Populism cannot be considered dictatorial when, especially after 1945, it has explicitly stressed the political legitimacy of democratic representation. Modern populism is not a form of mass dictatorship because of three connected historical reasons: 1) populism's contextually driven rejection of fascist dictatorial violence; 2) the fact that the leader is not entirely above the law, and his command is not fully equated with it or with the state; and 3) the issue of electoral representation and the dual notion of popular sovereignty that populism advances. These three reasons are eminently ideological and not merely a matter of style or strategy.

All in all, the malleability of populist authoritarian ideology in terms of left, neoliberal, and extreme right programs; its radical personalism and cult of the leader; and its antidemocratic ideas about its enemies should not be confused with ideological wishy-washiness. Populism can do many things—expand or reduce democratic participation; create a new capitalist class, or empower the traditional corporative powers; fight or defend racism —but its idea of democracy remains patently similar. It is a democracy managed by a leader who not only speaks in the name of the people but also takes their place symbolically. When populism becomes a regime, the leader acts in the name of the people. The package also includes the idea that the enemies of the people are the antipeople—in short, those who in not recognizing the unitary and delegative nature of the leader and movement are not true members of the nation. For populists, this is because the enemies are either members of the elites, simply badly informed citizens, or traitors to the popular will of the nation. After 1945, when these exclusionary views of leader, nation, and people (views that had hitherto been part and parcel of fascism) were combined with electoral procedures, the first populist regimes in history took shape. From then on, the adventures of modern postwar populism had been extremely diverse. We now turn to the diversity of populism in history and across the globe.

DEMOCRACY, NEOPOPULISM, AND NEOLIBERALISM

Modern postwar populism was a reformulation of fascism, especially with respect to political representation. When Carl Schmitt conceived his theory of dictatorship, he presented two ideal types: commissarial and sovereign. While the former comes forward to correct things in a time of emergency, the latter imposes radical, even revolutionary, change in the political system.[9]

Although Schmitt made clear that especially in modern times this typology disintegrated into actual histories that combined both forms of dictatorship, one could argue that fascist mass dictatorships were much more sovereign than commissarial in the sense that they created a new, purportedly epochal political order.

Populism also presented itself as an epochal change, but in practice it represented a return to democratic "normalcy." Populism is far away from the representational logic of mass dictatorship. In fascist theories of representation, the leader, people, and nation combine to make a unitary equation. The leader is not elected simply in the liberal democratic sense. He is believed to permanently represent the "will of the people." In short, dictatorship is at the root of the fascist form of representation. In contrast, after 1945 populism has held a much more ambivalent view of perennial forms of representation. In populism, democracy imposes limits on its own desires for total representation, even though there has been an enduring tendency from Vargas to Hugo Chávez to increasingly centralize power in the presidency. In fascist dictatorships, power, unmediated by any means of true electoral representation, is fully delegated to the leader. Fascism erases the democratic system of electoral representation, while populism has since 1945 reenacted democracy. Thus, if Hitler, the Chinese or the Argentine fascists proposed to destroy democracy, populism resurrected its legitimacy after the demise of fascism, albeit in an authoritarian manner. Fascist mass dictatorships eliminated electoral representation, while populist leaders like Perón or Vargas relegitimized it in an antiliberal and corporative sense.

Whereas in a populist democracy, a leader may cease to be the chief executive, either through constitutional limitations or more simply by being defeated in an election, no such situation pertains in fascist dictatorships. Populist leaders like Perón in Argentina and more recently Commander Hugo Chávez in Venezuela epitomize this situation well. When they encountered constitutional limits, both called for elections to reform the constitution, Perón in 1949 and Chávez in 2007.[10] The moment that the populist leader ignores democratic procedures, populism betrays its renunciation of dictatorship and becomes one. This for example was the case for Peruvian populist President Alberto Fujimori and his *autogolpe* (self-coup) of 1992.[11] When the leader does not acknowledge the possibility of stepping aside when faced with conditional limits, populism is unraveling and, in a sense, stops being populist.

Unlike fascism, when populism attempts to downplay constitutional checks and balances, it never supports the idea of a unitary executive with the total elimination of multiparty electoral politics and the separation of powers. Even Fujimori, after his self-coup, called for elections to legitimize his actions and leadership. Similar developments have occurred in Africa and Asia, where populism thrives as an outcome of the economic, social, and political failures attributed to democratization. For example, as Danielle Resnick explains, African populist leaders such as Jacob Zuma in South Africa (2009-present), Abdoulaye Wade in Senegal (2000–12), and Michael Sata in Zambia (2011–14) could only have emerged in the recently created democratic spaces for "contestation and debate" that opened up in the 1990s. As in other places where a multiparty system predominated, African populist politicians have used electoral mobilization to claim themselves the people's voice and then have addressed a real lack of popular participation.[12] This participatory electoral notion of democratic legitimacy would have been unthinkable for leaders like Franco and Mussolini. Especially in South Africa and Zambia, and in contrast to many other countries in the continent, where more authoritarian or dictatorial regimes prevailed, African populist leaders have combined populist and ethnic constituencies. Some scholars even define African populism as "ethno-populism," thereby connecting the African experience with Latin American countries like Bolivia. In Africa, populism emerged as a response to 1990s neoliberalism and technocratic politics. African ethno-populism has increased in countries where ethnic identity is not "unidimensional," and therefore can be combined with more expansive, and inclusive, conceptions of the people. As it does in Europe and Latin America, in Africa this populist inclusiveness has inevitably created constitutive outsiders who become the antipeople. Thus, as Nic Cheeseman and Miles Larmer argue, African populist leaders were able to "weave existing narratives of political marginalization based on ethnic identity and economic status into a common narrative of exclusion." Leaders like Sata, known as "King Cobra" for his harsh actions against political enemies, often combined plebiscitarian approaches with xenophobia, antielitism, and demonization of foreigners. Sata had an apocalyptic vision of his party as Noah's ark. His lemma was "get on the boat," and while focusing on the priorities of the urban poor, he also claimed to embody the people's will as a whole. Sata established an important alliance with the Catholic Church, and in a time of economic crisis, he did not question capitalism or "economic liberalization in general but rather asserted that foreign investors (particularly from India and China) did not have the interests of ordinary Zambians at heart." He denounced the elites and foreigners for appropriating the wealth of the people.[13]

Similarly, Wade in Senegal combined antielite discourse with calls for social change. In contrast, and like the Kirchners in

Argentina with the Peronist Party, Zuma contested his own party's neoliberal past while confronting manifold accusations of corruption. Zuma combined a vertical form of leadership with an antitechnocratic denunciation of the elites as enemies of the people. Like Morales in Bolivia, Zuma's Zulu ethnic identity was a key dimension of his populist strategy, but he did not make the African National Congress into an exclusionary party. Rather, at times he expanded its inclusionary reach, especially with respect to the youth.[14]

But if leaders like Zuma, Wade, and Sata have much in common with left-wing forms of populism like Chavismo or the leadership style of Morales in Bolivia, Alberto Fujimori of Peru was a neopopulist who embraced neoliberalism. Long thought of as contradictions, neoliberalism and populism have an important synergy, combining populist ideas of the people, the oligarchic enemies, and the nation with neoliberal austerity programs and promarket economic policies. Whereas Argentina's Carlos Menem refashioned the Peronist movement as a neoliberal front in the 1990s, in Peru and Colombia, neoliberal populism joined with an aggressive campaign against the two countries' left-wing guerrillas. Menem, and Collor de Melo in Brazil and Abdalá Bucaram in Ecuador appealed to apocalyptic notions of a neoliberal refoundation during times of economic and social crisis. Fujimori and Álvaro Uribe in Colombia (2002–10) also appealed to the hands of the market as social forces for the poor, along with the classical trope of populism as a response to a context of actual and imminent civil war. All these presidents mobilized a majority of citizens in support of their charismatic and at times messianic forms of leadership. Against the left and other enemies, they used plebiscitarian strategies as they translated democratic representation into populist delegation of power to the executive. With the exception of Collor and Bucaram, the presidents also used war as a means to strengthen their political positions. Uribe and Fujimori carefully presented their internal conflicts with the guerrillas as all-or-nothing wars, with the guerrillas portrayed as outsiders to the people, the leader, and the nation. Menem and Fujimori also tried to boost their political credentials by participating in the first Iraqi war (Menem) and in the brief war between Peru and Ecuador in 1995 (Fujimori).

The Israeli scholar Dani Filc has stressed Israeli right-wing leader Benjamin Netanyahu's (1996–99, 2009–present) similarities with Bucaram, Menem, and Fujimori. Although Netanyahu is not generally included in studies of populism, Filc makes a strong case for considering the Israeli leader a peculiar example of neoliberal populism. In my own view, leaders like Netanyahu are fellow travelers with populism in the same way that interwar, right-wing regimes and movements were fellow travelers with the fascists. They are close, and they even share significant anti-institutional patterns and the idea of politics as an all-or-nothing war against many enemies, but they are timid with respect to the cult of the leader and the logic of elites versus the people. Netanyahu does not inspire a strong personality cult in comparison with Menem or Berlusconi, but he has often used populist strategies and key vocabularies. The same can be said about leftist leaders like Lula in Brazil (2003–11). Lula, who enacted multiparty coalitions, clearly differed from leaders like Chávez or the Kirchners in terms of the main features of populism, including the radical myth of the leader and its personification of the people, populism's theological features and its political-religious aspects, and populism's attacks against the press. Together, these leaders from left to right were all, or continue to be, at times populist fellow travelers, constantly using or moving away from populist strategies.

In the same way that scholars of fascism talk about a logic of fascistization, a gravitational field that encompasses right-wing movements that were not typically fascist, the leaders discussed above displayed some populist traits while consciously avoiding others. Their experience cannot simply be conflated with the more typical examples of populism studied in this book.[15] Nonetheless, of all these leaders, Netanyahu is the one who is closest to the populist matrix.

Dani Filc sees "Bibi" Netanyahu as a remarkably apt example of populism's relation to war and ethnic-based politics. He considers the Israeli leader an emblem of exclusionary ethnic populism. Netanyahu's exclusionary notion of citizenship preserved but also undermined the relative inclusionary style of the right-wing Likud Party of the 1960s and 1970s. While the party's founder, Menachem Begin, had combined the inclusion of Jewish citizens with non-European backgrounds with the exclusion of Arab citizens, he also stressed that the Arab minority was entitled to all civil rights. In contrast, Netanyahu regularly accuses Israeli Arab citizens of posing a threat to national security without voiding their voting rights. Earlier in his career, in the 1990s, Netanyahu introduced himself as someone who did not belong to the party elites and was somehow identified with the poorest sectors of Israeli society. In this context, the Israeli scholar Uri Ram argues that the Likud's leader successfully combined populist antielitism with "populist Jewish traditionalism" and the continuous inclusion of Jewish minorities, settlers, and secular and religious nationalists. This coalition presented a new view of the people of Israel, at once inclusionary and exclusionary.

In 1999, Netanyahu typically identified his opponents as "the elites," who hate the people. The collective included in his use of the first-person plural "we" was conceived of as a victim. The elites were against the people: "They hate it. They hate Sephardim and Russians. They hate everyone who is not like them, everyone who is not with them: Ethiopians, Sephardim, Moroccans, and religious people. They hate them." For him, elites were antagonistic to the people, representing a "left" that for Bibi had forgotten what it meant to be Jewish. Netanyahu did not include the business elites in his idea of the enemy. For him the political elites and the left were often difficult to distinguish. As Filc indicates, *the left* was an especially vague term that could simultaneously encompass Ashkenazim who discriminated against Mizrahim, state employees and the unions, communist regimes in Europe, liberal Jews, academics, the media, foreign workers, and Arabs. Filc observes, "The Likud leader maintains the populist notion of the opposition pure people/corrupt elites. 'Us' is the true Jewish people." Similarly, Zeev Sternhell argues that today's Likud Party identifies its own policies with "historical rights," and regards those rights superior to human rights. Sternhell is one of the foremost experts on fascism—a historian, Holocaust survivor, Zionist, and former officer and war veteran in the Israeli Army, who was himself the victim of a bomb planted in 2008 by an Israeli right-wing extremist. For Sternhell, the positions of Likud confirm widely held illiberal views on what an electoral mandate means. "What they're saying in effect is, 'we are the majority, and we can do whatever we want.'" Assigning the majority a free pass led to calls for the exclusion of minorities. In the 2015 elections, Netanyahu warned Israelis that the Arabs were voting in large numbers, as if the exercise of a legal right by Arab citizens threatened his understanding of democracy. What he actually meant was that Palestinians who were Israeli citizens (20 percent of eligible Israeli voters in 2015) were not part of the ethnic collective majority that the populist leader favored. For him, Israeli Arabs are clearly a sort of antipeople who do not belong to his unitary notion of leadership, nation, and ethnicity. Avigdor Lieberman, an Israeli populist leader, and an extreme right-wing ally of Netanyahu, said that the leader "also knows that if the Arabs are voting in droves, only a strong Lieberman can stop them." Lieberman also said that "disloyal" Israeli Arabs should be beheaded. For the Israeli opposition leader Tzipi Livni, and as reported in the *Jerusalem Post*, "The premier had tried to turn the Israeli Left into the enemy of the state and deemed the position as 'unforgivable.' Livni stated that the maneuver had lead Netanyahu to victory, but she warned that it was also a move that leads to hatred and fear." When Netanyahu named Lieberman defense minister in 2016, Ehud Barak, a former Israeli prime minister, warned of the danger of fascism in Israel. He argued that the country had been "infected by the seeds of fascism." Interestingly, Barak seemed to echo the analysis of Zeev Sternhell, who asserted, "Israeli democracy has become increasingly eroded." He also warned that there were indicators of fascism. Sternhell reminded Israelis, "Democracy requires acceptance of the majority decision, but it does not mandate recognition of the rightness or the moral legitimacy of the majority." Following this point, which encapsulates a key dimension of populism, I would argue that right-wing populism is a better explanation than fascism for thinking about Lieberman's party and the striking similarities he and other politicians on the right have with the European xenophobic right. As is the case elsewhere, populism in Israel relies on combining democratic procedures with antidemocratic and antidiverse notions of the people.[16] As Filc argued, "Fear is construed along the border separating 'us' (the true people) from 'them' (the foreign enemy, Palestinians, and their domestic allies, who may vary over time)."[17]

Leaders like Recep Tayyip Erdogan in Turkey during the second decade of the century constantly played the politics of fear. In Erdogan's case, they did so against Turkish Kurdish citizens and other political minorities as a way to solidify strong executives, downplay the role of state institutions such as the judiciary, and buttress his electoral ethnic and religious majorities.

If Erdogan, Netanyahu, and Lieberman, as well as Donald Trump and the Republican "alt-right" in the United States, are not original in understanding democracy to be the exclusive domain of the electoral "silent" and ethnic majority, their concerns about electoral minorities exercising their rights put them closer to authoritarian leaders like Alberto Fujimori in Peru. More generally, neoliberal populists constantly invoked the name of the people to rule by decree, but they also called for elections to ratify even their most antidemocratic decisions. Authoritarianism *and* elections were both central to politicians who governed as if they were campaigning. As Kurt Weyland explains, "Fujimori, Menem and other neopopulist leaders such as Collor did maintain the populist political strategy that they had used in their electoral campaigns. They kept basing their government on a seemingly direct connection to their largely unorganized mass base; bypassing established parties and interest organizations; attacking the political class and other established elites; using opinion polls (the threat of) plebiscites, and other populist instruments for over-coming opposition; strengthening their personalistic leadership; concentrating power and reinforcing the majoritarian elements of constitutional arrangements; and transgressing liberal political norms and trampling on institutional rules."[18]

Similar populist situations appeared in Eastern European countries such as Poland and Ukraine, which mixed populist leaders with drastic neoliberal market reforms.[19] In Italy, Silvio Berlusconi, a playboy and billionaire, a mass media mogul and owner of AC Milan, one of Italy's most prized soccer teams, emerged in the context of a crisis of political representation. Berlusconi presented himself as an outsider who spoke for the needs of ordinary Italians. An anticommunist, he stated that he entered politics to fight "evil." Once he became the Italian premier, he undermined the division of powers, called the judiciary a "cancer," and enforced a plebiscitary form of power.

The names adopted by Berlusconi's political formations *Forza Italia* and *Il Popolo della Libertà*, the personalist vehicles for Berlusconism, combined soccer slogans with the unitary notion of Berlusconi and his followers as the people who stood for freedom. In this construction, there was no legitimate place for opponents. Did they stand against the people and freedom? This was exactly Berlusconi's point. Also known as Il Cavaliere, the Italian populist leader, who dominated Italian politics in the 1990s and 2000s, was an admirer of Margaret Thatcher and Ronald Reagan. In his terms as prime minister (1994–95, 2001–6 and 2008–11), he adapted neoliberalism to the Italian context. This generated impatience among European technocrats and the promarket press. Similarly, Argentina's Carlos Menem also tried to apply neoliberal austerity measures within the political culture of Peronism, which as in Italy case involved disregarding democratic institutions, amid personal scandals and corruption. Like Menem and Fujimori, Berlusconi stressed links within the right, including sectors identified with social nationalist ideas, and doing so constrained the full frontal application of shock austerity measures like those imposed in Margaret Thatcher's United Kingdom or General Augusto Pinochet's Chile. Berlusconi formed coalitions with the postfascists of the Alleanza

Nazionale and the xenophobic Lega. Like Menem, who always presented himself as *un vivo*, Berlusconi cultivated the ideal of himself as a man of the people, as the *furbo*, or the wise guy, who was always in on the joke. Typically, he would use the hand sign for "horns" behind the heads of others, including the Spanish foreign minister during a 2002 meeting in Spain. These gestures, plus his insistence that he would protect democracy against the left, that he stood for order and security, and that he would lower taxes and protect the ecosystem, along with his criticism of migrants, his intermittent defense of Mussolini, and his promise that he represented a true "freedom," made Berlusconi one of the most successful neoliberal global populists. Especially his idea of freedom applied to himself and his freedom to be the candidate who was, and represented, what the people wanted to be. As political theorist Nadia Urbinati argues, Berlusconi put forward an upside-down version of politics that juxtaposed "the audience imbecility of the many ... [with] the spectacle played by the few." Berlusconi promoted his populism as the true democracy of the people against the antipeople of the elites and the left. He considered them antidemocratic because they resisted the popular opinion and sovereignty of those that voted for him and his right-wing allies.[20]

Leaders like Berlusconi and Menem identified with the neoliberal tradition in politics, but they reformulated it in populist terms. Their public mingling with TV and football celebrities, as well as with *vedettes* and prostitutes, conveyed a political message about who they were and whom they stood for. In other words, their style represented their "transgression" of politics as usual. They projected their glamour, sexual promiscuity and misogyny as the fusion of elite and popular traditions. Menemists were famous for their culinary fusion of "pizza with champagne,"[21] a metaphor they used to explain their attempts to modernize the old politics of the elites in a way that mixed popular traditions with celebrity upper-class sensibilities. Berlusconism equally mixed authoritarian popular expectations with the rarified world of celebrity culture. For these leaders, liberalism was no longer a bad word, but their understanding and practice of liberalism equated with its most dehumanizing economic variants.

A man who had deeply profited from the old Italian political system, Berlusconi combined an extreme voluntarism with a projection of his messianic leadership and movement as a refoundation of Italian history and politics. Similarly, Menem, the "disciple" of Perón, explained that he was doing the things that Perón would have done in the new context of the Washington neoliberal consensus. In the election, he had asked Argentines to "follow me." Now in his inauguration 1989 speech, the conductor explained that he came for the people and he spoke from the people. His originality rested on the fact that he related austerity measures to popular sovereignty. In defending free market policies, he invoked the fatherland, God, and the people. He argued that these measures were needed for the sake of "national unity, and the sacred interest of Argentina and Latin America." Menem thought that Latin Americans could be fully integrated by his brand of neoliberal populism. He wanted to connect this new populism with the Peronist past: "The mandate of our general was to actualize our doctrine, our principles starting with our ideology, and to actualize our doctrine and our principles means repositioning Argentina in the context of all nations in the world from the starting point of a united people." For him, this actualization implied a new meaning for democracy that he understood also in terms of a style: "We are here to install a new style in the political life of the nation and I hope that it will propagate to all of Latin America. The rules that emerge from the people need to remain with the people and only work for the people." Menem's neoliberalism gave a new meaning to populist notions of democracy. He wanted to upgrade old Peronism while maintaining the "unity of the Argentine people."[22]

Menem imposed "severe austerity measures" at a time that he defined as a national economic "emergency." Argentina had experienced a major crisis and "hyperinflation," and Menem admitted that this was going to be painful to the people. But he said he acted in the name of the people and with a nationalist sense. This was a "major surgery" that was going to "extirpate at the root all intolerable and ancestral evils." Menem adopted neoliberalism in "the name of social justice."[23]

Most Peronists agreed at the time that Menem represented a historical continuity with Perón and Evita. Néstor Kirchner, a provincial governor in Patagonia, supported the Menemist privatization of Argentina's flagship oil company and even argued that, in listening to the people of his Patagonian province, Menem was the best Argentine president after Perón. Cristina Kirchner defended the privatization as an issue of "morality." In the 2000s, Néstor Kirchner and Cristina Kirchner denied their Menemist past and portrayed themselves as leaders of a new era diametrically opposed to the Menemism that had betrayed "the flags of the patria." However, at the time when Menem turned Peronism to the neoliberal right, Cristina Kirchner was also on board and openly stated that she voted and supported the president, that she "abhorred ... feminism," and that Argentina no longer risked being defeated by the "infamous *trapo rojo* [red rag] of the 1970s." When some years later, in the 2000s, she tried to embody the populist left, she questioned the so-called left that adopted the color red, while the true left was represented by

Argentines wearing the national colors. She also then implied that there were not differences between the Trotskyist left of the twenty-first century and the military agents of repression of the Dirty War. For her, there was no legitimate place either right or left beyond Kirchnerismo. History was at the service of the leaders who changed positions, but global contexts were equally significant. If during the time of neoliberalism there was one way to understand Peronism, when it turned to the left, there was no other legitimate space for the left. From this perspective, the non-Peronist right and left had no choice but to follow the leaders of the people and the nation.

In the 2010s, the Kirchner's nationalized the oil company that Menem had privatized, and Menem himself supported Kirchnerismo from his position in the senate.[24] But beyond these typical populist moments in the transformations of leaders like Menem and the Kirchners, what must be highlighted is the fluidity of populism: from its classical forms to its neoliberal and leftist versions, populism redefined itself in relationship to liberalism and dictatorship. This redefinition marked its radical differences with fascism.

THE LEADER AND THE PEOPLE

Fascism was a revolution against democracy. In contrast, after 1945, populism reformed the status quo, pushing an authoritarian form of democracy. This type of democracy had a dual nature. In speaking in the name of the people in a nonrevolutionary context, modern populism offered a democratic, anticommunist alternative. Populism attempted to democratize antiliberal politics during a time when fascism could no longer be considered sufficiently legitimate.

For General Perón, fascism could not be replicated. For a new epoch, a new truth was needed. Perón proposed a new form of "organic" democracy: "What is an organic government? It is an aggregation of solidly united forces that has at its head a man of state, who needn't be a genius nor a sage, but rather a man on whom nature has bestowed a special condition to span a complete panorama that others don't see."[25] The organic nature of the movement would lead to political supremacy in the long term: "Our aspiration is not to rule for six years but to secure sixty years of government."[26] But it was clear to all that this supremacy would be achieved by winning plebiscitary elections that confirmed the dual nature of the leader, who was at the same time an elected representative and a quasi-transcendental conductor of people. The "true index of power" could not be understood without the "conductor," and true success in politics could not exist without him. As Perón often said, "The people should know ... that the conductor is born. He is not made, not by decree nor by elections." He added, "It is essential that the conductor finds his own molds, to later fill them with a content that will be in direct relation, according to his efficiency, with the sacred oil of Samuel that the conductor has received from God."[27]

Likewise, the Colombian leader Gaitán wanted to replace a democratic "simulation" with "true democracy." In 1945, he called for a "moral and democratic restoration" to replace the "political nation" with the nation of the people. Democracy had defeated fascism, and with this defeat, the "victory of violence" was substituted for the triumph of "Christian civilization." Gaitán famously invoked God to say the divinity knew what was best for Colombia, just as he and his followers did.[28] Nonetheless, the leader was not exclusively conceived as a semigod whose power derived only from the sacred. The power of the leader emanated from his "umbilical" links with the people and with their common battle against the enemies of the nation.

In Venezuela, the populist leader Rómulo Betancourt, who was deeply critical of fascism and communism, presented his own third way. A former communist turned anticommunist, Betancourt explained that he had renounced his interwar communism in favor of his own national democratic option. This renunciation was the result of economic conditions, but it was also "a reflection" determined by a deep Venezuelan and Latin American identity that was the outcome of "my almost biological ascription to my land and my people." His was a movement for those who "have deep faith in Venezuela." His party was "the Party of the People," and his opponents were the "antipatria" [antifatherland]." In 1948, Betancourt stated, "I was, I am and I will be with the people and against their historical enemies." By appealing to history, Betancourt in fact referenced an epic, transhistorical fight between good and evil. Only the party and the government of the people, which stood for "social justice and national liberation" could represent "true democracy." Populism was defined by its rejection of historical dictatorships. The party had "returned" to the people their "usurped sovereignty." This model politically delegitimated opponents, who were nonetheless expected to participate in the democratic process. In fact, enemies were vaguely defined. They were "historical" insofar as they had always stood against the people. Most times, the enemies included communists and imperialists as well as the oligarchs and the political class.[29] In 1946, Gaitán told Venezuelans that the Betancourt's regime was the first stage, the gaining of political freedom, but democracy would remain formal if it were not followed by "the conquest of economic and social freedom." Also for Gaitán, the usual enemies included the fascists, plutocracy, oligarchy, and politics as usual. Politics was a battle, and he was "the captain of the Colombian multitudes," or as he also said in 1947, he was a "soldier," who had volunteered for "a mission on the battlefront." For Gaitán, "The people were superior to their leaders," and leaders could represent only "the voice of the people for the people." On the other side of the leader-people equations were the antipeople—those who had turned "their backs" to the people."[30] Similarly, for Perón the "Argentine drama" was a fight between the people and the "antipeople." The existence of the latter meant that the fight was "ideological," but for the populist leader, the transcendental nature of the fight also meant that this was a key moment in the history of Argentine emancipation. For a leader who was banned from his own country and was in exile at the time he uttered these words, such an extraordinary moment did not mean, however, moving beyond electoral procedures but rather calling for their reinstatement. Peronism called once again for the people's participation in the fight against social and economic limits to democracy. But without acknowledging any contradiction, Perón also stated, "Our enemies are in reality the enemies of the people."[31]

Peronism acted in the name of the people and of a united nation, and he advocated for full electoral rights for the citizens. Like other populisms, Peronists considered democratic elections were the primary way of defeating the enemy. But the links between the leader and the people also bypassed electoral forms and were believed to transcend the particular context and even the nation. The fight for a third way went beyond the two imperialisms, the two "spurious forces that emerged after the Second World War." For Perón, what was at stake was not only the destiny "of Argentina or of its people but also the destiny of the world and all of its peoples."[32] This idea of an all-or-nothing global confrontation with evil forces was reproduced many times in the years to come. If General Perón understood his own links with the people to be related to his own persona as a military man, Comandante Hugo Chávez identified himself as a Peronist: "I am deeply a Peronist with all my heart, because General Perón was a soldier of Latin America and of the people." He also presented himself as a "soldier of the people" who obeyed only them. Chávez stated, "Those who are not chavistas are not Venezuelans."[33]

These connections between the leader and the people followed an ideal of politics as creating what Andreas Kalyvas called the "politics of the extraordinary." In the case of populism, this meant advancing its own political moment as one that transcended more normal times as they generally functioned in history.[34]

These links also transcended issues of representation or specific policies or ideas. As Gaitán explained, no leader could effectively impose passions, thoughts, or determinations onto the people. The leader was not a man who could act on the masses in the same way that an artist provided perennial life to dead objects: "The leader of the great popular movements is the one who possesses the sensitivity and flexibility to capture and synthesize in a given moment the drives that exist in the agitated undercurrents of the collective soul." The leader was in short, an "antenna" who gathered at the top what emerged from below. He then synthesized popular demands from ethics to aesthetics.[35] A profound concern with the poor, and the mix of equalitarianism, nationalism, and rhetorical demonization of the enemy created an organized community that combined acclamation, delegation, and more traditional democratic procedures and institutions. Like Peronists, Colombians and Brazilians witnessed the transformation of liberal and fascist ideas of democracy into what their populist leaders (Gaitán and Vargas) understood as an organic form of democracy that moved the masses beyond liberalism and communism.

Fascism in history represented a theoretical and practical rejection of the idea of democratic representation, or of any democratic possibility, the natural result of which was establishment of dictatorship. After 1945, this idea of dictatorial representation was defeated, and junta dictatorial leaders such as Perón destroyed dictatorship from within.

Peronism was the first regime in history to engineer such a change from dictatorship to authoritarian delegative democracy.[36] Fascism had been defeated. Perón understood very well that the new order, his widely proclaimed third way between capitalism and communism, had to be framed as a democracy. In his 1947 "message to the world," Perón argued that it was not acceptable that "humanity should be destroyed in a holocaust of right-wing or left-wing hegemonies."[37]

Central to the Peronist third way was figuring out how to practice illiberal politics in a democratic key. All traditions were now up for grabs, and Perón took from left and right. Perón's was an attempt to continue the tradition of the anti-Enlightenment in the context of the Cold War. Perón was the strongman, the *caudillo*, who embodied a novel form of politics in power. He not only incarnated the people and the nation but a new postwar ideological synthesis to gain power in the name of the people and, in practice, to rule instead of them. Given the centrality of authoritarian leaders to any complete version of populism, it is surprising that for some scholars of populism, "The authoritarian characteristic of the strongman is not inherent to populism." This view depends on affirming the dual stereotype that Latin American is essentially the region of strongmen and that strongmen are naturally absent in Europe and the United States. In fact, Latin America does not exclusively own the populist notion of leadership. This is a global phenomenon, not a Latin American one.[38]

The same personalist attempts, but in a twenty-first-century context, were made by leaders such as Donald Trump and Marine Le Pen. Le Pen's presidential campaign in 2017 was clearly about affirming the embodiment of the French nation in her persona, as shown in her campaign clip, properly entitled "In the Name of the People." Against the right and the left, Le Pen claimed that she was the only candidate of the French people. It was in and through her own persona that her administration would be "French First." Le Pen echoed Trump's own slogan of America First. This was a slogan that in the United States was first used by fascist fellow travelers in the 1930s. If this fascist pedigree did not cause a problem for Trump, Le Pen in turn denied any role in the Holocaust for the French collaborators of the Nazis, who in truth had made possible the deportation of Jews to the camps. In both Le Pen's and Trump's cases, there was no difference between their idea of giving "first" priority to the country and to themselves. They were populist authoritarian leaders to the core. But in the history of populism, this politics of the populist strongman initially emerged after 1945, with the first populist regime.[39] In this sense, and to put it hyperbolically, Trump became the American Perón. That the most powerful country on earth became a global center of populism was striking to many observers, but in the United States as well the rise in inequality and the fusion of neoliberalism and technocracy were too significant to be ignored.

The Tea Party and Trumpism both represented an authoritarian American response to these global patterns. To be sure, Donald Trump's extremism echoed that of past Republicans leaders like Barry Goldwater and Richard Nixon—as well as independent candidates such as George Wallace—with Trump explicitly repeating Nixon's invocation of the "silent majority." For Nixon and Trump, that majority was clearly white, even if their framing was not as explicit as some of their most segregationist followers. Especially for many followers of Trumpism, the majority did not include the Western and Eastern seaboards of the country. In 1964, Goldwater displayed a similarly clear-cut antiurban and anti–East Coast sensibility. He actually said that if the East Coast were sawed off and floated away to the sea, the country would be better off.[40]

More so than in other histories of populism, race has been central to American populism. Nevertheless, for many global historians of fascism and populism, Trumpism was something entirely new and was a decidedly new low from the perspective of the threat on democracy. Its place at the top of the Republican ticket, and its winning of the presidency, signaled a new kind of American preeminence—in line with a strain of xenophobic right-wing populism that has been developing around the world.

During the campaign, mixing racism, religious discrimination, and antimigration and anti-integration rhetoric, Trump presented himself on the global stage as a new dominant world leader for the populist pack. His rhetoric also included calling for the imprisonment or expulsion of his opponent, Hillary Clinton. The "lock her up" chant was a prevailing theme of the campaign, as were the Trumpists' ritual calls for violence against Clinton at campaign events. At one presidential debate, Trump himself threatened her with jail time in the event he became the president, and he had also previously suggested that Clinton should be "deported."[41] Calls for political rivals and others to be imprisoned by acclamation have a specific history. Fascists (always) and populists (often) have both used prison to deal with the opposition.

In his leadership style, Trump is less like previous Republican candidates and more akin to the likes of Marine Le Pen in France, Recep Tayyip Erdogan in Turkey, and Nicolás Maduro in Venezuela. All of these powerful leaders were, in turn, reminiscent of historical figures like General Juan Perón in Argentina and Getúlio Vargas in Brazil, who converted fascist ideas into the populist form of electoral authoritarianism.

Leaders like Perón sent opponents to jail. They made a point of casting those they did not like—whether political opponents, the media, or the judiciary—as enemies rather than as interlocutors or sectors of society entitled to different opinions. Nonetheless, not all populists are the same, even those that arise in the same context. Perón, for example, remembered a conversation with Vargas, who told him he needed to follow a politics of conciliation at the time of his second presidency in the 1950s. Perón said that Vargas was wrong because "In politics first one needs domination, and then conciliation comes as a result of it." In the same instance, and with respect to the people's "international" consciousness, Perón stated that he knew "my people wanted what I wanted."[42]

The idea of a leader who is the proverbial subject, who knows about everything and has decided to ignore what he does not know, was especially powerful in the theory and practice of Trumpism. Perón's idea of a leader who thinks and decides for the people, and whose legitimacy is reassured but not created by the votes, was put forward similarly by Donald Trump many years later, when he stated that there was a direct link between natural intuition, predestination, action, and legitimation. He argued, "I am a very instinctual person but my instinct turns out to be right." The inner self provided a truth that was a natural knowledge emanating from the leader incarnated in the people. Trump stated, "I happen to be a person that knows how life works. I said I was going to win the election, I won the election." In populism, the triumph of the will was confirmed by electoral means. And when the moment of regime formation finally arrived, owning the power of decision was itself a form of legitimation, or as Trump put it, "I can't be doing so badly, because I am president, and you're not." Trump identified democracy as the moment of his election as the leader of the country. But elections such as his own were not just another chapter in the electoral history of the country. In a speech toward the end of his successful campaign, Trump stated that he defended the people against a "global power structure" and against the national media and political elites: "This is not simply another four-year election. This is a crossroads in the history of our civilization that will determine whether or not we the people reclaim control over our government." According to this fiction, it was the leader who, in returning power to the people, took it away from their enemies. Trumpism was the last reverberation of a long history of absolute democratic claims by populist leaders who aspired to embody the victory of civilization.[43]

Likewise, classical Latin American populist leaders presented their politics as those of fighting for the true people's representation in the context of a civilizational apocalyptic fight between good and evil. The idea of incarnation led to the proclamation of the leader's indispensability, even to the extent that the election of the leader represented the last opportunity for the nation. The sense of emergency was a result of the projection of friend-enemy positions and military strategies onto the opponents. As Trump's claimed, "For them it's a war, and for them nothing at all is out of bounds. This is a struggle for the survival of our nation, believe me. And this will be our last chance to save it on November 8 — remember that." Trump told his followers that his election marked "our independence day." Perón had similarly identified his leadership with a long history of military conquerors who were, like him, conductors of the people: "The history of the world, through the examples of Alexander, Julius Cesar, Frederick or Napoleon, shows that victory belongs to those that know to lift and conduct the people." Perón identified his own election with a second "independence" and maintained that, "God put me on earth for the independence and the freedom of the Argentine people."[44]

The leader was predestined to serve the people by becoming them. The idea that the body of the leader no longer mattered, or to put it differently that his leadership replaced personal needs with the people's desires, was taken to its fullest logical conclusion by Vargas, who killed himself in the name of the people and against their internal and external enemies. In his famous testament, written just before his personal and political suicide in 1954, Vargas defined himself as a "slave" of the Brazilian people. He took the first step in the "path of eternity." He was leaving "life to enter history." His "holocaust" was going to keep the people united, and his "name would become the flag of your fight." Just as he had given the people his "life," he now offered them "his death."[45] Much later on, the deaths of Néstor Kirchner (2010) and Hugo Chávez (2013) were also widely interpreted by their successors as political sacrifices. As with Vargas, and later Eva Perón, the myths surrounding them were put to practical use to add another layer of legitimacy to the dual nature of populist sovereignty.

To be sure, the deaths of Kirchner and Chávez were not political, in the sense that heart failure and cancer are by definition apolitical. But their deaths were widely presented as the sacrificial acts of devoted leaders, who put the interests of the people before or beyond the physical needs of their own bodies. When Eva Perón died of cancer, the Peronist regime officially proclaimed, "The secretariat of information of the Presidency fulfills its extremely painful obligation to inform the people of the Republic that at the hour 20.25, the Señora Eva Perón, Spiritual Leader of the nation has passed away." After her death, every single day, all radio programs stated, "It is 8:25 pm, the time when Eva Perón passed into immortality." In her last speech, Eva Perón famously said to a multitude that she would gladly give her life for the people. She said, "I know God is with us" and against the "arrogant oligarchy." She asked the people to remain "faithful to Perón" and against the enemies from within and from without. And she concluded her political life by uttering these words: "I never wanted and I do not want anything for me. My glory is and always will be the emblem of Perón and the flag of my people. Even when I leave behind the remnants of my life, I know you will pick up my name and will take it as a flag to victory."[46]

Many years later, probably with Eva Perón famous speech in mind, Ernesto Laclau, the most important intellectual of Kirchnerismo, defined the mourning for Néstor Kirchner as "perhaps the most immense expression of collective grief in Argentina history." But he also insisted that, after his death, Kirchner transcended a mere symbolic nature to become something more transcendental. He also stated that Kirchner's widow now occupied Néstor Kirchner's place: "Cristina is not alone.... She is followed by an entire people." For Laclau, the "personification of power" in Cristina Kirchner offered "more democratic guarantees than the dilution of power." The Kirchners represented "the concentration of a name" in a series of processes for democratic change.[47]

The legacy of the leader transcended his life and became one with the people and the new leader. The constant references to a transcendental dead Chávez who presided from the sky in Venezuela took on a more extreme tone, but the logic was the same. Chávez himself had said that precisely because of the fact that he embodied the people even in death he will remain with the people, "I am like Nietzsche's eternal return.... I come from many deaths.... Even when I am gone I will remain with you on these streets and under this sky.... Chávez is now an entire invincible people." After Chávez' death, his successor Nicolás Maduro, typically stated that Chávez was now "the child, the man and the woman. We are all Chávez."[48]

From beyond the grave, populism worked in tandem with political resurrection.

In terms of populist style and ideology, these populist leaders died as they had lived—in the name of the people and in a total fight against their imagined and real internal and external enemies. All populists claim to talk for the masses and against the elites, just as Trump declared, "I am your voice." But in practice, they replace the voices of the citizens with their own singular voice. Decrying a diverse plurality of American voices, the American right showed the world that America and Trumpism were writing a new chapter in the long global history of authoritarian challenges to democracy.

While rooted in fascism, this American populist chapter was very different from fascism. It did not proposed politics as dictatorship. With modern populism, the illiberal politics of the masses returned to the politics of electoral representation. These politics had many populist articulations—classical populisms in Latin America; free market populism; left-wing neo-populisms in Latin America, Europe, and beyond; extreme right wing populism; among others—but historically they generally used the name of the primordial and total leader to imagine and actualize a democracy that surpassed more ordinary politics of representation.

DEMOCRACY IN THE NAME OF THE FATHER

As an ideology, populism in history often blended a vertical understanding of the political with a notion of irreducible enemies, a unique national identity, and even a unique form of thinking. Ideas could be controlled by, and even reduced to, the changing dictum of the leader. Theological notions were combined with unitary conceptions of people, leader, and nation. Cristina Kirchner even created a "Secretariat of National Thinking" in 2014. Maduro formed "the Vice Ministry for the Supreme Social Happiness of the People" in 2013. Maduro wanted to transcend the "welfare state," meaning forms of social advancement within capitalism, and also connect social work with heaven, from where Chávez was supposed to be watching.[49] When both institutions were created, the invocation of the names of the deceased leaders Kirchner and Chávez was obsessively and ritually asserted, happiness, and thinking could not be dissociated from the names that had incarnated the people. The Argentine secretariat for national thinking brought together politicians and scholars, who were close to, or often worked with or received funds from, the Argentine administration. It also invoked connections among populists globally by inviting key leaders of the Podemos Party and organizing a 2015 international forum on the thought of the key theorist of populism Ernesto Laclau.

Laclau, the most significant theorist of populist democracy, unwillingly became a philosopher of power. In time, his name became synonymous with populist politics and the concept of populism itself. As Beatriz Sarlo has observed, Argentine populists did not engage with his highly specialized Lacanian-Schmittian vocabulary and work, but he was celebrated as the preeminent theorist of Argentina's early twenty-first-century populism.[50] Laclau's name itself came to speak for many demands. In translating Laclau for the wider public, many populist intellectuals engaged with Laclau's theory of the symbolic and simplified his theory of democratization as accomplished through the politics of naming the leader. For example, the secretariat of national thinking adapted Laclau's idea of the antagonist-populist rupture to the oldest traditions in Argentine history, establishing a clear frontier between the name Kirchnerismo and "barbarism." In this apocalyptical framework, a simplification that radicalized Laclau's political theology, the power of the Kirchners was opposed to a more sinister "real and traditional power." The "eternal forms of power" had been attacked by a name that provoked a "refoundation of politics."[51]

Never reaching the secretary's hyperbolic elevation of the Kirchner name, and also never accepting a public position that was offered to him by the Kirchners, nonetheless in his public appearances, Laclau performed the need to defend a populist moment that for him and many admirers had become unified with his own theories of populism as the only path to democracy.

In his academic work, Laclau himself had argued that populist moments of transformation were intrinsic to the name of the leader. He argued, for example, that only the leader could fully and purely represent the democratic homogeneity he advocated for:

> The construction of a popular subjectivity is possible only on the basis of discursively producing tendentially empty signifiers. The so-called "poverty" of the populist symbols is the condition of their political efficacy—as their function is to bring to equivalential homogeneity a highly heterogeneous reality, they can only do so

on the basis of reducing to a minimum their particularistic content. At the limit, this process reaches a point where the homogenizing function is carried out by a pure name: the name of the leader.[52]

In his public appearances in Argentina, he stressed the centrality of the Kirchner name. Laclau was last interviewed for an Argentine newspaper psychoanalytic series of interviews called *Politicians on the Sofa,* where he defended the Kirchners, as well as his own theoretical approach. In his last years, Laclau found it difficult to integrate his criticism of power with a new defense of the established regimes in Argentina and Venezuela. He had become an organic intellectual of the populist government but was also an increasingly symptomatic defender of its more dubious facts. In other words, he failed to distinguish between populism as his ideal of democracy and the ambiguous democratic realities of Peronist populism as a regime. In response to the question of how he felt about the Kirchners' having become millionaires, a question that in Argentina became really important because of the Kirchners' dubious inability to explain how or why they had become immensely richer during their presidencies, Laclau playfully said that he also wanted to be rich. He also approved of Soccer for Everyone,[53] a program in which the Kirchner government had invested important state funds to make professional soccer free "for the people" to watch. Standing with soccer star Diego Maradona, Cristina Kirchner defended the program as an "act of democratization." To promote watching professional sport as an affirmation of democracy was one thing, but even more striking was declaring it an act against dictatorship. The president argued that before Kirchner, *fútbol* had been disappeared just like many Argentine citizens had been during the Dirty War of the 1970s. Speaking to the people, she said that private TV had "kidnapped your goals ... as they had kidnapped 30.000 Argentines." This was the context of Laclau's support for the Soccer for Everyone program.[54]

Laclau, the theorist of the underdog, found himself in the uncomfortable position of praising power. Given the complexity of his own theoretical model, his simplification and adaptation of it to fit the ambiguities of Kirchnerismo are perplexing. This was a process of construction in the sense that he also used his model to speak in the name of the people. This radical constructivism was quite far from the historiographical approach that had defined his early academic career as a historian. What made this possible, as Arato observes, was that for Laclau, the people are constructed from a section of the citizens, which then become the whole. Thus, the leader is essential in providing the newly invented people with the "empty signifier" of the leader's name. In this sense, Arato argues that Laclau "explicitly advocates not only the construction of 'the people' in an entirely voluntaristic manner, but filling the empty space of power by leadership incarnating a subject that does not exist."[55]

From Spain to Argentina and beyond, Laclau was celebrated, and he felt the need to support his political hosts even when he was engaged in academic conferences in Argentina. But Laclau also was able to insert some criticisms of Kirchnerismo as insufficiently polarizing, for example, when he stated that Kirchnerismo "had a populist vocation," but it was short of populism in its deeds. Laclau was critical of the lack of a clear friend-enemy demarcation in Kirchnerismo, especially in the sense of establishing an "internal frontier" that would effectively divide the "popular" camp from the other camp. Laclau argued that classical Peronism had done this, as had Evo Morales's and Hugo Chávez's, in Bolivia and Venezuela, respectively, where the leaders were also indispensable. Laclau defended strong executives against parliamentarianism.[56] In his essay "The Legacy of Néstor Kirchner," Laclau argued that Kirchner stood against reactionaries, representing the popular will against the status quo. Kirchner presented a choice between "the corporative Argentina of the past or popular Argentina." Laclau stated, "It is on the threshold of this confrontation that the name of Néstor Kirchner will always remain a liminal and path breaking sign. It will no longer be a flag for the fights, it has been transformed into something most important, in a symbol for our consciousness."[57]

After Laclau's death in 2014, President Cristina Kirchner said that the critics of Laclau were rooted "in stupidity and ignorance." They ignored, she said, that Argentina had been divided in two since its independence in 1810. Laclau's last book, where he reflects on his own Marxist background but without sufficiently analyzing the extent of his own attempts to link Peronism and Marxism, Laclau reads Argentine history after 1955 through the prism of Peronism, radically opposing it to dictatorship and downplaying its dictatorial, militaristic, and neofascist tendencies. In his view, Peronism had been the site for the creation of a new left "national and popular and entirely different from the traditional liberal left." What was absent from this picture was the persistence of a nonliberal and non-Peronist left and, more generally, the complexities of Argentine history. What was present was Laclau's theory of populism as the only form of politics and the consequential idea that Argentina's left-wing populism homogenously represented democracy in the country.[58] This reduction of history to experience, and of history to theory, also applied to more recent events. For Laclau, Kirchner, like Chávez or Morales, had represented his own thinking through their political actions, but for many populist followers, his theoretical thinking was linked to the voices of the people and their populist leaders.

At Argentina's state conference on Laclau, the minister of culture argued that Laclau was a "decisive thinker that got out of what is merely academic and he knew how to listen to the great Latin American popular traditions." For these politicians, Laclau also spoke in the name of the people. The meeting took place in the monumental Kirchner Cultural Center in Buenos Aires, a fact of great symbolic importance according to Chantal Mouffe, the theorist and widow of Laclau, who stressed Laclau's "identification with Néstor."[59] The Kirchner Center was the most symbolic moment of the Kirchner name being inscribed in Argentina's political and actual landscape. But it was not unique, just bigger than many other eponymous Kirchner sites. Locations, symbols, and objects with the name Kirchner proliferated in Argentina even before the leader died. They included national buildings, streets, a police station, an airport, a gas pipeline, cafeterias, highways, the "Néstor Kirchner Center of Studies," stadiums, the 2011 national soccer tournament, tunnels, neighborhoods, cultural centers, bus stations, hospitals, and bridges.[60]

In terms of continuities with a long Peronist tradition, the most symbolic of these sites of populist naming was the Néstor Kirchner student hostel, which was located on Carlos Menem Street in La Rioja Province. The reductionism of an ideology centered around the political desires of the leader led to the imposition of the leader's name across the country. There was a Peronist precedent to this. In Perón's time, two provinces (Chaco and La Pampa) were named after Juan and Eva Perón. When Eva Perón died, the city of La Plata was renamed after her. A similar obsession with proper names can be seen in leaders like Trump and Berlusconi. Typical murals for Berlusconi reproduced his name a thousand times and included the words, "We are all with Silvio," meaning that all Italians were in a sense little Berlusconis and that the body of the king, as Hobbes would have it, contained the people. Trump also projected his name as the reflection of his ideology. His mixing of business and populism was preceded by his commercial fixation on naming towers, beef, casinos, wine, and clothing after himself. He launched his campaign from the famous Trump Tower, one of the many towers bearing the Trump name that populate New York City. Among them is the skyscraper named "Trump World Tower," an icon of affluent skyline disruption located at the United Nations Plaza. The fact that Trump had positioned his luxury building proximal to the United Nations building acquired new meanings when Hillary Clinton launched her own presidential campaign at Roosevelt Island's "Four Freedoms Park." This monument to Roosevelt's antifascism faces both the United Nations and the Trump building. In 2015 and 2016, these commercially named buildings in New York, a city which stands as a global icon of cosmopolitanism and cultural diversity, became fully politicized as symbols of a leader who stood against globalization and multiculturalism.

Born and raised in New York, Trump represented a view of populism in the city that set the United Nations and minorities in opposition to traditions of segregation and discrimination. Here it is worth remembering that the business Trump had inherited from his father was also rooted in serious accusations of racial discriminations against African Americans, as the antifascist singer Woody Guthrie, the author of the American anthem of inclusion "This Land is your Land," and a tenant of the Trumps in the early 1950s, sang about the president's father: "I suppose that Old Man Trump knows just how much racial hate / He stirred up in that bloodpot of human hearts / When he drawed that color line / Here at his Beach Haven family project / Beach Haven ain't my home! / No, I just can't pay this rent!"[61]

It was precisely in the postwar years that a new modern populism began its ascendance in American politics, first with McCarthyism and later with the presidential candidacies of Barry Goldwater and the Alabama governor George Wallace. Wallace, the candidate of "law and order," had criticized his predecessor for being "soft on the nigger question." In 1963, he attacked a government that he saw as desiring to turn politicians into the category of a "master of the people" and as "being the opposite of Christ." He stressed the need to maintain "segregation now! Segregation tomorrow!" Wallace defended racism "in the name of the greatest people that have ever trod this earth." By the people he meant American whites. Famously, Wallace had argued that New York City was not precisely an example for the rest of the country: "In New York City you can't walk in Central Park at night without fear of being raped, or mugged, or shot."[62]

It was precisely this idea of Central Park as the place that signaled what was wrong with the country that first brought political notoriety to a then young populist-in-the-making. The context was the "Central Park Five" case in 1989. As CNN explained, "The case involved five teenage boys of color, who were wrongly accused and convicted of beating and raping a woman in Central Park. Trump purchased full-page ads that ran in several New York City newspapers that read, 'Bring Back The Death Penalty. Bring Back Our Police!'" The wrongly accused men "were later exonerated in 2002, when another man confessed to the crime and DNA backed up his confession." In 1989, in reference to this case, Trump argued, "The ad's basically very strong and vocal, they are saying bring back law and order. And I'm not just referring to New York, I'm referring to everything." He stated "Maybe hate is what we need if we're gonna get something done." This early combination of "law and order," and racist arguments could be considered a *populist* rehearsal and would later be the trademark for his successful ran for the presidency. Following a long-standing tradition that Argentine jurist Roberto Gargarella aptly calls "penal populism," Trump called for harsh measures against crime that were supposed to be rooted in the will of the people. Populist leaders imagine the people want them as their primary law givers and judges. Trump justified himself by stressing a wide popular support for his actions, but of course the "people" were never consulted in practice.[63]

If American populism throughout its history has combined its politics of resentment with the notion of the working people as a white "silent majority" that either potentially or implicitly rejected cosmopolitan city realities, and the minorities that lived and worked in them, not all populisms embraced this typically American type of populist exclusion. In other words, not all populists identify the demos with the ethnos, the people and the race, but all of them identify the people with the workers and producers and the antipeople with those that either do not work or do not work enough. This "producerism" is a key component of the populist understanding of the people.

Generally, populist leaders personify by name the united people, whom they place in opposition to the antipeople—the elites and traitors they fought against. In a 2013 speech symbolically delivered at the Piazza del Popolo (the People's Square) in Rome, Berlusconi rhetorically renamed it People of Freedom Square after his own party. He argued that the speech was for a new Italy, and he spoke for those without political representation. According to Berlusconi, he and his followers were the legitimate Italian people. He told those "that are with me ... all of us, together, we represent Italians of good will, good sense, of good faith. We represent the Italy that works and produces. The Italy of women and men that want to remain free. We are the people of freedom." Berlusconi argued, "We are the best Italy and we are the majority of Italy." Berlusconi finished his speech in typical populist fashion. He quoted Gandhi, described his neoliberal economic proposals, conflated his persona with his party and freedom, and announced that he was symbolically hugging each follower. The followers responded by shouting over and over that Berlusconi was their only love, and singing the anthem "Meno male che Silvio c'è," or "Thank Goodness That Silvio Exists." The anthem was first introduced in a TV spot in 2008, where an ethnically homogeneous group of Italians representing different classes of workers, with the young specially featured, repeatedly sang the phrase "At least there is Silvio." The 1990s aesthetic of the spot combined a melodic cheesiness with images of multitudes embracing a long Italian flag, but Berlusconi himself was absent from the picture. The invocation of his name conveyed that he was more an omniscient parental equation of people and nation than an ordinary citizen. The people followed, and invoked the name of, the leader to ensure there was no other legitimate form of political representation beyond Berlusconi. In other speeches, Berlusconists represented their slogan "We are all with Silvio" by wearing Berlusconi masks.[64] From Berlusconi's frame of reference, there was no legitimate place for the supposed minority of those who did not support Il Cavaliere's multiclass conflation of the country and people. The message was that they represented poor sense, bad faith, and even oppression.

General Perón had also argued that the people "are the humble men of all conditions. They are the only class of Argentine we recognize: the class of people that work." Also for Perón, the ones who did not work, the ones whom by inference he could not recognize as Argentines, were linked to the political opposition. They were the antipeople— "anti-Peronist … antirevolutionary and retrogrades of reaction."[65] Here the enemy appears once again as the enemy of freedom, a freedom that for Perón was always under attack from the *demoliberalismo*.

Later, for Menem, Fujimori, and Berlusconi, the enemy of freedom was the left. Similarly, Trump and Marine Le Pen accused their enemies of following dated ideologies and putting forward proposals that would undermine democracy, while Cristina Kirchner identified all people who charged her with intolerance with the extreme left, the extreme right, and the military dictatorship. While Perón, George Wallace, and many other cold war populists explicitly denied they were fascists, the new populists like Marine Le Pen, Trump, or Erdogan actually presented their own enemies as "totalitarian" Nazis or fascists.[66]

Wallace famously rebuked protesters accusing him of being fascist by stating, "I was killing fascists when you punks were in diapers." Even when he was the leader of dictatorship in 1944, Perón published in the main opposition newspaper a detailed explanation of "why the Argentine government is not fascist." The conductor, who was not yet elected, nonetheless expressed "his faith in democratic institutions" and stressed the fact that the regime held extremely high popular support. For Peronism, if the people supported the regime, that meant those against it were enemies of the nation as a whole, representing a "nefarious epoch," in which democracy existed only in "appearance" but not in reality.[67] Chavismo also reproduced the classical Peronist ideological points about the people and the regime as One and the antipeople as opposition. For Comandante Chávez, the project of the opposition was "an enemy of the Venezuelan people."

Chávez argued against the "democracy of elites," saying "representative democracy is counterrevolutionary. A government enclosed within four walls expropriates the people's sovereignty and is counterrevolutionary." In 2009, after winning a reelection referendum, and in announcing his new candidacy for reelection in 2012, Chávez juxtaposed the truth of the people's victory and the dignity of the fatherland against the lies of the opposition. He vowed never to return to the "indignity of the past," to which the opposition wanted to return. He promised to "open the gates of the future." At times, he identified the opposition with prehistoric times, proclaiming "the man of the future is Chávez."[68]

From the populist left to the populist right, democracy needed to be distanced from its liberal representative version. One important dimension in this idea of the enemy as those standing against freedom and democracy was that, while these populist leaders often claimed the recuperation of a fictional, departed golden past to identify themselves, their nations, and their people with the present and the future, the enemies were always marked as holdovers from a decadent past that no longer corresponded with the will of the people. In short, they were enemies identified with a dated political system that stood against true democracy. The independent media became the perfect example of a regime of empirically based truth and a notion of check and balances that the populists put in question. In this context, a deep suspicion, and at times a demonization, of the independent press was coupled with a populist strategy to use and manipulate the independent media—to publicize its political spectacles while also enforcing its ideological notion of politics as a battle over media power, especially against the independent media. The independent media were thus presented as a key enemy of the leader of the people. Here populism was also following and reformulating the experience of fascism.

FROM CLASSIC PROPAGANDA TO THE NEW MEDIA LANDSCAPE

In the transition to mass democratic politics, classical versions of populism followed on the footsteps of fascism. They shared a view of the media as the key vehicle for propaganda. In populism, the media's primary role was to aestheticize politics, which meant rearranging what had previously been fascist personalist propaganda in a democratic key. In contrast with fascism, the populist version of politics as spectacle worked in tandem with electoral procedures, and never replaced them altogether. There are limits to populist media acclamation. Postwar Peronist propaganda, for example, relied on the overpowering concept of Juan and Eva Perón as the parents of the people, but it also stressed the fact that their regime was repeatedly reelected. A variety of media were used under Peronism, including newspapers, movies, radio, and magazines. The compulsive repetition of the leader's words and images, by himself and by many other "little Peróns," displaced the need to offer complex explanations of programs or ideas. From the perspective of the populist leader, the doctrine existed to root out, and eventually correct, the unbelievers. The realizations of the leader were more important than abstract theory. Perón asserted that "The doctrine is the final aim because it is incarnated in the collective soul of the community" But in fact, the doctrine existed to affirm a solid belief in whatever Perón had said or done. He constantly actualized the ideology of the movement through his control of his own words and images and, increasingly, of the national media.[69]

Similarly, in the 1990s, populist leaders vilified the media, using state media, and in Berlusconi's case his own media empire, to provide a clear and controlled message. Like Perón and many others, these neoliberal populist leaders demonized the independent media, even suggesting at times that the media were their main enemies. And like any enemy, the media could be defeated by populist democracy, as Carlos Menem argued after his presidential victory in 1995. Similar situations unfolded with populist leaders such as Chávez and Erdogan. Some of their efforts to control words and images, and to silence the independent press, were rather "traditional." But everything changed when new channels of communication, including social media, became available. Most populist leaders have excelled at using modern technologies to establish direct links with the citizens, bypassing the mediation of the press. This has been especially, but not exclusively, useful for leaders in the opposition.

In his successful bid for the presidency, Trump was able, surprisingly and successfully, to combine sustained attention from the independent press with more direct means of electronic communication, especially Twitter. Talking about the press, Trump stated, "They're trying desperately to suppress my vote and the voice of the American people." Since Trump's populist schema conceived of him as the embodiment of the nation and its people, he could understand the critical responses of the media to his own acts against women, immigrants, and other minorities only as attempts to curtail American sovereignty. In this sense, Donald Trump's campaign perfectly executed the populist playbook. If populist leaders who are not yet in power define themselves in terms of their hostility toward independent media, even while they use them to spread their messages, they often shift away from instrumental use of the media to active, explicit attacks on media autonomy when they are in charge of the government. Even the possibility of an electoral loss must be attributed to a broad, -antidemocratic conspiracy of media elites "rigging" the system to block the will of the people, who are incarnated in his or her candidacy. Trump's appeal was in part owing to the powerful lies circulating between him and his supporters. The latter's belief in them was apparently impervious to empirical disproof produced by a fact-checking media that Trump regarded as an elite enemy of the people.

Populists overemphasize the importance of the media by placing it at the center of politics. As we argue with Pablo Piccato and Fabián Bosoer, populists see politics as spectacle, a cultural battle between those who defend the interests of the "true" people of the nation and the media, elites, and minorities that guard antinational interests. Freedom of expression is acceptable just as long as it means the leader is giving voice to "the common man."[70] On the basis of a postfascist view of democracy, in which authoritarianism and demonization replace tolerance and open dialogue, Trump blamed political criticism on the existence of a free press. This is why he came to view the independent press as a key adversary of his own politics. Internet blogs and other nontraditional media enabled Trump to bring the messengers of the right into full view. He returned to a premodern conception of the press as conveyors of bias, and made the CEO of *Breitbart*, the alt-right, white supremacist website, the director of his campaign. The *New York Times, Washington Post,* CNN, and other media outlets were frequently the main fodder for his attacks.[71]

For Argentines, Trump was singing an old familiar song. For ten years, the former presidents Néstor Kirchner and Cristina

Fernández de Kirchner launched an offensive against critical media, choosing *Clarín,* one of the most important newspapers in the country, as their main target. They blamed the newspaper for all the problems they had governing, even distributing T-shirts and socks bearing the slogan *"Clarín* is lying" and constantly declaring that *Clarín* was crooked. Moving from demonization to practice, they used the Argentine IRS to harass the newspaper with audits and, eventually, antimonopoly laws that benefited media owned by friends of the populist leaders. Similar methods were used in countries like Venezuela and Ecuador in the first two decades of the twenty-first century.[72]

Populist aggression toward the autonomy of the press does not mean that populists refuse to use it as yet another vehicle to promote politics. Criticizing the press attracts its attention. When populists reach government, the dialogue between those in power and the opposition tends to be replaced with a reinvigorated focus on the press as a key enemy of the government, the leader, and the nation.

Thus, in recent and present-day versions of populism, the strategy of accusing the press of acting as agents for distributing the propaganda of the leader's enemies has been combined with the use of new Internet communication technologies, especially twitter, that stress the links between authoritarian leaders and their "followers." As Beatriz Sarlo observes, if politics is increasingly complex and multipolar, politics as it works in the social networks tends to be seen in binary terms. In this sense, social media and populism are perfect for each other.[73] Populists are disposed to regard independent reporters as deeply suspect, and even as enemies, and technology allows them to bypass the press to connect directly with their followers. This unprecedented, unmediated access to their supporters allows populist leaders to distinguish themselves from politicians and highlight their hostility toward politics as usual. The new technologies do not favor debate or open access to ideas but rather acutely downplay the relevance of key democratic institutions like a free press. The idea that the unmediated, and unquestioned, voice of the leader represents the truth works in tandem with the fantasy that traditional media have nothing to offer the public except lies.

Media and citizens' participation in politics are essentially intertwined. For populism, this synergistic relationship needs to be subsumed under its political imperative. As the Argentine media scholar Silvio Waisbord maintains, acute sensitivity toward the media is part of the DNA of populism. Its main contradiction is related to the dual need to speak for the majority of the people and a pyramidal structure of communication that affirms the word of the leader.[74] Especially because it is so successful in bypassing the scrutinizing function of independent journalism, populism affirms that it is the voice of the "silent majority." In theory, the lionized voice of the leader promotes people's participation in politics. In practice, the people's voice is a monologue by the leader that is free of journalistic mediations.

Populism's effective use of new media highlighted ideological ambiguities but also left them unquestioned. In this sense, populism's principles were affirmed through and by these technologies, just as liberal dogmas were. The uncritical and unreflective nature of the so-called twenty-four-hour news cycle was not invented by populism, but populism thrived under it to defeat neoliberalism. The result was an overall absence of detailed proposals and programs. As Jean Comaroff argues,

> Under late liberal conditions, when the old coordinates of left, right, and center seem profoundly unmoored, it is increasingly difficult to set these popular faces apart, in any thoroughgoing sense.

The ambiguous politics of populist leaders in contemporary Latin America, for example, might not be unprecedented, building as it does on the legacies of figures such as Perón and Bolívar. But it also seems to present an ever more intense, confusing amalgam of the progressive and the proto-fascist, having taken its current form in particular historical circumstances—among them, the advent of worldwide policies of deregulation, the extension of electronic media into ever more expansive and ever more personal realms of existence, and the mutation of a politics of class into identity-based movements and born-again theologies of one kind and another.[75]

A media regime that catered to identity, nation, and the sacred was a key factor in the success of populism.

The new populist uses of technology, including the leader's ability to "block" leader-identified undesirables who interfered with the message, did not strengthen the public's access to democracy but instead drummed out conflicting opinions. These synthetic messages did not require, and even prevented, analysis and explanations, making it even easier to conflate slogans and policies and to mock or demonize the enemies without having to face debate or scrutiny. When it comes to populism-by-Twitter, meaningful citizen participation in a leader's decisions is a mirage. As Umberto Eco noted, in both fascism and "Internet populism ... citizens do not act; they are only called on to play the role of the People."[76]

As with fascism, the populist spectacle of the people should not be conflated with populism at large. Style and aesthetics cannot be equated simply with an understanding of political ideology. New media technologies have been added to the populist repertoire, but its foundational approach to politics has not changed. In other words, in a changing media landscape, populism has adapted its media strategy, but the effect—replacing a diversity of voices with a singular one—is the same as it was before the array of innovative technologies became available.[77] Affirming a notion of sovereignty that relies on legitimacy conferred by elections, a leader who owned the truth and a vertical form of propaganda to sacralize him or her has always been central to the populist vision of democracy.

THE GODS OF POPULISM

Populism shares with the past century's other big isms—liberalism, communism, and fascism—the idea of popular sovereignty as the main source of legitimation for the political. In other words, in all these isms, the leadership is theoretically defined as the representative of the people by the people. Thus, populism, fascism, liberalism, and real socialism agree that the people are the main legitimating force for political representation. Of course, these political philosophies have historically differed on their theories and practices of representation. Fascism and real socialism proclaim the popular nature of the leadership to have mythical or teleological foundations. They do not need elections to confirm dictatorial revolutionary rule. In contrast, populism is closer to liberalism in its emphasis on electoral forms of representation. Unlike fascism, or real socialism, liberalism and populism stand rhetorically against dictatorship. In all these political ideological formations, and their contextual ramifications, the leader and the system are legitimized because the people want them, or so their interpreters declare. They disagree in practice in how to make that possible because liberalism and populism ultimately focus on electoral representation, while fascism and real socialism eschew electoral procedures to confirm the legitimacy of the leader, who is nonetheless presented as the ultimate and permanent representative of the people.

But if postwar populism and Cold War liberalism have historically shared a methodology of political representation rooted in democratic means, they belonged to significantly different ideological and intellectual traditions.

In theory, all these modern political isms equated democracy with mass participation. But the ideal of democratic expansion held by liberalism and communism was based in the tradition of the Enlightenment, while the fascist and populist versions were explicitly anti-Enlightenment. In fascism, and also to some extent in certain versions of populism, popular sovereignty was conceived as a rejection of the legacies of the French Revolution. Thus, if we focus on the theory, populism might be considered closer to dictatorship than it has been in practice. And yet one cannot understand ideas without accounting for their political experiences in history. Both dimensions affected and changed each other constantly, turning modern postfascist populism first, into a reformulation, and second, into a renunciation, of fascism.

More specifically, the constant interaction between democratic realities and authoritarian tendencies led postwar populism to present a dual source of legitimation: the leader is the leader because of electoral representation, but populist political theology also requires a firm belief in the leader as a transcendental, charismatic figure whose legitimacy goes beyond electoral representation.

Perón was represented as just such a Godlike figure. He often presented himself as working in tandem with the Lord by way of spreading the word, or as he said in 1953, by "preaching." Like many populist leaders of regimes who came after him, Perón used the sacred to validate his own persona and leadership.

According to him, he was "also helping God" to reveal his own mercy and greatness.[78] In Peronism, formal religion and political religion were simply conflated, but the spheres of God and the leader were not. The conductor was the political leader, not God. Christianity was elevated by Peronism but not through the Church. In this case, rhetorical conflation led in fact to the Peronization of Christianism. As Eva Perón, Perón's famous wife, maintained when she announced the coming of a Peronist Christmas in 1946, "I come from the people, like General Perón, and I am delighted to have arrived in this Christmas of the good *pan dulce* [sweet bread] of Perón and the *sidra* [hard cider] of Perón, to all the homes that Perón has reestablished to their Christian heights."[79] As I have argued elsewhere, the religious dimensions of the Peronist populist doctrine were intimately linked with the alleged religious nature of Perón's leadership. At one point, Peronist ideology identified a kernel of truth in these exaggerations. The constant blurring of the profane and the sacred was continuously pushed to its limits. As Eva Perón told her close advisor, the hardcore clerico-fascist Father Virgilio Filippo, and others in 1951, Perón was the God of the Argentines.[80] Like fascist leaders, Perón acted as a temporal analogy to the sacred. He was the one who bore the cross in the name of the nation and the people.

Notions of popular sovereignty lay at the center of these populist theologies. In practice, these dual forms of representation engendered unitary notions of the people, intolerant views, attacks on freedoms of expression, and even plebiscitary and delegative notions of democracy, but they did not lead to the demise of democracy itself. In this context, the populist leader is leader because of the faith the people are supposed to have in her or his leadership. The leaders act as the personification of the popular will, and not only because they were elected by the people. This logic of extreme identification crisscrossed the populist universe and its history. The transformation of the leader into the people makes him or her a transcendental figure unlike any other human and renders the former homogeneous and akin to the latter. In France, the slogan of the National Front literally equated the leader with the people: "Le Pen, le peuple." In Colombia, Gaitán famously said, "I am not a man, I am a people."[81] The leader is sacralized, and his theory of representation is partly a form of representation of the will of the people by means of popular repossession of the leader's self. The people possess the leader, or so he says. In this view, his own persona is no longer important, which explains the ease and eagerness with which populist leaders refer to themselves in the third person. General Perón stated, "I am only a man for a cause. I am not interested in Perón nor have I ever been interested [in Perón], or I have been interested in him only to the extent that Perón could serve the cause."[82]

As we have seen, the case of Hugo Chávez is especially symptomatic. He in fact argued, "I feel I am incarnated in the people." He multiplied his name and projected it onto the nation and its people. Not only was he speaking in the name of the people, but his name *was* the name of the people: "Chávez is Venezuela."

In 2012, Chávez told Venezuelans that they were "the people of Chávez." Explaining this Trinitarian idea of the leader, people, and nation, Chávez often talked about the three components of his nation as indistinct. He said, "I am no longer Chávez, Chávez became the people [Chávez se hizo un pueblo]." He also said that "Chávez became the essence of the nation." This process of transubstantiation meant that every Venezuelan was a little Chávez, insofar as they were all components of the national people of the leader. "I am not Chávez, you are Chávez, we are all Chávez, I am no longer myself. In truth, Chávez is a people." Like Perón, Gaitán, and many others, Chávez asserted a clear link between himself, the nation's history, and God. He asked Christ to give him his crown and cross. Chávez also stated in 2012, "I am convinced that God helps Chávez and his friends."[83]

The Chavista Movement clearly saw itself as a radical political religion with its own prayers and recitations. In the construction of Chávez's leadership, there was a synthesis between the *libertador* Simón Bolívar and Jesus. Carlos de la Torre explains, "His political movement, the new constitution and even Venezuela were renamed as 'Bolivarian.' Chávez constantly invoked 'Jesus as 'my commander in chief' and as 'the Lord of Venezuela.'" De La Torre notes that the conflation of the populist leader with formal religion was even personified by the leader himself on national television in 2012: "Chávez compared his agony with cancer with the passion of Christ. Following Christ's invocation to his Father when he felt abandoned in the cross, Chávez prayed out loud, Give me life ... Christ give me your crown of thorns. Give it to me that I bleed. Give me your cross ... Give me life because I still need to do things for this people and motherland. Do not take me. Give me your cross, your thorns, your blood. I will carry them, but give me life. Christ my Lord. Amen."[84]

When Chávez died in 2013, Nicolás Maduro, his proclaimed "son" and "apostle," wanted to have him embalmed, as Perón had done with Eva Perón's corpse. But instead of mentioning Evita, Maduro linked the dead leader with other famous mummified leaders, such as Ho Chi Minh, Lenin, and Mao. The purpose of mummifying the leader was to establish his singular place with respect to the rest of dead citizens, who got rather traditional forms of burial. In any case, lack of proper planning voided this choice, and Chávez was buried like every other Venezuelan.

The Venezuelan attempt to mummify the leader is a symptomatic example of how in the populist imaginary the leader belongs to the people, even in death. Making a case for the future embalming of Chávez, Maduro said, "The body of our commander in chief will remain embalmed in the Museum of the Revolution. It will remain in a special manner in order for it to be displayed in [a] crystal case and the people will have him forever."[85]

When he entered politics in 1994, Berlusconi claimed to be "appointed by God."[86] Berlusconi also once argued, "I am the Jesus Christ of politics ... I sacrifice myself for everyone." In Argentina, Cristina Kirchner argued that it was important to fear only God but also to fear her a "little bit."[87] The leader, by being the leader, prevented an apocalyptic situation. Above all, the sacred idea of the leader mixed electoral representation with messianic notions of predestination. For example, Donald Trump equated his Republican primary voters and his own candidacy with the will of the American people. He even argued that he was going to unify them into a single voice. He did replace their voice with his voice, but the result was a repossession of the people by the leader. Collectively, the people remained a passive actor, for whom he would "fight" and "win." He spoke for a "silent majority" that could not defend itself, or even speak. He told "people who work hard but no longer have a voice- I am your voice."[88]

Trump combined messianic undertones typical of the American political tradition with rhetorical praise for violence against members of the opposition. A noted Trump supporter, who was a Republican senator at the time, presented the choice of Trump as one between life or death for the Republican Party. The idea of the leader as being somehow closer to God than other mortals was reformulated in the 2015–16 presidential campaign. Trump told religious leaders that gaining the presidency was going to get him to heaven. In Trumpism, the sacred was entangled with the American entrepreneurship ideal as represented in the charisma and "brain power" of the populist leader. Trump introduced himself as the leader of a nation and a people of winners, but he also deferred to God as the ultimate owner of property.[89]

Trump established parallel lanes of meaning between his own real estate deals, the sacred, and the politics of the American present and near future. North of the Rio Grande, twenty-first-century populism reformulated a long-standing American populist combination of extreme individualism, religion, racism, anti-institutionalism, materialism, and "hard work" with a newly established form of political and business predestination. Trump proffered himself as both the embodiment of the nation and the personification of the spirit of capitalism. He wanted to be seen as a living myth. As the preeminent scholar of political myth Chiara Bottici argued, Trump's slogan, "Make America Great Again" echoed the fascist "mythologem of 'greatness-decline-rebirth.'" This narrative plot enabled the populist leader "to single out those who are the perceived cause of the decline, target them as guilty and thus channel and fuel hostility toward them."[90] Here old fascist myths were recombined with a xeno-phobic, populist right-wing American tradition that wanted a society ruled by the wealthy. This was the context in which, as Judith Butler suggested, Trump was approaching a fascist situation.[91] In fact, Trump's populism in practice was not far from a neoliberal, elitist idea of a ruling class whose power derives from their wealth, but it was fused with old fascist political myths of sacred leadership and populist ideas of popular sovereignty, along with the exclusion of the antipeople.

In this regard, Trump was close to the Italian populist Silvio Berlusconi. Part of their appeal was that each combined a self-presentation of himself as a "man of the people" with the rarified world of a billionaire. This appeal was embellished with religious undertones. According to this conception, the leader is more special than his people, as if this were divinely predestined. If this sounds religious, that's because it is. Sacred forms belonging to the privacy of religious faith are a key component of the populist political theology.

Unlike fascists, the faith of populists is confirmed by electoral results. But like fascists, populists adopt religious forms (language and rituals), and they endorse the idea of the leader as a divine figure who is never wrong. For Chávez, the idea of himself as a Godlike figure connected him to Jesus and implied a radical idea of the enemy as impious. Similarly, in Turkey, as the Turkish scholar Ertug Tombus suggests, Erdogan mixed two political theologies (formal religion and populism), especially after the coup attempt of July 2016. While Tombus stresses the connections between the fascist and populist understanding of the political, as well as the transnational character of both, some scholars working on Muslim nations resort to the presentation of an "Islamic populist" Other. But is it really the case that populism is so different in Islamic politics that we should talk about an Islamic populism?

ISLAMIC POPULISM?

In many studies of politics and Islam, populism becomes the way to differentiate a big part of the world from the West. Populism, these studies claim, is a natural outcome of the democratic weakness of politics in Islam. These scholars tend to speak of a compact "Islamic" form of politics, in which the tendency toward populism is naturalized and almost appears by default. In my view, the merging of these two theologies (Islam, or for that matter any religion, and populism) does not warrant the creation of the new category "Islamic populism." The use of the term *Islamic populism* often conflates the extremely different experiences of countries like Turkey, Egypt, Iran, Morocco, Tunisia, and Indonesia. While Turkish populism emerged out of a multiparty system, other countries like Indonesia and Egypt presented very different authoritarian and democratic contexts.

Islamic populism is a misnomer that inflates populist politics and identifies populism with any Islamic critique of the elites or in some cases with mass politics in Muslim countries. Even if the merging of Islamic and populist themes is a singular manifestation of populist politics in Muslim countries, the term *Islamic* does not explain much about forms of populism that often resemble "non-Muslim" contexts in European, African, or Latin American cases more than they do each other. As with the term *Islamo-fascism, Islamic populism* blurs the continuities within the global history of populism at the same time that it obscures converging histories of political Islam around the world. In addition, public uses of Islamic populism exemplify efforts to present populism as a perversion, or deformity, of "real," normative democracy. In this case, the implication is that Muslims cannot handle full-blown democratic governance, a claim with a very long and gory colonial history.[92]

More generally the use of the term avoids the key distinctions between left and right wing forms of populism across the political spectrum (including also the Middle East) and tends to stress and even confirm stereotypical assumptions about Islam and the West, often confusing the populist domestication and synchronization of religion with actual formal religions.

The scholar of populism Vedi R. Hadiz, who defends the use of the term, nonetheless provides a very specific periodization of the concept and argues that one such convergence of populism and Islamic politics is a shared identification of the notion of *umma*, or a community of Muslim believers that conceives of the people as whole. But as he also astutely observes, the *umma* often adopts a national connotation rather than a universal one. It is exactly this national dimension that illuminates the particular ways a transnational understanding of political theology is adopted and lived in specific periods and countries.

In his excellent study of populism in Algeria, the Algerian scholar Lahouari Addi insists precisely on the permanence of the notion of populism in Algeria from the country's independence during the Cold War to the 1990s, but he also stresses its very different contextual variations. Algerian forms of populism, either secular or Islamic, have more in common with each other than they do with other transnational examples. The same, of course, can be said of the Peronist experience in Argentina and of other national cases that are part of the same national histories. But if in Argentina Peronism encompassed different currents, from anti-imperialism to corporativism to neoclassical populism and neoliberalism, in Algeria populism was adopted and reformulated by different and even opposing currents. All of them claimed to be the incarnation of the people, but Algerian populism, rather than being only a top-down structure, mobilized its citizens, increasing their political participation while eventually redefining who were the common enemies of the people. As Addi cogently argues, the contents of populism changed in different historical periods, but a mythical idea of the people remained. At the time of the anticolonial battles for independence, its contents were all inclusive and suited the common enemy of the people, that is, the colonial power. After independence, populism was devised as a means to conserve power. Popular participation was significantly reduced, and the representatives of the people were those who "indefinitely spoke in their name." At the same time, these leaders defined who was and who was not part of the people. This situation eventually led to the rulers being opposed by those in whose names they ruled. The rule of the FLN unified the people, increasingly excluding their actual participation in the political process. Addi highlights how the crisis of an authoritarian populism can create or lead to another. What is highly suggestive is that Addi's historical analysis of populism in power explains the populism of the political movement, the Islamic Salvation Front (FIS), that took shape in the late 1980s. This was a result of Algerian history and its populist political culture, specifically its secular populism, rather than of the outcome of generic or essentialist Islamic notions. Thus Addi shows that by 1988, in a time of social and economic crisis, when the country was allowing for a democratic political process with multiparty elections, the FIS Party, which was radically opposed to the power of the ruling populist elites, revindicated the "agonizing populism of the FLN," though one reformulated in a religious manner. The FIS revived populism in a very different moment of Algerian history, presenting "itself as a movement with the ambition of making concrete the political program of the FLN" and also its "promises." From its secular moment in history to its religious one, Algerian populism exhibited similar traits, including a mythical conception of the people, voluntarism, the cult of the state, a "moral anchoring of its political values," the idea of the incarnation of the people, and a denial of conflict within society. For Addi, the Algerian case shows the political uses of Islam are not new but have been reformulated at different times. Islam was "a political resource," but the nature of the Algerian conflict over democracy was not religious but essentially political in nature. This key point should also restrain the often ahistorical uses of the notion of Islamic populism.

All in all, Addi stresses how Algerian forms of populism ultimately were impediments to the enhancement of democracy, and yet as in Thailand, Argentina, and other non-Muslim societies, the FIS version of populist democracy was finished in 1992 by an antipopulist military dictatorship.[93] Independent of the specific religion invoked, in Algeria and in Argentina, but also in countries as different as Turkey, Israel, Egypt, Indonesia, Italy, Hungary, the United States, and Venezuela, the will of the people was used interchangeably with the will of God.

MACHO POPULISM

At the start of the twenty-first century, populist ideals of sexuality became more explicit, and less decorous, than in the past. While Perón had also represented the ideal of Argentine masculinity as a key dimension of Peronism, he had set up clear demarcations between genders. He had highlighted the central civic duty of women as mothers, whose task was to educate men. A case in point was the nationalist Peronist Oscar Ivanissevich. He declared, "The Peronist is a person with a defined sex who admires beauty with all his senses."[94] The ideal of Peronist beauty was defined by a traditional and baroque view of culture that avidly assimilated contemporary popular elements that at times transformed it. Some more recent right-wing populist leaders have articulated a stereotyped and even more reactionary version of the role and image of women in society.

Like Berlusconi and the Latin American neoliberal populists of the 1990s, the presidents Carlos Menem in Argentina and Abdalá Bucaram in Ecuador, Trump put forward a *machista* model of leadership combining sexism, misogyny, and the power of money. Similarly, authoritarian views on gender and sexuality appeared in leftist Latin American populism, such as in Ecuador's Correa, while other populisms of the left and the right were simply not engaged in these forms of discrimination or, like Argentina in the 2000s, opposed them. It would be problematic to explain, as some generic scholars of populism do, these differences through the stereotypes of an "emancipated" or progressive North versus "patriarchal" Latin America.[95]

Gender and sexual repression, for example, the highly repressive attempts to ban Muslim women from wearing the veil in some European countries, appear in some form in most populisms of the right. From Trump to Berlusconi and to Menem and Bucaram, some key examples of the populism of the right have favored very traditional and even repressive female stereotypes and gender distinctions, while in countries like Argentina or Bolivia, populists of the left have promoted substantial legal changes to advance gender and sexual equality. In any case, the macho aspect of populist leaders who mix aggressive capitalism and entrepreneurship with repressive gender attitudes seems to transcend regions and continents. The populism of Trump, Berlusconi, Bucaram, and many others supports popular sovereignty, delegation of power, and a highly repressive take on gender.

Constant vulgar references to male and female genitalia, and the serial objectification of women (the leaders counted their female "conquests" and stressed the size of their genitalia, among other things), were proffered as examples of their denunciation of politics as usual. In a presidential primary debate, Trump "guaranteed," and even boasted about, the size of his penis. In a disclosed recording from 2005, which came to define Trump's macho-populist ideology, the Republican standard bearer "bragged in vulgar terms about kissing, groping and trying to have sex with women." He thought his special celebrity status allowed him license to behave toward women as he wanted and without their consent. As Joseph Biden, then vice president of the country argued when the tape came out, "Such behavior is an abuse of power. It's not lewd. It's sexual assault." In his own words, Trump celebrated his macho persona as defined by his unrepressed desire to do what he wanted to women. He stated that "because he was 'a star,' … he could 'grab them by the pussy' whenever he wanted."[96]

Another icon of macho populism, Silvio Berlusconi, made vulgar references to the body of the German chancellor, Angela Merkel, and serially boasted of his sexual prowess. Berlusconi rationalized it was "better to have a passion for beautiful women than to be gay." Menem defined himself as only "half libertine," saying he had not had many extramarital relations, "just the normal" standard for men. The Philippine leader, Rodrigo Duterte, linked his connection to the people with his sexual prowess: "If I can love 100 million and one [Filipinos], I can love four women at the same time." As a self-proclaimed man of the people, he claimed, "This is how men talk." The idea that speaking in the name of the people meant enforcing gender and sexual discrimination led him to insult the American ambassador with homophobic slurs and state that he had also wanted to rape an Australian missionary, who had been raped and murdered in a 1989 prison riot. In 2016, Duterte once again asserted that his connection to the people protected him from criticism when he called

Barack Obama, the American president at the time, a "son of a bitch." The Philippine leader described an American leader's questioning of his own deeds as president, especially his serious human rights violations, as a colonialist erosion of both national sovereignty and the intrinsic bond he had with the people: "Who is this man? I do not have any master, except the Filipino people, nobody but nobody."[97] Unlike most populist leaders, Duterte used rhetoric regarding the practice of violence that invoked analogies between him, fascism, and the Holocaust. He claimed, "Hitler massacred 3 million Jews ... there's 3 million drug addicts. There are. I'd be happy to slaughter them," thus obscuring the fact that Nazism was responsible for the death of six million Jews and connecting his actions to both the precedent of fascist violence and its apocalyptic connotations. In 2016, he told reporters that his critics suggested he was "a cousin of Hitler." Duterte remarked, "If Germany had Hitler, the Philippines would have ...," and then pointed to himself. "You know my victims," he told reporters, "I would like [them] to be all criminals to finish the problem of my country and save the next generation from perdition."[98]

If extreme in his approach to violence compared to the standards set by Chávez, Trump, Menem, and Bucaram, Duterte showed he shared their attitudes on sexuality and their very conservative stances on reproductive rights and the family. In short, they all have macho populism in common.

Bucaram compared his "big balls" to the smaller genitalia of politicians in the opposition. He also made Lorena Bobbitt (who became famous for having castrated her abusive American husband) an honorary guest of the president. This vulgarity and macho obsession with genitalia are not random and speak volumes about a particular trend in recent populism. Chávez also used phallic imagery when he proposed at a 2006 UN meeting that "we need a political Viagra" against political impotence. He had earlier told the "elite" to take Viagra against the people. The leader and his people represented a form of virility that blurred distinctions between public and private life. In 2000, he told his wife on his national TV program to be ready for sex that night: "Marisabel, be ready, tonight I will give to you what is yours."[99]

Carlos de la Torre explains that these leaders present their own virility as a form of resistance against the "effeminate elites." In their objectifying references to female ugliness and beauty, they claim to express what all males think but cannot say. Their acts and bodies, according to these leaders, affirm the masculinity of the people ("the people" in this context includes only their male followers). The result is the upholding of stereotypes. De la Torre notes that this "vindication of a machista popular culture accepts and reproduces an authoritarian culture based on the subordination of women." Leaders like Bucaram, by "staging male sexual dreams such as seducing ladies from high society or dancing with attractive models on television, was symbolically democratizing the access by all men, especially common men, to the gender privileges of elite men. In this way, he was broadening the authoritarian male pact of domination."[100]

The subordination of women, and this populist type of machismo, has not been prevalent in other cases of populism, but it has been prominent in Argentina, in Italy, in Ecuador, in the Philippines, and in the United States, where Trump mixed these ideas and styles with racist statements and proposals regarding Muslims and Hispanics, a disregard for the rule of law and the separation of powers, and a deep antagonism toward other candidates and independent journalism. These features connect populist authoritarianism with the fascist past. Trump, like many of his predecessors, delivered the message that his followers expected. As Pablo Piccato and I argue, Trump's followers shared with "the early supporters of fascism a deep suspicion of the other, of people of different ethnic and religious backgrounds. Trump's followers want a country that looks, believes, talks, eats and drinks the same. They want to go back to a country without diversity, which never existed except in the reactionary images of the past. This idea derives from a longstanding fear of difference and nationalism that in Europe caused much destruction. Against a meaningful democracy, where all people who are living in the country can participate, Trump's supporters want a similarly reduced version of America."[101]

A big divide between the fiery right-wing American and Europopulist rhetoric against Muslims and real fascism is the latter's rise to power and the actual physical elimination of a perceived enemy. According to an Italian historian of fascism, Trump's populism appeared to be a more "peaceful" version of fascism. One might make similar points about Pegida and Lepenism.[102] Under a fascist dictatorship, the treatment of the enemy is not at all peaceful, and it takes place with total disregard for the rule of law. Once fascist politicians reach power, they switch from racist statements to the suppression of the other. Fascism not only talks about the enemy but eliminates it from the political process. Trump was a perfect example of the continuities but also the differences between populism and fascism. As a candidate, he never advocated or put forward a dictatorial view of the United States. In other words, he represented an authoritarian populist version of democracy.

The presidential candidacy of Donald Trump was unique in world history, not because of Trump's idiosyncratic nature and his histrionic behavior, but in the sense that he presided from the center over what used to be the politics of the margins. He accomplished this by being the populist leader of a party that used to be to the right of the political center, as well as by bringing to the American mainstream politics that generally receive massive support in other regions of the world like Latin America, Israel, the Arab countries, Austria, Hungary, and the Philippines. If the populist and racist traditions that preceded and opposed the civil rights movements were prominent in his American background, the forces of fascism and populism were also part of Trump's global pedigree. Perhaps Trump himself ignored these authoritarian genealogies, but he nonetheless represented them in a nearly absolute way—putting racism at the center of his politics, making a case for religious exclusion, and proposing mass deportation of immigrants. This new American populism has already left its mark on the history of the country and the world. Once again, democracy has changed from within. Global authoritarian projects for democracy are here to stay, precisely because, as the history of why and how fascism became populism tells us, they were never out of the picture.

Epilogue

Populism Recharged

> After having razed the garden and profaned the
> chalices and the altars, the Huns entered the
> monastery library on horseback and trampled the
> incomprehensible books and vituperated and burned
> them, perhaps fearful that the letters concealed
> blasphemies against their god, which was an iron
> scimitar.
>
> Jorge Luis Borges, *The Theologians* (1949)

I

Modern postwar populism had a fascist starting point, and yet populism is not fascism. In fact, after 1945, especially in Latin America, and later in the rest of the world, fascism often became populism—not the other way around. As this book has shown, while populism was often historically constituted as a repudiation of fascism, it also represented its democratic reformulation. Historically located somewhere between fascism and liberalism, populism, when it finally became a regime, constantly drew on the residues of the former to challenge the latter. At the same time, it continued to engage in democratic electoral processes. This postfascism did bring back the engagement with democracy early fascists had adopted before they destroyed the democratic system. The upshot was a revamped authoritarianism that transformed the dictatorial tradition of classical fascism into *an antiliberal and intolerant form of democracy.*

Populism cannot be understood without appreciating its complex history, and theories of populism suffer when they rely on simplistic definitions of a populism that is hemmed in by tight borders. Often uninformed by global perspectives, such theories ignore the protean nature of the populisms that have been continually emerging since World War II, as well as the major historical and theoretical significance of the times when populists reached power and established regimes. My goal has been to return populism to its diverse history, from the Global South to the dominant North.

Historically, postfascist populism was the revitalization of an authoritarian view of democracy, and its translation into a regime, that is itself founded in a fascist imaginary. In the second decade of our new century, a new populist incursion is covering large parts of the world. It has come back with a vengeance, and in unexpected places. For many, this has been a terrible shock, but the return of populism is part of a broader history of authoritarian conceptions of democracy that have always sat uncomfortably alongside democracy's more egalitarian expressions. Compounding the shock, this recharged populism has seized much of the terrain of the geopolitical center, and a more open and diverse conception of democracy has been threatened in the process. This too is not new, but populism's latest political gains—and potential geopolitical repercussions—are unprecedented. To the delight of many, and to the horror of many others, populism now lives in the White House.

II

How American is the new American populism? Regarding it from the often-neglected perspective of the Global South, some in the United States have finally recognized how similar America is to the rest of the world. Indeed, with the election of Donald Trump, the United States has instantly become the epicenter of global populism, a development that helps legitimate all other populisms. Just as Rome and Berlin became models for the fascists, so too did the xenophobic campaign of Donald Trump soon became a model—and a source of validation—for populists worldwide. Populist leaders of the right like Silvio Berlusconi, Marine Le Pen, Nigel Farage, and Geert Wilders, as well as some left-leaning populists positioned between the right and the left, such as Cristina Kirchner, praised Trumpism and its voters for standing against traditional forms of democratic representation and their purportedly "elite," and excessively "liberal" and "cosmopolitan," culture. In France, Le Pen crowed that Trump's win "made possible what had previously been presented as impossible. This is really the victory of the people against the elites." The Trump victory was for her part of "a global revolution."[1]

And yet American populism has not in fact been the driving force behind populism worldwide. It is, rather, populism's latest and arguably most stunning incarnation. Even in the context of American history, Trump is an expression of the long history of racism and xenophobia, which accompanied both the strides made in the civil rights movement and the many waves of immigration into America as economic recession (or simply the vagaries of the globalized economy) hit the rest of the world. Trump's victory intensified the intolerance toward difference that has for many years been front and center in the Republican

Party and in its Tea Party Movement. Trump has moved this tradition further to the right.

Globally, populism represented an authoritarian response to an extended crisis of democratic representation. For its adherents, populism replaced reason with faith in a Godlike leader, who purportedly knew what the people felt, feared, and wanted. In this sense, it "represented" them far better than any conventional democratic leader or institution. The idea of truth, moreover, was reformulated as a matter of ideological, often visceral, faith, rather than as a function of observation, rational discernment, and corroboration. With its trinitarian conception of sovereignty (nation, leader, people), populism posed a special threat to more secular, as opposed to theological, understandings of democracy.

From a global historical perspective, the metropolitan centers looks more and more like the margins, or periphery, of the world. This is especially true of the United States, a country that has always been ambivalent about the relationship between politics and the sacred, no matter its formal doctrine of separation of state and church.

No sustained political movement or initiative has ever been able to settle the question of American populism ideologically. Rather it has always reflected the intermittent power and appeal of authoritarian populist politics that were very much tied to particular social, economic, and political developments. In the United States, there is little historical or institutional memory that consciously links today's populists to their early forbears, or that lends perspective to the key issue of American populism's intimate connection to a preeminently white conception of the nation, especially, but not only, since 1945. The history of the early populist movement of late nineteenth-century America is today known in any meaningful way to only a handful of scholars and their students, while more recent American populists are not generally thought of in terms of their connections to other postwar populisms.

As of 2017, American populism has become the most consequential postfascism of the new century. After decades of largely disavowing populism as foreign to its own political culture, the United States has now assumed the role of populism's global leader, which Argentina held after 1945. The idea of Perón as the uncontested man of the people was a key element not only of Peronism but in the creation of modern postwar populism. The extraordinary personality cult of Trump echoes this dynamic. Populism rests on the idea of the leader as a transcendental figure. He is the voice of the people, and he knows better than they do what they really want. General Perón also saw himself as the Godlike personification of the people. His wife, Eva Perón, explained that "Perón is a God for all of us, to the extent that we do not conceive of the sky without Perón. Perón is our sun, Perón is the water. Perón is the life of our country and the Argentine people."[2] Time will tell if America will abide such an elevated, even mystical, conception of a redemptive national leader.

III

Populism is both genetically and historically linked to fascism. One might argue that it is an heir to fascism—a postfascism for democratic times, which combines a more narrow commitment to democracy with authoritarian, antidemocratic impulses.

The identification of people, leader, and nation as one was of course central to fascism. Unlike populism, however, fascism initially exploited, but then contemptuously discarded, democratic

procedures. When it was in power, it was not significantly medi-
ated or limited by the legitimacy conferred by genuine, multiparty
elections. In both fascist dictatorship and populist democracy, the
leader is constructed as the representative and embodiment of
the people, or as the personification of the people, the nation, and
the nation's history. While both fascist mass dictatorships and populist democratic regimes paint a portrait of a leader who potentially knows better than the people what they really need, however, the two differ starkly.

As long as postwar populist leaders did not interfere with
elections, they represented nonliberal, or even antiliberal, multiparty democratic regimes. Faith in the populist leader nonetheless went well beyond winning the popular vote (however narrow the electoral margin). That faith was also formed on the basis
of the leader's personification of the people. This duality is a key
feature of populist theory and its historical practice. The leader's
aura both preceded and transcended the electoral moment, pro-
jecting a mythical order that stood against liberalism. Postwar
populism's practice of democracy, therefore, was both a response
to and a critique of the liberal order. After the dictatorial era of
classical fascism, classical populism reconnected electoral
democracy with anticommunism and antiliberalism. Democratic
populism was an unexpected fulfillment of the long-standing
and reactionary anti-Enlightenment tradition that, even so, was
historically contingent. Like fascism, it arose from an illiberal
tradition that had penetrated important sectors within civil society. It was an experiment in democratic politics and a response
from within illiberalism to the dictatorial form of the political.[3]

As secularized forms of the sacred, fascism and populism put
forward the political trinity of leader, nation, and people, as their
main source of legitimation. Both represent a political theology

that extends beyond the ways the sacred always informs politics. Within these movements, there is no contradiction between the people and the nation and the representation of the people in the persona of the leader. Both ideologies believe in personification as representation, which means, in effect, that achieving the will of the people is fully delegated to the leader. The trinitarian myth of representation rests on the notion that somehow a single leader is the same as a nation and its people—a conflation of one person and two concepts. In fascism, this idea of personification does not require any rational or procedural mediation, such as electoral representation.

For Italian fascists, their movement and regime were an "authoritarian democracy" because "The demos, that is all of the people, circulates in the state." Similarly, Hitler had argued in 1935 that the "state is the only organization of popular life." Fascists distinguished between democracy as the rule of the people and liberalism as a dated and problematic form of representation—technocratic, inefficient, alienated from the "people" and the national will, and prone to capture and manipulation by particular, often "elite," interests. Dictatorship was the practical consequence of this distinction. Populism accepted the idea that liberalism blocked the true will of the people but also reformulated it. Dictatorship was now left behind, but the fascist residues of populism affected how democracy was both engaged with and reconsidered. The new populist charge against representation had been anticipated by many fascists. As the Romanian fascist leader Horia Sima argued, the will of the people could express itself at a given moment in political parties or in "democracy but nothing impedes it from also finding other forms of expression."[4]

Fascism was similarly conceived in Argentina under the failed Uriburu dictatorship (1930–32). The Argentine dictator explained that fascism represented a shift toward republican foundations and away from democratic ones. The republic was more relevant than democracy itself. "The word Democracy with a capital D no longer has meaning for us.... This doesn't imply that we are not democrats but more sincerely how much we hope that at some point a democracy in lowercase, but organic and truthful, replaces the dislocated demagogy that has done us great harm." As part of his global search for forms of popular expression that could replace electoral democracy, Uriburu identified his choice with the fascist dictatorial model.[5]

With populism, on the other hand, electoral democracy became a key part of the political equation after 1945. A former dictatorial strongman himself before 1945, Juan Perón now believed that an "organic" form of electoral democracy should replace *demoliberalismo* in the postwar era. The will of the people could now also be represented in elections. The leader made the popular will organic again. Otherwise, these "inorganic masses" were "susceptible to being manipulated by foreign professional agitators."[6] In the populist sense, the agency of the masses had to be communicated in and through elections, but once this agency had been translated into votes, the leader became the only one who could channel the will of the people. Without their leaders, the masses would be lost or, even worse, might become inauthentic supporters of the will of the antipeople.

In its classical, postwar form, populism became a chimera between two distinct traditions of representation: the electoral and the dictatorial. This combination constituted the new populist modernity. The fact that early Cold War Latin American populists combined both forms of political representation had to do with context and ideology. The dual nature of populism eventually accommodated democratic and dictatorial traditions, the Enlightenment and the anti-Enlightenment, electoral representation and political theology. The postwar result of this synergy was not mass dictatorship but a new, authoritarian form of democracy.

The first populist regimes were born at the Latin American margins, but in less than a century, populism had moved to Washington, DC. This was the result of a long, truly global historical process, whereby a defeated fascism of dictatorship radically reformulated itself as democratic populism. In the early twenty-first century, populism seemed to come from nowhere. But in fact it had gradually moved to center stage from the global sidelines. As this book has shown, understanding the populism that has belatedly become central in the United States, and also in Europe, requires knowledge of its history on the periphery.

As a global manifestation of antipolitics, populist leaders typically replaced traditional politicians, but they did so without extending meaningful forms of decision making to the citizens. In the name of fighting the elites, the political heads changed, but ironically the elitism remained. Power remained in the persona of the new leader, never reaching the citizens, at least not in any systemic and sustained way. The populist leaders replaced old politics, impersonating the people and doing the thinking and deciding for them. The notion of a leader who was smarter and much better than his or her people defines the history of populism in power. Historically, populism without leadership remains an incomplete form. From *peronismo* to *trumpismo,* this ideology of authoritarian democracy both grew out of and differed from fascism, depending on where it took root, but the fundamentals remained: populists desperately need enemies of the people to confirm the fiction that they speak and act in the name of the national community.

Understanding its complex history helps us explain the persistence of modern populism and its formidable ability to undermine democratic tolerance and oppose pluralistic forms of popular sovereignty. Populism's past challenges to egalitarian forms of democracy continue in the present and are now threatening the future of our own democratic times.

ACKNOWLEDGMENTS

This book is an outcome, and in many ways a synthesis, of two decades of cumulative historical research on fascism and populism. Having published five specialized books on these topics, I intend this new work to be a more global historical take that, although it works with primary sources, also substantially relies on significant works by many other colleagues and scholars of fascism and populism. I thank all of them, but I am especially indebted to those who have participated with me in cosmopolitan conversations across borders and oceans over the years. First, for their comments and readings, I am grateful to Andrew Arato, Ben Brower, Luis Herrán Ávila, Sandra McGee Deutsch, Pablo Piccato, Paul Gillingham, and Nadia Urbinati. Muchas gracias también to Fabián Bosoer and Carlos de la Torre for their readings. I also want to thank Paul Corner, Antonio Costa Pinto, Geoff Eley, Oz Frankel, Valeria Galimi, Aaron Jakes, Andreas Kalyvas, Natalia Mehlman Petrzela, Raanan Rein, Alberto Spektorowski, Ertug Tombus, Enzo Traverso, Jeremy Varon, Angelo Ventrone, and Hans Vorländer. Thanks also go to Giulia

Albanese, Melissa Amezcua, Nick Fox, José Alves Freitas Neto, Étienne Balibar, Michele Battini, Martin Baumeister, Luis Fernando Beneduzi, Richard Bernstein, Chris Bickerton, Ernesto Bohoslavsky, Judit Bokser Liwerant, Chiara Bottici, Jonathan Brown, Amy Chazkel, Manuela Consonni, Faisal Devji, Patrizia Dogliani, Hugo Drochon, Tanya Filer, Carlos Forment, Alessio Gagliardi, Roberto García Ferreira, Carol Gluck, Amos Goldberg, Rebekka Habermas, Tanya Harmer, Ágnes Heller, Daniel Kressel, Dominick LaCapra, Simon Levis Sullam, Daniel Lvovich, Tracie Matysyk, Andrea Mammone, Will Milberg, Dirk Moses, Jose Moya, Tim Muller, Nara Milanich, Xosé Núñez Seixas, Julia Ott, Elias Palti, Matteo Pasetti, Enrique Peruzzotti, Caterina Pizzigoni, Sven Reichardt, Gema Santamaria, Leonardo Senkman, David Sheinin, Héctor Raúl Solís Gadea, Michael Steinberg, Ann Laura Stoler, Dan Stone, and Kurt Weyland.

Like all my other books, this one is connected to my teaching. Recent events precipitated its writing, but for whatever it's worth my perspective is that not of a newcomer forced to write on the theme of the day but of a student, teacher, and researcher, who over two decades has become a specialist on a topic that sadly is even more urgent than before. In fact, I have been teaching the main arguments of this book for several years, initially at Brown University and then at the New School for Social Research and at Eugene Lang College. I want to thank all the students who took my courses on fascism and populism. More recently, in 2016, I taught a seminar on fascism and populism at the Technische Universität Dresden and presented on these topics at Columbia University, the University of Texas at Austin, Northwestern University, and Brown University in the United States; the Hebrew University of Jerusalem and the University of Tel Aviv; the University of Macerata and Università Ca'

Foscari in Venice; the Universities of Padova and Bologna; the University of Guadalajara in Mexico; Trent University in Canada; the University of Cambridge; the University of Lisbon; and the Universidad de la República in Montevideo, among others. My thanks to those who attended those lectures and engaged in multiple conversations.

Parts of chapters 1 and 2 were published in very different form in 2008 and 2014 in the journal *Constellations*. The arguments in chapter 3 were initially developed for my contribution to the *Palgrave Handbook of Mass Dictatorship* (2016), edited by Paul Corner and Jie-Hyun Lim.

I will always be thankful to my ideal editor, Kate Marshall, for suggesting that this book was possible and whose advice and editorial work made it much better. I also want to thank Bradley Depew at UC Press for his exceptional editorial work, as well as Dore Brown, Ann Donahue, Alex Dahne, and Tom Sullivan. I thank Luis Herrán Ávila for preparing the index.

I want to remember my Argentine professors José Sazbón and Tulio Halperín Donghi. Their influence and ideas remain critical to me. I also want to remember my abuela, Luisa Guelman, who passed away in late 2016 at 106 years old. Her long, memorable life corresponded with all the political and ideological transformations analyzed in this book. She was born in 1910, and since I was a student at the Universidad de Buenos Aires, she shared her insights from the interwar years, times that some years ago looked very different from our own. Now that this is no longer the case, it is important for me to remember that she lived long enough to witness the uncanny resemblance of the new century to the first decades of the last. She often liked to tell the story of the day that she was expelled from her University of Buenos Aires' classes during the 1930 coup in Argentina, when fascist forces wanted to leave Argentine secular and democratic traditions behind. Predictably, one of their first steps was to interrupt the life of the universities. My abuela, then, lived through all the metamorphoses of fascism and populism in history as they were experienced in Argentina and in the world, including their most recent reverberations in 2016.

As with my previous books, my family gave me their full support, and I could not have written this one without them. I want to thank my parents, Norma and Jaime, and my brothers, Diego and Inés. My wife, Laura, and my daughters, Gabriela and Lucia, were always there for me, and my gratitude for them has no borders.

NOTES

PREFACE TO THE PAPERBACK EDITION

1. On this topic, see also Mabel Berezin, "Fascism and Populism: Are They Useful Categories for Comparative Sociological Analysis?," *Annual Review of Sociology* 45 (2019).

2. See my books *Transatlantic Fascism: Ideology, Violence and the Sacred in Argentina and Italy, 1919–1945* (Durham, NC: Duke University Press, 2010); and *The Ideological Origins of the Dirty War: Fascism, Populism, and Dictatorship in Twentieth Century Argentina* (New York: Oxford University Press, 2014).

3. I have made minor changes and small updates for the Spanish (2018) and Turkish and Italian (2019) editions.

4. Saagar Enjeti and Benny Johnson, "Exclusive: Trump Warns Antifa—You Could Be in Big Trouble," *Daily Caller*, November 14, 2018, https://dailycaller.com/2018/11/14/trump-antifa-opposition-mobilize/. On the history of antifa, see Marc Bray, *Antifa: The Antifascist Handbook* (New York: Melville House, 2017).

5. Bernard Harcourt, "How Trump Fuels the Fascist Right," *New York Review of Books*, November 29, 2018, www.nybooks.com/daily/2018/11/29/how-trump-fuels-the-fascist-right/. See also Federico Finchelstein, "Trumpism Is Spreading in Latin America," *Washington Post*, September

18, 2018; "Jair Bolsonaro's Model Isn't Berlusconi: It's Goebbels," *Foreign Policy,* October 5, 2018; and "Why Far-Right Populists Are at War with HHHHistory," *Washington Post,* April 23, 2019.

6. On this topic, see Andrea Mammone, "A Daily Revision of the Past: Fascism, Anti-Fascism, and Memory in Contemporary Italy," *Modern Italy* 11, no. 2 (2016): 211–26.

7. Ishaan Tharoor, "Trump Deploys the Fascist Playbook for the Midterms," *Washington Post,* November 2, 2018.

8. See David Leonhardt and Ian Prasad Philbrick, "Trump's Corruption: The Definitive List," *New York Times,* October 28, 2018.

9. For example, according to Harvard historian Moshik Temkin, historians should not concern themselves with Trumpism's connections to "foreign dictators of the past" because "things rarely repeat themselves." See Moshik Temkin, "Historians Shouldn't Be Pundits," *New York Times,* June 26, 2017. In a similar vein, Corey Robin argues, "For all the talk of increasing authoritarianism and Republican hegemony, there are signs that the United States is more open and freer today—and the Republicans less hegemonic—than it has been in a while." See Corey Robin, "If Authoritarianism Is Looming in the US, How Come Donald Trump Looks So Weak?," *Guardian,* January 13, 2018.

10. In the last populist proposal for the left, Chantal Mouffe rather mysteriously does not talk much about the past of Latin American left-wing populism. In fact, she specifically sets it aside on page 10 of her new book. See Chantal Mouffe, *For a Left Populism* (New York: Verso, 2018). Mouffe and Ernesto Laclau have presented Chavism and Argentine Kirchnerism as worthy of emulation in Europe. For a critique of this argument for Europe, see Eric Fassin, *Populisme: le grand ressentiment* (Paris: Textuel, 2017); and Nadia Urbinati, *Me the People: How Populism Transforms Democracy* (Cambridge, MA: Harvard University Press, 2019). For a similar critique respecting Latin America, see Carlos de la Torre, *Populismos* (Barcelona: Tibidabo, 2017).

PROLOGUE

1. See Federico Finchelstein, "An Argentine Dictator's Legacy," *New York Times,* May 28, 2013. I thank Professor Hans Vorländer, the foremost

expert on Pegida, and a renowned scholar of democracy and populism, for inviting me to teach about populism and fascism at the prestigious Technische Universität Dresden and for his explanations of Pegida, which took place soon after this unusual encounter with the sources.

2. On the center and the margins, see Étienne Balibar, *We, the People of Europe? Reflections on Transnational Citizenship* (Princeton, NJ: Princeton University Press, 2004), 2.

3. See, for example, Giovanni Gentile, *Che cos'è il fascismo* (Florence: Vallecchi, 1925); Leon Trotsky, *Fascism: What It Is, How to Fight It* (New York: Pioneer, 1944), and the early populist T.C. Jory, *What Is Populism? An Exposition of the Principles of the Omaha Platform Adopted by the People's Party in National Convention Assembled July 4, 1892* (Salem, OR: R.E. Moores, 1895).

4. On the anti-Enlightenment, see Zeev Sternhell, *The Anti-Enlightenment Tradition* (New Haven, CT: Yale University Press, 2010).

5. Andrew Arato, *Post Sovereign Constitution Making: Learning and Legitimacy* (Oxford: Oxford University Press, 2016), 283, 295.

6. On fascist notions of truth as detached from empirical observation, see Federico Finchelstein, "Truth, Mythology, and the Fascist Unconscious," *Constellations* 23, no. 2 (2016): 223–35.

7. See Jorge Luis Borges, "Palabras pronunciadas por Jorge Luis Borges en la comida que le ofrecieron los escritores," *Sur* 142 (1946): 114–15; "L'illusion comique," *Sur* 237 (1955): 9–10; "Leyenda y realidad," in *Textos Recobrados III, 1956–1986* (Mexico: Debolsillo, 2015), 287–89.

INTRODUCTION

1. See Eric Hobsbwam, *The Age of Extremes: The Short Twentieth Century 1914–91* (London: Michael Joseph, 1994), 133.

2. For a paradigmatic example of the tendency to see populism as a right-wing, European, and entirely new political phenomenon, see Tzvetan Todorov, *The Inner Enemies of Democracy* (Cambridge: Polity, 2014), 139, 142.

3. See Cristiano Lima, "CIA Chief Calls Trump Nazi Germany Comparison 'Outrageous,'" *Politico,* January 15, 2017, www.politico.com /story/2017/01/cia-brennan-trump-nazi-germany-233636.

4. Andrea Mammone, "Don't Be Fooled by 'Moderate' Marine Le Pen: Front National's More Toxic Than Ever," *Guardian,* April 10, 2015. On PEGIDA and the German right, see Hans Vorländer, Maik Herold, and Steven Schäller, *PEGIDA: Entwicklung, Zusammensetzung und Deutung einer Empörungsbewegung* (Wiesbaden: Springer, 2016). On AFL (Alternative for Germany), see Nicole Berbuir, Marcel Lewandowsky, and Jasmin Siri "The AfD and Its Sympathisers: Finally a Right-Wing Populist Movement in Germany?," *German Politics* 24, no. 2 (2015): 154–78.

5. Because this book was finished before Trump's inauguration, the analysis of Trumpism is restricted mostly to his populist campaign. Some initial dimensions of Trumpism as a regime are addressed in A. Dirk Moses, Federico Finchelstein, and Pablo Piccato, "Juan Perón Shows How Trump Could Destroy Our Democracy without Tearing It Down," *Washington Post,* March 22, 2017; Federico Finchelstein and Pablo Piccato, "Trump y sus ideas sobre la ciencia," *Clarín* (Argentina), March 17, 2017; Pablo Piccato and Federico Finchelstein, "La ofensiva de Trump contra la sociedad civil ¿Qué sigue?," *Nexos (Mexico),* March 1, 2017; Federico Finchelstein, "Com Trump, Washington se torna a capital mundial do populismo," *Folha de S. Paulo (Brazil),* February 7, 2017.

6. James P. Pinkerton, "A Manifesto for the 60 Percent: The Center-Right Populist-Nationalist Coalition," *Breitbart,* September 16, 2016, www.breitbart.com/big-government/2016/09/11/manifesto-60-percent-center-right-populist-nationalist-coalition/; Scott Morefield, "Why Populism Is Replacing Conservatism, and Why It Is Winning," *Breitbart,* June 17, 2016, www.breitbart.com/2016-presidential-race/2016/06/17/populism-replacing-conservatism-winning/; John Hayward, "'Trump Could Be the Next Hitler!' Says the Increasingly Fascist Left," *Breitbart,* June 3, 2016, www.breitbart.com/big-government/2016/06/03/six-years-obamacare-liberals-suddenly-worried-fascism/.

7. Carl Hulse, "Donald Trump's Advice to Panicked Republicans: Man Up," *New York Times,* June 9, 2016, 14.

8. Ashley Parker, "Trump Pledges to 'Heal Divisions' (and Sue His Accusers)," *New York Times,* October 23, 2016, 23; "Trump Calls Himself a Victim of 'Smears' as Allegations Grow," *New York Times,* October 14, 2016, 15; Patrick Healy and Maggie Haberman May, "Donald Trump,

Bucking Calls to Unite, Claims 'Mandate' to Be Provocative," *New York Times,* May 11, 2016, www.nytimes.com/2016/05/12/us/politics /donald-trump-campaign.html.

9. See Robert Paxton, interview by Isaac Chotiner, "Is Donald Trump a Fascist? Yes and No," *Slate,* February 10, 2016, www.slate.com /articles/news_and_politics/interrogation/2016/02/is_donald_trump_ a_fascist_an_expert_on_fascism_weighs_in.html; and Robert Paxton, interview by Amy Goodman, "Father of Fascism Studies: Donald Trump Shows Alarming Willingness to Use Fascist Terms & Styles," *Democracy Now!,* March 15, 2016, www.democracynow.org/2016/3/15 /father_of_fascism_studies_donald_trump; Robert O. Paxton, interview by Marc Bassets, "Con Trump tenemos una especie de cuasifascismo populista, no un fascismo plenamente desarrollado," *El País,* June 6, 2016, internacional.elpais.com/internacional/2016/06/05 /estados_unidos/1465162717_340531.html.

10. Dylan Matthew, "I Asked 5 Fascism Experts Whether Donald Trump Is a Fascist. Here's What They Said," *Vox,* May 19, 2016, www .vox.com/policy-and-politics/2015/12/10/9886152/donald-trump-fascism; Peter Baker, "Rise of Donald Trump Tracks Growing Debate over Global Fascism," *New York Times,* May 18, 2016, www.nytimes .com/2016/05/29/world/europe/rise-of-donald-trump-tracks-growing-debate-over-global-fascism.html; Jan Werner Müller, "Trump Is a Far Right Populist, Not a Fascist," *Al Jazeera America,* December 26, 2015, http://america.aljazeera.com/opinions/2015/12/trump-is-a-far-right-populist-not-a-fascist.html. Similar objections were made by historians of European fascism such as Serge Bernstein in France. See his "Non, Donald Trump n'est pas fasciste mais ...," *Le Obs,* March 1, 2016, http://tempsreel.nouvelobs.com/monde/elections-americaines/20160301 .OBS5614/non-donald-trump-n-est-pas-fasciste-mais.html.

11. For the opposing view, see Federico Finchelstein and Pablo Piccato, "A Belief System That Once Laid the Groundwork for Fascism," *New York Times,* December 9, 2015, www.nytimes.com/roomfordebate /2015/12/09/donald-trumps-america/a-belief-system-that-once-laid-the-groundwork-for-fascism?smid = tw-share; and Federico Finchelstein and Fabián Bosoer, "Is Fascism Returning to Europe?," *New York Times,* December 18, 2013. See also the insightful interventions by Ruth

Ben-Ghiat, "An American Authoritarian," *Atlantic,* August 10, 2015, www
.theatlantic.com/politics/archive/2016/08/american-authoritarianism-under-donald-trump/495263/; and Carlos De la Torre, "¿Sobrevivirá la democracia americana a Trump?," *El País,* October 11, 2016.

12. Federico Finchelstein, *Transatlantic Fascism* (Durham, NC: Duke University Press, 2010).

13. See Zeev Sternhell, *The Birth of Fascist Ideology: From Cultural Rebellion to Political Revolution,* with Mario Sznajder and Maia Asheri (Princeton, NJ: Princeton University Press, 1994); Emilio Gentile, *Fascismo: Storia e interpretazione* (Rome-Bari: Laterza, 2002); Robert Paxton, *The Anatomy of Fascism* (New York: Knopf, 2004); Geoff Eley, *Nazism as Fascism: Violence, Ideology, and the Ground of Consent in Germany 1930–1945* (New York: Routledge, 2013); and Finchelstein, *Transatlantic Fascism.*

14. See Miguel Reale, "Nós e os fascistas da Europa," in *Obras Políticas* (Brasilia: UnB, 1983), vol. 3, 223–33.

15. See Reto Hofmann, *The Fascist Effect: Japan and Italy, 1915–1952* (Ithaca, NY: Cornell University Press, 2015), 64.

16. On postfascism and Peronism, see Finchelstein, *Transatlantic Fascism,* 168, 170. For a discussion of postfascism for other Latin American cases, see Sandra McGee Deutsch, "Fascismo, Neo-Fascismo, ou Post-Fascismo?," *Dialogos* 12, no. 3 (2009), 19–44. For Europe, see, among others, Nicola Tranfaglia, *Un passato scomodo: Fascismo e postfascismo* (Bari: Laterza, 1999); Roger Griffin, "The 'Post-Fascism' of the Alleanza Nazionale: A Case Study in Ideological Morphology," *Journal of Political Ideologies* 1, no. 2 (1996): 123–45; Tamir Bar-On, *Where Have All the Fascists Gone?* (Aldershot: Ashgate, 2007), 137; and Enzo Traverso, *Les nouveaux visages du fascisme* (Paris: Textuel, 2017).

17. See Zeev Sternhell, *Neither Right nor Left: Fascist Ideology in France* (Berkeley: University of California Press, 1986); and Zeev Sternhell, "Le fascisme en France: Entre refoulement et oubli," *Lignes* 50, no. 2 (2016).

18. For some key studies of populism, see Nadia Urbinati, *Democracy Disfigured: Opinion, Truth, and the People* (Cambridge: Harvard University Press, 2014); Carlos de la Torre, *Populist Seduction in Latin America* (Athens: Ohio University Press, 2010); Ernesto Laclau, *On Populist Reason* (London: Verso, 2005); Raanan Rein, "From Juan Perón to Hugo

Chávez and Back: Populism Reconsidered," in *Shifting Frontiers of Citizenship*, ed. Mario Sznajder, Luis Roniger, and Carlos Forment (Boston: Brill, 2012), 289–311; and Andrew Arato, *Post Sovereign Constitution Making: Learning and Legitimacy* (Oxford: Oxford University Press, 2016).

19. Juan Domingo Perón, *Memorial de Puerta de Hierro* (Buenos Aires: Honorable Congreso de la Nación, 2001), 65.

20. On this topic, see Roger Griffin, "Interregnum or Endgame? The Radical Right in the 'Post-Fascist' Era," in *The Populist Radical Right*, ed. Cas Mudde (London: Routledge, 2017), 15.

21. "Fini in Israele 'Il fascismo fu parte del male assoluto,'" *La Repubblica*, November 24, 2003.

22. On the great recession, see Carles Manera, *The Great Recession* (Brighton: Sussex Academic Press, 2013); and Anwar Shaikh, *Capitalism: Competition, Conflict, Crises* (New York: Oxford University Press, 2016).

23. Urbinati, *Democracy Disfigured*.

1. WHAT IS FASCISM IN HISTORY?

1. See Zeev Sternhell, *The Anti-enlightenment Tradition*, trans. David Meisel (New Haven, CT: Yale University Press, 2009).

2. See Angelo Ventrone, *Grande guerra e Novecento* (Rome: Donzelli, 2015), 222–25.

3. Mike Cronin, "The Blueshirt Movement, 1932–5: Ireland's Fascists?" *Journal of Contemporary History* 30, no. 2 (1995): 319.

4. João Ameal, *A Revolução da Ordem* (Lisbon: S.L., 1932), cited in "Lecturas," *Acción Española* (December 16, 1932): 109; "Reglamentos de los camisas azules," *Bandera Argentina* (February 22, 1933). See also Felipe Yofre, *El fascismo y nosotros* (Buenos Aires: Liga Republicana, 1933), 18, 40; Carlos Ibarguren, *La inquietud de esta hora: Liberalismo, corporativismo, nacionalismo* (Buenos Aires: Libreria y Editorial La Facultad, 1934); Folleto Luis F. Gallardo, *La Mística del Adunismo* (Buenos Aires: 1933), 15, in *Archivo General de la Nación* (AGN); Archivo Uriburu, Legajo 26; and also the speech by Argentine fascist leader Juan P. Ramos in *AGN*, Archivo Agustín P. Justo, Caja 45, doc. 146.

5. See Miguel Reale, "Nós e os fascistas da Europa," in *Obras Políticas* (Brasilia: UnB, 1983), 3:222–33; Jorge Vigón, "Actualidad

internacional," *Acción Española* (May 1, 1933): 423; Jorge Vigón "El éxito del Congreso Antifascista," *Acción Española* (June 16, 1933), 84.

6. See the following works by George L. Mosse: *Masses and Man: Nationalist and Fascist Perceptions of Reality* (New York: H. Fertig, 1980); and *The Nationalization of the Masses: Political Symbolism and Mass Movements in Germany from the Napoleonic Wars through the Third Reich* (Ithaca, NY: Cornell University Press, 1991).

7. Richard J. Evans, *The Coming of the Third Reich* (*London: Allen Lane, 2003*), 184–86. See also Wolfgang Schieder, "Fatal Attraction: The German Right and Italian Fascism," in *The Third Reich between Vision and Reality: New Perspectives on German History 1918–1945*, ed. Hans Momsen (Oxford: Berg, 2001); Alexander De Grand, *Fascist Italy and Nazi Germany* (New York: Routledge, 1995); Philippe Burrin, *Fascisme, nazisme, autoritarisme* (Paris: Seuil, 2000).

8. See Max Horkheimer and Theodor W. Adorno, *Dialectic of Enlightenment* (Stanford, CA: Stanford University Press, 2002). On Freud, see Federico Finchelstein, *El Mito del fascismo: De Freud a Borges* (Buenos Aires: Capital Intelectual, 2015).

9. Benito Mussolini, "La significazione," *Il Popolo d'Italia*, October 25, 1919; Benito Mussolini, "Un programma," *Il Popolo d'Italia*, February 26, 1920. See also Dino Grandi, *Le origini e la missione del fascismo* (Bologna: Capelli, 1922), I, 52–57, 58–62, 66–71; and the declarations by Mussolini on the people and democracy in "Lo spirito e il compito del fascismo," *L'Idea Nazionale*, May 24, 1924.

10. Emilio Gentile, *Le origini dell'ideologia fascista (1918–1925)* (Bologna: Il Mulino, 1996), 4–6. See also the interesting study by Augusto Simonini, *Il linguaggio di Mussolini* (Milan: Bompiani, 2004).

11. For the best example of this trend, see Denis Mack Smith, *Mussolini's Roman Empire* (New York: Penguin, 1977). For a criticism of this argument, see Zeev Sternhell, "How to Think about Fascism and Its Ideology," *Constellations* 15, no. 3 (2008): 280–90.

12. Antonio Gramsci, *Socialismo e fascismo: L'Ordine Nuovo 1921–1922* (Turin: Einaudi, 1978).

13. Benito Mussolini, "Dopo l'adunata fascista: Verso l'azione," *Il Popolo d'Italia*, October 13, 1919; Benito Mussolini, "Logica e demagogia," *Il Popolo d'Italia*, October 26, 1919; Benito Mussolini, "I volti e le

maschere," *Il Popolo d'Italia,* March 3, 1920; Benito Mussolini, "Dopo un anno. Il fascismo," *Il Popolo d'Italia,* March 26, 1920; Benito Mussolini, "Fatti, non parole!," *Il Popolo d'Italia,* March 30, 1920; Benito Mussolini, "Nella foresta degli 'ismi,'" *Il Popolo d'Italia,* March 31, 1920; Benito Mussolini, "Panglossismo," *Il Popolo d'Italia,* April 11, 1920; Benito Mussolini, "Verso la reazione!," *Il Popolo d'Italia,* April 29, 1920. See also Tabelloni murali, Mostra della Rivoluzione Fascista (MRF), B 91, F 154, Sala dotrinna SF 2, Archivio Centrale dello Stato. Italy.

14. See Ruth Ben Ghiat, *Fascist Modernities: Italy, 1922–1945* (Berkeley: University of California Press, 2001). For the notion of reactionary modernism, see Jeffrey Herf, *Reactionary Modernism: Technology, Culture, and Politics in Weimar and the Third Reich* (Cambridge: Cambridge University Press, 1984).

15. See Walter Benjamin, "The Work of Art in the Age of Mechanical Reproduction," in *Illuminations,* ed. Hannah Arendt, trans. Harry Zohn (New York: Schocken, 1969). 241. On Benjamin's notions of fascism, see also Walter Benjamin, "Theories of German Fascism," *New German Critique* 17 (1979): 120–28. For contemporary arguments that aestheticize and decontextualize fascism and victimization in ways that Benjamin would never have dreamed of, see Slavoj Žižek, *Did Somebody Say Totalitarianism? Five Interventions in the (Mis)use of a Notion* (New York: Verso, 2002); Giorgio Agamben, *Remnants of Auschwitz: The Witness and the Archive* (New York: Zone Books, 1999).

16. Paxton explains them as "the warmth of belonging to a race now fully aware of its identity, historic destiny, and power; the excitement of participating in a vast collective enterprise; the gratification of submerging oneself in a wave of shared feelings, and of sacrificing one's petty concerns for the group's good; and the thrill of domination." Robert Paxton, *The Anatomy of Fascism* (New York: Knopf, 2004), 17.

17. Simonetta Falasca-Zamponi, *Fascist Spectacle: The Aesthetics of Power in Mussolini's Italy* (Berkeley: University of California Press, 1997). See also Falasca-Zamponi's insightful essay "Fascism and Aesthetics," *Constellations* 15, no. 3 (2008); Mabel Berezin, *Making the Fascist Self: The Political Culture of Inter-war Italy* (Ithaca, NY: Cornell University Press, 1997).

18. See, for example, Volt [Vincenzo Fani Ciotti], *Programma della destra fascista* (Florence: La Voce, 1924), 49–51.

19. "Ma fuse e confuse nella sostanza." See Benito Mussolini, "Blocco fascista anticagoiesco delle 'teste di ferro'!," *Il Popolo d'Italia*, October 24, 1919.

20. See Benito Mussolini, "Sintesi della lotta politica," in *Opera omnia di Benito Mussolini*, vol. 21 (1924; repr., Florence: La Fenice, 1956), 46.

21. See Antonio Gramsci, "La guerra è la guerra," in *Socialismo e fascismo: L'Ordine Nuovo 1921–1922* (Turin: Einaudi, 1978), 55.

22. See Federico Finchelstein, *Fascismo, Liturgia e Imaginario: El mito del general Uriburu y la Argentina nacionalista* (Buenos Aires: Fondo de Cultura Económica, 2002), 144. On Latin American fascism, see the pathbreaking works of Sandra McGee Deutsch, *Las Derechas: The Extreme Right in Argentina, Brazil, and Chile 1890–1939* (Stanford, CA: Stanford University Press, 1999); Alberto Spektorowski, *Argentina's Revolution of the Right* (Notre Dame, IN: University of Notre Dame Press, 2003); Franco Savarino, "Juego de ilusiones: Brasil, México y los 'fascismos' latinoamericanos frente al fascismo italiano," *Historia Crítica* 37 (2009): 120–47; João Fábio Bertonha, *Sobre a Direita: Estudos Sobre o Fascismo, o Nazismo e o Integralismo* (Maringá, Brazil: Editora da Universidade estadual de Maringá, 2008); Hélgio Trindade, *O nazi-fascismo na América Latina: Mito e realidade* (Porto Alegre, Brazil: UfrGs, 2004).

23. Yitzhak Arad, Israel Gutman, and Abraham Margaliot, eds., *Documents on the Holocaust* (Lincoln: University of Nebraska Press, 1999), 134.

24. On fascist antisemitism, see Michele Sarfatti, *Gli ebrei nell'Italia fascista: Vicende, identità, persecuzione* (Turin: Einaudi, 2000); Renzo De Felice, *Storia degli ebrei italiani sotto il fascismo* (Turin: Einaudi, 1993); Marie-Anne Matard-Bonucci, *L'Italie Fasciste et La Persécution des Juifs* (Paris: Perrin, 2007); Valeria Galimi, "Politica della razza, antisemitismo, Shoah," *Studi Storici* 1 (2014): 169–182; Simon Levis Sullam, *I Carnefici Italiani: Scene dal Genocidio Degli Ebrei, 1943–1945* (Milan: Feltrinelli, 2015).

25. See Emilio Gentile, *Le religioni della politica: Fra democrazie e totalitarismi* (Rome-Bari: Laterza, 2001). Moreover, at times fascism established strong links with institutional religions and, in the Argentine case, presented itself as the political representative of God. On Argentine clerico-fascism, see Loris Zanatta, *Del estado liberal a la nación católica: Iglesia y Ejército en los orígenes del peronismo* (Bernal, Argentina: Universidad Nacional de Quilmes, 1996); and Finchelstein, *Transatlan-*

tic Fascism (Durham, NC: Duke University Press, 2010). On the notion of clerico-fascism, see also Enzo Collotti, *Fascismo, Fascismi* (Milan: Sansoni Editore, 1994).

26. See Richard J. Evans, *The Coming of the Third Reich*, 184–86. On the centrality of the fascist vision of gender and masculinity, see George L. Mosse, *Nationalism and Sexuality: Respectability and Abnormal Sexuality in Modern Europe* (New York: H. Fertig, 1985); George L. Mosse, *The Image of Man: The Creation of Modern Masculinity* (New York: Oxford University Press, 1996). See also Victoria De Grazia, *How Fascism Ruled Women: Italy 1922–1945* (Berkeley: University of California Press, 1992).

27. On the conceptual history of totalitarianism, see Enzo Traverso, *El Totalitarismo: Historia de Un Debate* (Buenos Aires: Eudeba, 2001); Anson Rabinbach, "Moments of Totalitarianism," *History and Theory* 45 (2006): 72–100; Ruth Ben-Ghiat, "A Lesser Evil? Italian Fascism in/and the Totalitarian Equation," in *The Lesser Evil: Moral Approaches to Genocide Practices in a Comparative Perspective*, ed. Helmut Dubiel and Gabriel Motzkin (New York: Routledge, 2004); Emilio Gentile, "Fascism and the Italian Road to Totalitarianism," *Constellations* 15, no. 3 (2008): 291–302.

28. Benito Mussolini, "La dottrina del fascismo," in *Opera omnia di Benito Mussolini*, vol. 34 (1932; repr., Florence: La Fenice, 1967), 119–21. In English, see also Benito Mussolini, *Fascism: Doctrine and Institutions* (Rome: Ardita, 1935).

29. On this topic, see Hannah Arendt, "Ideology and Terror: A Novel Form of Government," *Review of Politics* 15, no. 3 (1953): 303–27.

30. See, for example, Segreteria Particolare del Duce, Carteggio riservato, B 50 251/RF "Avanti!" Pietro Nenni (1931), Archivi Fascisti, Archivio Centrale dello Stato, Italy; Dossier France, Daniel Guerin, F Delta 721, 51/1, Vingt Ans d'Histoire Allemande, Bibliothèque de documentation internationale contemporaine, Nanterre, France; Piero Gobetti, *On Liberal Revolution* (New Haven, CT: Yale University Press, 2000), 226; G.L. "1935," *Cuaderno di 'Giustizia e libertá'* 12 (1935): 4–5.

31. Paxton, *Anatomy of Fascism*, 104.

32. See Matteo Pasetti, *L'Europa Corporativa: Una Storia Transnazionale tra Le Due Guerre Mondiali* (Bologna: Bononia University Press, 2016); Antonio Costa Pinto and Francisco Palomanes Martinho, eds., *A*

Onda Corporativa: Corporativismo e Ditaduras na Europa e América Latina (Rio de Janeiro: Editora da Fundação Getulio Vargas, 2016).

33. In this regard, Slavoj Žižek seems to shift from argument into hyperbole. For him, the rationalist background of communism explains the "emancipatory potential" of Stalinism. Slavoj Žižek, *Did Somebody Say Totalitarianism? Five Interventions in the (Mis)use of a Notion* (New York: Verso, 2001), 131.

34. On the idea of listening to reason, see Michael Steinberg, *Listening to Reason: Culture, Subjectivity, and 19th- Century Music* (Princeton, NJ: Princeton University Press, 2004). On the Nazi appropriation of Beethoven, see David B. Dennis, *Beethoven in German Politics, 1870–1989* (New Haven, CT: Yale University Press, 1996). I want to thank Eli Zaretsky for sharing his thoughts about *The Lives of Others* with me.

35. One may find a similar presentation in Gary Oldman's character's gruesome killings while he listened to Beethoven in Luc Besson's *The Professional* (1994). The killer in Mary Harron's *American Psycho* (2000), who listens to Phil Collins while massacring people, may be seen as an ironic downplaying of this aesthetic movement.

36. A different trend, developed by Marxist social scientists, continued the more structural line of analysis without sufficiently exploring its interconnected historical processes. The best example of this approach is Nicos Poulantzas, *Fascism and Dictatorship: The Third International and the Problem of Fascism* (London: NLB, 1974).

37. Renzo De Felice, *Mussolini il Revoluzionario 1883–1920*, vol. 22 (1965; repr., Turin: Einaudi, 1995); Renzo De Felice, "Il fenomeno fascista," *Storia Contemporanea* 10 (1979); Emilio Gentile, "Fascism in Italian Historiography: In Search of an Individual Historical Identity," *Journal of Contemporary History* 1, no. 2 (1986): 183.

38. This stance was nonetheless increasingly stressed, becoming what Norberto Bobbio has defined as a "strong anticommunist passion" embodied in De Felice's historical narrative. See Norberto Bobbio, "Revisionismo nella storia d'Italia, " in *Italiani, amici, nemici*, ed. Norberto Bobbio, Renzo De Felice, and Gian Enrico Rusconi (Milan: Reset, 1996), 57. With regard to researching fascism globally, De Felice, and historians like him, never considered this exercise either essential

or indispensable and was careful to remark, with increasing emphasis throughout his vast work, the Italian specificity of the fascist phenomenon compared with German Nazism or other radical-wing movements. Other historians at the time presented a more comparative view. See, for example, Eugen Weber, *Varieties of Fascism: Doctrines of Revolution in the Twentieth Century* (New York, 1964); Walter Laqueur and George Mosse, eds., *International Fascism, 1920–1945* (New York: Harper and Row, 1966); S.J. Woolf, ed., *European Fascism* (New York: Vintage Books, 1969); Walter Laqueur, ed., *Fascism: A Reader's Guide* (Berkeley: University of California Press, 1976). For an overview of the historiography, see Wolfgang Wippermann, *Faschismustheorien: Die Entwicklung der Diskussion von den Anfängen bis heute* (Darmstadt, Germany: Primus, 1997); Emilio Gentile, *Fascismo: Storia e interpretazione* (Rome: Laterza, 2002).

39. On this topic, see Enzo Traverso, *El Totalitarismo*.

40. Zeev Sternhell, "Fascism: Reflections on the Fate of Ideas in Twentieth Century History," *Journal of Political Ideologies* 5, no. 2 (2000). It is possible to observe this particular Cold War continuity in De Felice's work. In 1969, De Felice argued that the theory of totalitarianism "with respect to our problem, undoubtedly poses suggestive aspects giving rise to many questions; but—at the same time—offers important elements for the study of historical interpretation of fascism as a phenomenon, elements which should not be underestimated." De Felice suggested that, in order to understand the historical reality of fascism, one should have to analyze its totalitarian forms. See Renzo De Felice, *El Fascismo: Sus interpretaciones* (Buenos Aires: Paidós, 1976), 120; Renzo De Felice, *Il Fascismo: Le interpretazioni dei contemporanei e degli storici* (Rome-Bari: Laterza, 1998), 36. See also Emilo Gentile, "Renzo De Felice: A Tribute," *Journal of Contemporary History* 32, no. 2 (1997), 149; Emilo Gentile, *La via Italiana al totalitarismo* (Rome: La Nuova Italia Scientifica, 1995), 114–17.

41. See, for example, Roger Griffin, "The Primacy of Culture: The Current Growth (or Manufacture) of Consensus within Fascist Studies," *Journal of Contemporary History* 37, no. 1 (2002): 21–43; Stanley G. Payne, "Historical Fascism and the Radical Right," *Journal of Contemporary History* 35, no. 1 (2000): 111; Roger Griffin, ed., *International Fascism:*

Theories, Causes and the New Consensus (London, 1998); Roger Eatwell, "Towards a New Model of Generic Fascism," *Journal of Theoretical Politics* 4, no. 2 (1992).

42. Stanley G. Payne, *A History of Fascism 1914–1945* (Madison: University of Wisconsin Press, 1995), 461.

43. Gilbert Allardyce, "What Fascism Is Not: Thoughts on the Deflation of a Concept," *American Historical Review* 84, no. 2 (1979): 369.

44. Gentile, *Fascismo*, 9–10.

45. Paxton, *Anatomy of Fascism*, 23, 218.

46. See Ernst Nolte, *La guerra civil europea, 1917–1945: Nacionalsocialismo y bolchevismo* (Mexico: FCE, 1994, originally published as *Der europäische Bürgerkrieg 1917–1945: Nationalsozialismus und Bolschewismus*, Berlin: Propyläen, 1987). See François Furet and Ernst Nolte, *Fascism and Communism* (Lincoln: University of Nebraska Press, 2001). For Nolte and the *Historikerstreit*, see *Forever in the Shadow of Hitler? Original Documents of the Historikerstreit, the Controversy Concerning the Singularity of the Holocaust*, ed. and trans. Truett Cates and James Knowlton (Atlantic Highlands, NJ: Humanities Press, 1993). For analyses of this debate, see Dominick LaCapra, *Representing the Holocaust: History, Theory, Trauma* (Ithaca, NY: Cornell University Press, 1994), 49–50, 53, 106, 190; Dominick LaCapra, *History and Memory after Auschwitz* (Ithaca, NY: Cornell University Press, 1998), 55–59, 64–65; María Pía Lara, *Narrating Evil: A Postmetaphysical Theory of Reflective Judgment* (New York: Columbia University Press, 2007); Matthew G. Specter, *Habermas: An Intellectual Biography* (Cambridge: Cambridge University Press, 2010).

47. On Nolte as a pioneer for generic historians, see Aristotle Kallis, "Fascism—A 'Generic' Concept?," in *The Fascism Reader*, ed. Aristotle Kallis (London: Routledge, 2003), 46.

48. Ernst Nolte, *Three Faces of Fascism: Action Française, Italian fascism, National Socialism* (New York: Mentor, 1969), 51, 81.

49. Nolte, *Three Faces of Fascism*, 529, 540.

50. Zeev Sternhell, "How to Think about Fascism and Its Ideology," *Constellations* 15, no. 3 (2008): 282.

51. Zeev Sternhell, *La Droite révolutionnaire (1885–1914): Les origines françaises du fascisme* (Paris: Gallimard, 1997), x.

52. Sternhell, *La Droite révolutionnaire*, xxxii.

53. Zeev Sternhell "Fascism: Reflections on the Fate of Ideas in Twentieth Century History," *Journal of Political Ideologies* 5, no. 2 (2000): 139.

54. Sternhell, *La Droite révolutionnaire*, x.

55. See Zeev Sternhell, *The Birth of Fascist Ideology: From Cultural Rebellion to Political Revolution*, with Mario Sznajder and Maia Asheri (Princeton, NJ: Princeton University Press, 1994), 9, 12; Zeev Sternhell, *Neither Right nor Left: Fascist Ideology in France* (Berkeley: University of California Press, 1986), 27; Sternhell, *La Droite révolutionnaire*, ix-lxxvi; Zeev Sternhell "Fascist Ideology" in *Fascism: A Reader's Guide. Analyses, Interpretations, Bibliography*, ed. Walter Laqueur (Berkeley: University of California Press, 1976), 315–71.

56. Zeev Sternhell, "How to Think about Fascism and Its Ideology," *Constellations* 15, no. 3 (2008): 281, 282.

57. George L. Mosse, *The Nationalization of the Masses: Political Symbolism and Mass Movements in Germany from the Napoleonic Wars through the Third Reich* (1975; repr., Ithaca, NY: Cornell University Press, 1996), 214. Page numbers refer to the 1996 edition.

58. It is important to note that many insights into intellectual, cultural, and mythological practices that appear in one way or another in the texts of Mosse can be identified with the historiographical line stemming from De Felice. The most remarkable case in this context is that of Emilio Gentile's important book *Il culto del littorio* (Rome: Laterza, 1993). Gentile also recognized, without having to relinquish the idea of the specificity of Italian fascism, the innovative historiographical importance of both Mosse and De Felice, in his book on the origins of fascist ideology (*Origini dell' ideologia fascista*), 2; George Mosse, *Intervista sul Nazismo: A cura di Michael Ledeen* (Rome: Laterza, 1977), 89–90.

59. George Mosse, *The Fascist Revolution: Toward a General Theory of Fascism* (New York: Howard Fertig, 1998), x-xvii, 42.

60. Enzo Traverso, "Interpreting Fascism: Mosse, Sternhell and Gentile in Comparative Perspective," *Constellations* 15, no. 3 (2008): 310.

61. For example, Stanley Payne presents seven reasons for fascism's lack of authenticity in Latin America: 1) minimal political mobilization, 2) nationalism without territorial ambitions, 3) military predominance, 4) impossibility of autarchy in dependent and underdeveloped countries, 5) elitist client/patron relations, 6) multiracial nature of society, and 7)

weakness of the left before 1960. Whereas points 1, 2, 5, and 7 are simply wrong with respect to South American countries like Argentina, Bolivia, Chile, or Brazil, it would be possible to ascribe point 3 to Spanish fascism or points 4 and 5 to Italian fascism, especially in the southern half of the Italian peninsula. Further, if we replace "race" with "ethnicity," we could easily present Nazi Germany before the Holocaust as a multiethnic society with regard to point 6. See Payne, *History of Fascism*, 340; and his earlier *Fascism: Comparison and Definition* (Madison: University of Wisconsin Press, 1980), 167–76. See also Alistair Hennessy, "Fascism and Populism in Latin America," in *Fascism: A Reader's Guide. Analyses, Interpretations, Bibliography*, ed. Walter Laqueur (Berkeley: University of California Press, 1976), 255–94; Finchelstein, *Transatlantic Fascism*, 183.

62. For example, Roger Griffin, a noted scholar of fascism, views fascism as a "consciously constructed ideal type of fascism which sets up to be more heuristically useful to academic research than existing ones." See Roger Griffin, *The Nature of Fascism* (New York: Routledge, 1991), 12; and Stanley Payne, *A History of Fascism 1914–1945* (Madison: University of Wisconsin Press, 1995), 4. For a criticism of Griffin in this regard, see Daniel Woodley, *Fascism and Political Theory: Critical Perspectives on Fascist Ideology* (London, 2010), 8–13.

63. Payne, *History of Fascism*, 14; Roger Griffin, *Modernism and Fascism: The Sense of a Beginning under Mussolini and Hitler* (London, 2007), xv, 332; Griffin, *Nature of Fascism*.

64. See Griffin, *Nature of Fascism;* Griffin, *Fascist Century* (New York: Palgrave Macmillan, 2008). See also Payne, *History of Fascism;* and his earlier *Fascism: Comparison and Definition* (Madison: University of Wisconsin Press, 1980), 167–76; Paxton, *Anatomy of Fascism;* Roger Eatwell, "On Defining the 'Fascist Minimum': The Centrality of Ideology," *Journal of Political Ideologies* 1 (1996): 303–19.

65. Benjamin Zachariah, "A Voluntary Gleichschaltung? Indian Perspectives Towards a Non-Eurocentric Understanding of Fascism," *Transcultural Studies* 2 (2014): 66–67.

66. The most recent symptomatic example of this resistance to global approaches to fascism outside Europe can be found in the teleological and highly repetitive digressions expressed in David Roberts's *Fascist Interactions: Proposals for a New Approach to Fascism and Its Era,*

1919–1945 (New York: Berghahn Books, 2016). For my criticism of other historiographical examples outside Europe, see Finchelstein, *Fascismo, liturgia e imaginario*, 9–27.

67. See Constantin Iordachi, "Comparative Fascist Studies; An introduction," in *Comparative Fascist Studies: New Perspectives*, ed. Constantin Iordachi (London: Routledge, 2010), 41; Zachariah, "Voluntary Gleichschaltung?, 63–100. See also Benjamin Zachariah, "Rethinking (the Absence) of Fascism in India, c. 1922–45," in *Cosmopolitan Thought Zones: South Asia and the Global Circulation of Ideas*, ed. Sugata Bose and Kris Manjapra (Houndmills, Basingstoke, UK: Palgrave Macmillan, 2010), 178–209.

68. Benjamin Zachariah, "At the Fuzzy Edges of Fascism: Framing the Volk in India," *South Asia: Journal of South Asian Studies* 38, no. 4 (2015): 641.

69. Federico Finchelstein, *Transatlantic Fascism* (Durham, NC: Duke University Press, 2010), 4, 39.

70. See Sebastian Conrad, *What Is Global History?* (Princeton, NJ: Princeton University Press, 2016), 3, 44–45, 78–79. On transnational and comparative history, see, for example, Daniel Rodgers, Frederick Cooper, Pierre-Yves Saunier, Michael Werner, and Bénédicte Zimmerman, "Penser l'histoire croisée: Entre empirie et réflexivité," *Annales. Histoire, sciences sociales* 58 (2003): 7–36; and Gunilla Budde, Sebastian Conrad, and Oliver Janz, ed., *Transnationale Geschichte: Themen, Theorien, Tendenzen* (Göttingen: Vandenhoeck and Ruprecht, 2006).

71. Rebekka Habermas, "Lost in Translation: Transfer and Non-transfer in the Atakpame Colonial Scandal," *Journal of Modern History* 86 (March 2014): 48, 49.

72. See Reto Hofmann, *The Fascist Effect: Japan and Italy, 1915–1952* (Ithaca, NY: Cornell University Press, 2015), 7. On Japanese fascism, see also Rikki Kersten, "Japan," in *The Oxford Handbook of Fascism*, ed. R.J.B. Bosworth (Oxford: Oxford University Press, 2009), 526–44.

73. Silvio Villegas, *No hay enemigos a la derecha* (Manizales: Arturo Zapata, 1937), 80, 86, 144, 145. I want to thank Luis Herrán Ávila for sharing this source with me.

74. See José Vasconcelos, "El Fulgor en la tiniebla," *Timón*, March 23, 1940; "En Defensa propia: Los protocolos de los sabios de Sión,"

Timón, May 25, 1940; and "Otro fantasma: El nazismo en la América española," *Timón,* May 4, 1940. These articles were published in Itzhak M. Bar-Lewaw, ed., *La Revista "Timón" y José Vasconcelos* (Mexico: Edimex, 1971), 77–79, 138–40, 146–49.

75. See Jean Meyer, *El Sinarquismo: ¿Un Fascismo Mexicano? 1937–1947* (Mexico: Joaquín Mortiz, 1979).

76. See Tirso Molinari Morales, *El fascismo en el Perú* (Lima: Fondo Editorial de la Facultad de Ciencias Sociales, 2006), 300–3.

77. See Giulia Albanese, *Dittature Mediterranee: Sovversioni fasciste e colpi di stato in Italia, Spagna e Portogallo* (Rome: Laterza, 2016), 210, 211; Sven Reichardt, "Violence, Body, Politics: Paradoxes in Interwar Germany" in *Political Violence and Democracy in Western Europe, 1918–1940,* ed. Chris Millington and Kevin Passmore (Houndmills: Palgrave, 2015), 62–96.

78. See Albanese, *Dittature Mediterranee,* xxi, xxii; Finchelstein, *Transatlantic Fascism;* Miguel Ángel Perfecto, "La derecha radical Argentina y España: Relaciones culturales e interdependencias," *Studia Historica Historia Contemporánea* 33 (2015); Constantin Iordachi, *The Comparative History of Fascism in Eastern Europe: Sources and Commentaries* (London: Bloomsbury, 2017). On global fascism, see Stein Ugelvik Larsen, ed., *Fascism outside Europe: The European Impulse against Domestic Conditions in the Diffusion of Global Fascism* (Boulder, CO: Social Science Monographs, 2001).

79. As Kiran Klaus Patel and Sven Reichardt maintain, "Transnational processes of exchange and adaptation that began in or led to Nazi Germany have been largely neglected. Transnationalism and Nazism seem incompatible, and transnational history continues to concentrate on peaceful forms of exchange between similarly structured societies" ("The Dark Side of Transnationalism Social Engineering and Nazism, 1930s–40s," *Journal of Contemporary History* 51, no. 1 [2016]: 6). Christian Goeschel also perceptively proposes moving beyond a homogenizing notion of transfer: "It is time to clarify our terminology and think more concretely in terms of a history of fascist entanglement, a history that examines both mutual influences amongst fascist regimes and their interconnectedness rather than simply looking at transfers. The 'fascist entanglement' perspective also examines

the significance of transfers and does not assume that all crossovers were necessarily equally important for the actors involved, paying close attention to friction amongst the actors" ("Italia Docet? The Relationship between Italian Fascism and Nazism Revisited," *European History Quarterly* 42, no. 3 [2012], 490). See also the important earlier essay by Ruth Ben-Ghiat, "Fascist Italy and Nazi Germany: The Dynamics of an Uneasy Relationship," in *Art, Culture, and the Media in the Third Reich*, ed. Richard Etlin (Chicago: University of Chicago Press, 2002), 257–86; and Benjamin Martin, *The Nazi-Fascist New Order for European Culture* (Cambridge: Harvard University Press, 2016).

80. Zachariah, "Voluntary Gleichschaltung?," 63.

81. César Pico, *Carta a Jacques Maritain sobre la colaboración de los católicos con los movimientos de tipo fascista* (Buenos Aires: Francisco A. Colombo, 1937), 7–8, 13–14, 20, 21, 36, 40–41, 43.

82. See José Maria Pemán, "Pasemos a la escucha," *Sol y Luna* 4 (1940): 91.

83. Faisal Devji, *The Impossible Indian: Gandhi and the Temptation of Violence* (Cambridge: Harvard University Press, 2012), 21; Markus Daechsel, "Scientism and Its Discontents: The Indo-Muslim 'Fascism' of Inayatullah Khan al-Mashriqi," *Modern Intellectual History* 3, no. 3 (2006): 452–53; Hofmann, *Fascist Effect*, 46.

84. Federico Finchelstein, *The Ideological Origins of the Dirty War: Fascism, Populism, and Dictatorship in Twentieth Century Argentina* (Oxford: Oxford University Press, 2014).

85. See Reto Hofmann, *Fascist Effect*, 136–42. On the Cold War in Latin America, see Tanya Harmer, "The Cold War in Latin America," in *The Routledge Handbook of the Cold War*, ed. Artemy M. Kalinovsky and Craig Daigle (Abingdon: Routledge, 2014); Tanya Harmer, *Allende's Chile and the Inter-American Cold War* (Chapel Hill: University of North Carolina Press, 2011). See also Gilbert M. Joseph, "Latin America's Long Cold War," in *A Century of Revolution: Insurgent and Counterinsurgent Violence during Latin America's Long Cold War*, ed. Greg Grandin and Gilbert M. Joseph (Durham, NC: Duke University Press, 2010); Virginia Garrard-Burnett, Mark Atwood Lawrence, and Julio E. Moreno, eds., *Beyond the Eagle's Shadow: New Histories of Latin America's Cold War* (Albuquerque: University of New Mexico Press, 2013).

86. Andrea Mammone, *Transnational Neofascism in France and Italy* (Cambridge: Cambridge University Press, 2015), xix.

87. See Luis Herrán Ávila, "Anticommunism, the Extreme Right, and the Politics of Enmity in Argentina, Colombia, And Mexico, 1946–1972" (PhD diss., The New School for Social Research, 2016); and his article "Las guerrillas blancas, anticomunismo transnacional e imaginarios de derechas en Argentina y México, 1954–1972," *Quinto Sol* 19, no. 1 (2015); Daniel Gunnar Kressel, "The Hispanic Community of Nations: The Spanish-Argentine Nexus and the Imagining of a Hispanic Cold War Bloc," *Cahiers des Amériques latines* 79, no. 2 (2015): 115–33. See also Leandro Pereira Gonçalves, "Plínio Salgado e a Guerra Fria: Uma análise entre Brasil e Portugal no âmbito das Guerras Coloniais," *Cahiers des Amériques latines* 79, no. 2 (2015): 31–54; Odilon Caldeira Neto, *Sob o signo do sigma: Integralismo, neointegralismo e antissemitismo* (Maringá: EDUEM, 2014); Ernesto Bohoslavsky and Stéphane Boisard, "Les droites latino-américaines pendant la guerre froide (1959–1989)," *Cahiers des Amériques latines* 79, no. 2 (2015): 17–30; the essays in Olivier Dard, ed., *Organisations, Mouvements et partis des Droites Radicales au XXᵉ siècle* (Bern: Peter Lang, 2016); Matteo Albanese and Pablo del Hierro, *Transnational Fascism in the Twentieth Century: Spain, Italy and the Global Neo-Fascist Network* (London: Bloomsbury, 2016).

88. See Jorge Luis Borges, "Deutsches Requiem," in *Obras Completas* (Buenos Aires: Emecé, 1996), 1:581; Jorge Luis Borges, *Labyrinths: Selected Stories and Other Writings* (New York: New Directions, 1964), 147. On Borges and Zur Linde, see Finchelstein, *El Mito del fascismo*.

89. I thank Ben Brower for sharing his reflections on the relationship of physical violence to "symbolic violence." On this topic, see also Étienne Balibar, "Outlines of a Topography of Cruelty: Citizenship and Civility in the Era of Global Violence," *Constellations* 8, no. 1 (2001); Étienne Balibar, *Violence and Civility* (New York: Columbia University Press, 2015); Richard J. Bernstein, *Violence: Thinking without Banisters* (Cambridge: Polity, 2013); Martin Jay, *Refractions of Violence* (New York: Routledge, 2003). On fascism, see also Angelo Ventrone, *La seduzione totalitaria* (Rome: Donzelli, 2003); Francisco Sevillano Calero, *Exterminar: El terror con Franco* (Madrid: Oberon, 2004); Sven Reichardt, "Fas-

cismo e teoria delle pratiche sociali: Violenza e comunità come elementi di un praxeologico di fascismo," *Storiografia* 12 (2008).

90. See Finchelstein, *El Mito del fascismo.*

91. On antifascism and its view of fascism, see Benedetto Croce, *Scritti e discorsi politici, 1943–1947,* 2 vols. (Bari: Laterza 1963), 1:7, 2:46, 357. See also Renzo De Felice, *Interpretations of Fascism* (Cambridge, MA: Harvard University Press, 1977), 14–23; Enzo Collotti, ed., *Fascismo e antifascismo* (Rome: Laterza, 2000); Leonardo Paggi, "Antifascism and the Reshaping of the Democratic Consensus in Post-1945 Italy," *New German Critique* 67 (1996); Manuela Consonni, *L'Eclisse dell'Antifascismo* (Rome: Laterza, 2015); Hugo García, "Transnational History: A New Paradigm for Anti-fascist Studies?" *Contemporary European History* 25, no. 4 (2016): 563–72; Hugo García, Mercedes Yusta, Xavier Tabet, and Cristina Clímaco, eds., *Rethinking Anti-fascism: History, Memory and Politics, 1922 to the Present* (New York: Berghahn, 2016).

92. Jean Améry, *At the Mind's Limits* (Bloomington: Indiana University Press, 1980), x.

93. Chaim Kaplan, *Scroll of Agony: The Warsaw Diary of Chaim A. Kaplan* (New York: Collier Books, 1973), 280–81.

94. Primo Levi, *The Black Hole of Auschwitz* (Cambridge: Polity, 2005), 8, 33, 72.

95. Ian Thomson, *Primo Levi* (London: Hutchinson, 2002), 26–27.

96. On notions of the enemy, see Finchelstein, *Transatlantic Fascism;* Angelo Ventrone, *Il Nemico Interno: Immagini, parole e simboli della lotta politica nell'Italia del Novecento* (Rome: Donzelli, 2005).

97. There are some significant exceptions among historians of fascism that have explored the connections between fascism and Nazism and the Holocaust. I see this chapter as providing an elaborate complement to these works. See, for example, Tim Mason, *Nazism, Fascism and the Working Class* (Cambridge: Cambridge University Press, 1995); Mosse, *Fascist Revolution;* Geoff Eley, *Nazism as Fascism: Violence, Ideology and the Ground of Consent in Germany 1930–1945* (New York: Routledge, 2013).

98. Saul Friedländer, "Nazism: Fascism or Totalitarianism," in Charles S. Maier, Stanley Hoffmann, and Andrew Gould, ed., *The Rise of the Nazi Regime: Historical Reassessments* (Boulder: Westview Press,

1986), 30. See also Saul Friedländer, *Memory, History, and the Extermination of the Jews of Europe* (Bloomington: Indiana University Press, 1993), 26; Friedländer, "Mosse's Influence on the Historiography of the Holocaust," in *What History Tells: George L. Mosse and the Culture of Modern Europe*, ed. Stanley G. Payne, David J. Sorkin, and John S. Tortorice (Madison: University of Wisconsin Press, 2004), 142.

99. Friedländer pushes his point radically enough to limit any kind of comparison. In his critique of the work of the German historian Wolfgang Schieder, Friedlander argues, "And a point, on which it seems useless to dwell, Nazi anti-Semitism has been compared to the 'racism' of Italian fascists toward Africans, slaves, and the Germans of southern Tyrol" ("Nazism," 27). For a more nuanced approach, see Ian Kershaw, *Hitler, the Germans and the Final Solution* (New Haven, CT: Yale University Press, 2008), 345.

100. For important works on these connections, see A. Dirk Moses, ed., *Empire, Colony, Genocide: Conquest, Occupation, and Subaltern Resistance in World History* (New York: Berghahn, 2008); Bashir and Amos Goldberg, "Deliberating the Holocaust and the Nakba: Disruptive Empathy and Binationalism in Israel/Palestine," *Journal of Genocide Research* 16, no. 1 (2014): 77–99; Dan Stone, *History, Memory and Mass Atrocity: Essays on the Holocaust and Genocide* (London: Vallentine Mitchell, 2006); Donald Bloxham, *The Final Solution: A Genocide* (Oxford: Oxford University Press, 2009).

101. Matthew P. Fitzpatrick, "The Pre-History of the Holocaust? The Sonderweg and Historikerstreit Debates and the Abject Colonial Past," *Central European History* 41, no. 3 (2008); Edward Ross Dickinson, "The German Empire: An Empire?" *History Workshop Journal* 66 (2008); Olivier Le Cour Grandmaison, *Coloniser, exterminer: Sur la guerre et l'état colonial* (Paris: Fayard, 2005); Isabel Hull, *Absolute Destruction: Military Culture and the Practices of War in Imperial Germany* (Ithaca: Cornell University Press, 2005); Joël Kotek, "Sonderweg: Le génocide des Herero, symptôme d'un Sonderweg allemand?" *La Revue d'histoire de la Shoah* 189 (2008); Jürgen Zimmerer, "The First Genocide of the Twentieth Century: The German War of Destruction in Southwest Africa (1904–1908) and the Global History of Genocide," in *The Holocaust: Lessons and Legacies*, ed., Doris L. Bergen (Chicago: 2008), 34–64; Donald Bloxham, *The Final Solution: A Genocide*

(Oxford: Oxford University Press 2009); Benjamin Brower, "Genealogies of Modern Violence, Arendt and Imperialism in Africa 1830–1914," in *The Cambridge History of Violence,* ed. Louise Edwards, Nigel Penn, and Jay Winter, vol. 4 (Cambridge: Cambridge University Press, 2017).

102. See Hannah Arendt, *The Origins of Totalitarianism* (New York: Meridian, 1959) 158–84; Hannah Arendt, "The Seeds of a Fascist International," in *Essays in Understanding, 1930–1954,* ed. Jerome Kohn (New York: Harcourt Brace, 1994), 147.

103. See Raul Hilberg, *The Destruction of the European Jews* (New York: Holmes and Meier, 1985) 660–79; Susan Zuccotti, *The Italians and the Holocaust: Persecution, Rescue, and Survival* (New York: Basic Books, 1987); Simon Levis Sullam, *I Carnefici Italiani: Scene dal Genocidio degli ebrei, 1943–1945* (Milan: Feltrinelli, 2015).

104. I borrow the concept "laboratories of fascism" from Enzo Traverso's key work *The Origins of Nazi Violence.*

105. See Lloyd E. Eastman, "Fascism in Kuomintang China: The Blue Shirts," *China Quarterly* 49 (January–March 1972): 4.

106. Antonio Costa Pinto, *Os Camisas Azuis e Salazar—Rolão Preto e o Fascismo em Portugal* (Porto Alegre: EDIPUCRS, 2016), 110. On Portuguese fascism and its international connections with other fascisms, see also Nuno Simão Ferreira, "Alberto de Monsaraz e a vaga dos nacionalismos político-autoritários europeus do pós-I Guerra mundial: Um rumo até o fascismo?" *Lusíada História* 4 (2007): 7–75.

107. See Federico Finchelstein, "Truth, Mythology and the Fascist Unconscious," *Constellations* 23, no. 2 (2016): 227.

108. Ibid., 225.

109. Ventrone, *La seduzione totalitaria,* 138–139, 153, 185.

110. See Primo Levi, *The Drowned and the Saved* (New York: Vintage, 1989), 105. On Levi's identification of Nazism with fascism, see Primo Levi, *Conversazioni e interviste 1964–1987* (Turin: Einaudi, 1997), 245, 250.

111. On the negative sublime, see the following works by Dominick LaCapra: *History and Memory after Auschwitz* (Ithaca, NY: Cornell University Press, 1998), 27–30; *Representing the Holocaust: History, Theory, Trauma* (Ithaca, NY: Cornell University Press, 1994), 100–110; *Writing History, Writing Trauma* (Baltimore: Johns Hopkins University Press, 2001), 94.

112. For some examples see Sergio Panunzio, *Diritto, forza e violenza: Lineamenti di una teoria della violenza* (Bologna: Capelli, 1921), 17; Curzio Suckert (Malaparte), *L'Europa Vivente: Teoria Storica del Sindicalismo Nazionale* (Florence: La Voce, 1923), xlviii, 1–5, 22–25, 34, 111–19; Curzio Malaparte, *Italia barbara* (Turin: P. Gobetti, 1925). For an early criticism of fascism's appreciation of violence "for its own sake," see Rodolfo Mondolfo, *Per la comprensione storica del fascismo* (Bologna: Capelli, 1922) i–iii, xv, xxxiv–xxxv; Rodolfo Mondolfo, "Forza e violenza nella storia (Aprendo la discussione)," in *Diritto, forza e violenza: Lineamenti di una teoria della violenza,* ed. Sergio Panunzio (Bologna: Capelli, 1921), viii, xi, xiii, xv, xvii, xvii, xviii, xix.

113. MRF B 93 F, 159 SF 1, Archivio Centrale dello Stato, Italy. Mussolini said, "I don't give a damn" (*me ne frego*)—the proud motto of the fighting squads scrawled by a wounded man on his bandages is not only an act of philosophic stoicism; it sums up a doctrine that is not merely political: it is evidence of a fighting spirit that accepts all risks. It signifies a new style of Italian life. The Fascist accepts and loves life; he rejects and despises suicide as cowardly. Life as he understands it means duty, elevation, conquest; life must be lofty and full; it must be lived for oneself but above all for others, both nearby and far off, present and future" (Benito Mussolini, "La dottrina del fascismo," in *Opera omnia di Benito Mussolini,* vol. 34 [Florence: La Fenice, 1967], 119–21).

114. MRF B 93 F, 159 SF 1, Archivio Centrale dello Stato, Italy.

115. See, for example, tabelloni murali, MRF B 93 F 158; MRF B 91 F, 154 Sala Dotrinna SF 2, tabelloni murali," Archivio Centrale dello Stato. Italy.

116. See *Acción Española,* Antología, March 1937, 366; Finchelstein, *Origins of Dirty War,* 45; James P. Jankowski, "The Egyptian Blue Shirts and the Egyptian Wafd, 1935–1938," *Middle Eastern Studies* 6 (1970): 82; Eastman, "Fascism in Kuomintang China," 9–10.

117. Villegas, *No hay enemigos a la derecha,* 224; Constantin Iordachi, "God's Chosen Warriors," in *Comparative Fascist Studies,* ed. Constantin Iordachi (London: Routledge, 2010), 345–47

118. See Benito Mussolini, "Vivere pericolosamente," in *Opera omnia di Benito Mussolini,* vol. 21 (1924; repr., Florence: La Fenice, 1960), 40.

119. See Benito Mussolini, "La dottrina del fascismo" in *Opera omnia di Benito Mussolini*, vol. 34 (Florence: La Fenice, 1967), 119–21. For a more specific Fascist self-understanding of the state as shown in the "permanent" fascist exhibition of 1942, see MRF B, 91 F, 154 Sala Dotrinna SF 2, tabelloni murali, "Lo Stato Fascista"; "I Codici di Mussolini," Archivio Centrale dello Stato, Italia.

120. See Ann Laura Stoler, "On Degrees of Imperial Sovereignty," *Public Culture* 18, no. 1 (2006): 135.

121. Bruno Biancini, *Dizionario Mussoliniano Mille Affermazioni e Definizioni Del Duce* (Milan: Hoepli, 1939), 45, 88.

122. For a study of this notion within other forms of contemporary imperialism that embrace the idea of a "war without an end," see Ellen Meiksins Wood, *Empire of Capital* (London: Verso, 2005), 143–51. Meiksins Wood does not mention that fascism may have been the first imperialism to embrace this notion of war, thus making it a precedent to its contemporary followers.

123. MRF B, 93 F, 155 SF 1 Impero. See also Collez, Muss #92; #47, Archivio Centrale dello Stato, Italy.

124. Benito Mussolini, "La dottrina del fascismo," in *Opera omnia di Benito Mussolini*, vol. 34 (Florence: La Fenice, 1967), 119–21.

125. On the Fascist International, see Michael Ledeen, *Universal Fascism: The Theory and Practice of the Fascist International, 1928–1936* (New York: H. Fertig, 1972); Davide Sabatini, *L'internazionale di Mussolini: la diffusione del fascismo in Europa nel progetto politico di Asvero Gravelli* (Rome: Edizioni Tusculum, 1997); Marco Cuzzi, *L'internazionale delle camicie nere: i CAUR, Comitati d'azione per l'universalità di Roma, 1933–1939* (Milan: Mursia, 2005).

126. See Hannah Arendt, "Ideology and Terror: A Novel Form of Government," *Review of Politics* 15, no. 3 (1953), 303–27; *The Origins of Totalitarianism*, 158–84; Hannah Arendt, "The Seeds of a Fascist International," in *Essays in Understanding 1930–1954*, ed. Jerome Kohn (New York: Harcourt Brace, 1994), 147.

127. See Sternhell, *Birth of Fascist Ideology*; Sternhell, *Anti-enlightenment Tradition*. See also by Sternhell, *Histoire et Lumières: Changer le Monde par la Raison* (Paris: Albin Michel, 2014); "Fascism and Its Ideology," 280–90.

128. I thank my colleague Andreas Kalyvas for his suggestions and insights on the birth of Athenian democracy.

129. Peter Fritzsche, "The Role of 'the People' and the Rise of the Nazis," in *Transformations of Populism in Europe and the Americas: History and Recent Tendencies,* ed. John Abromeit, Bridget Maria Chesterton, Gary Marotta, and York Norman (London: Bloomsbury, 2016), 37; Geoff Eley, "Conservatives-Radical Nationalists-Fascists: Calling the People into Politics, 1890–1930," in *Transformations of Populism in Europe and the Americas: History and Recent Tendencies,* ed. John Abromeit, Bridget Maria Chesterton, Gary Marotta, and York Norman (London: Bloomsbury, 2016), 74; Ismael Saz, *España contra España: Los nacionalismos franquistas* (*Madrid: Marcial Pons,* 2010), 53; António Costa Pinto, *The Nature of Fascism Revisited,* Social Science Monographs (New York: Columbia University Press, 2012), 1–27. See also Peter Fritzsche, *Rehearsals for Fascism: Populism and Political Mobilization in Weimar Germany* (New York: Oxford University Press, 1990); Eley, *Nazism as Fascism;* Sven Reichardt, "Fascist Movements" in *The Wiley-Blackwell Encyclopedia of Social and Political Movements,* ed. David A. Snow, Donatella della Porta, Bert Klandermans, and Doug McAdam (New York: Wiley, 2013), 2, 457; Pierre Milza, "Mussolini entre fascisme et populisme," *Vingtième Siècle* 56 (1997); Sandra McGee Deutsch, *Las Derechas,* 315, 329–31, 339; Alberto Spektorowski, *The Origins of Argentina's Revolution of the Right* (Notre Dame, IN: University of Notre Dame Press, 2003); Victor Lundberg, "Within the Fascist World of Work: Sven Olov Lindholm, Ernst Junger and the Pursuit of Proletarian Fascism in Sweden," in *New Political Ideas in the Aftermath of the Great War,* ed. Anders G. Kjøstvedt and Alessandro Salvador (London: Palgrave MacMillan, 2016), 199–217; Daniel Knegt, "French Intellectual Fascism and the Third Way: The Case of Bertrand de Jouvenel and Alfred Fabre-Luce," in *New Political Ideas in the Aftermath of the Great War,* ed. Anders G. Kjøstvedt and Alessandro Salvador (London: Palgrave MacMillan, 2016), 41–65.

130. Pinto, *Nature of Fascism Revisited,* xix.

131. Matteo Pasetti, *L'Europa Corporativa: Una Storia Transnazionale tra Le Due Guerre Mondiali;* Antonio Costa Pinto and Francisco Palomanes Martinho, eds., *A Onda Corporativa: Corporativismo e Ditaduras na Europa e América Latina.*

132. "Il corporativismo è l'economia disciplinata, e quindi anche controllata, perché non si può pensare a una disciplina che non abbia un controllo. Il corporativismo supera il socialismo e supera il liberalismo, crea una nuova sintesi." See Benito Mussolini, *Opera omnia di Benito Mussolini*, vol. 26 (Florence: La Fenice, 1958), 95.

133. Pinto, *Nature of Fascism Revisited*, xii.

134. Matteo Passetti, "Neither Bluff nor Revolution: The Corporations and the Consolidation of the Fascist Regime (1925–1926)," in *In the Society of Fascists: Acclamation, Acquiescence, and Agency in Mussolini's Italy*, ed. Giulia Albanese and Roberta Pergher (Basingstoke: Palgrave Macmillan, 2012); Alessio Gagliardi, *Il corporativismo fascista* (Rome: Laterza, 2010). On fascist corporatism, see also Philip Morgan, "Corporatism and the Economic Order," in *The Oxford Handbook of Fascism*, ed. R.J.B. Bosworth (Oxford: Oxford University Press, 2019), 150–65.

135. António Costa Pinto, "Fascism, Corporatism and the Crafting of Authoritarian Institutions in Interwar European Dictatorships," in *Rethinking Fascism and Dictatorship in Europe*, ed. António Costa Pinto and Aristotle A Kallis (Basingstoke, UK: Palgrave Macmillan, 2014), 87.

136. See "En un mitin, en Cáceres, el señor Primo de Rivera afirma Falange Española quiere que haya justicia social y nación," *La Nación* (Madrid), February 5, 1934, 2); Carlo Costamagna, "Teoría general del Estado corporativo," *Acción Española*, May 16, 1933, 468.

137. See *AGN*, Archivo Agustín P. Justo. Caja 49 doc.166. See also the following works by Gustavo Barroso: "Capitalismo, Propriedade e Burguesia," in *O que o Integralista Deve Saber* (Rio de Janeiro: Civilização Brasileira, 1935); *O Espírito do Século XX* (Rio de Janeiro: Civilização Brasileira, 1936).

138. Leopoldo Lugones, *El Estado equitativo (Ensayo sobre la realidad Argentina)* (Buenos Aires: La Editora Argentina, 1932), 11

139. Leopoldo Lugones, *Política revolucionaria* (Buenos Aires: Anaconda, 1931), 52, 53, 65–66; Lugones, *El Estado equitativo*, 9, 11.

140. J. Hurtado de Zaldivar, "El Décimo tercero aniversario de la fundación de los Fascios," *Acción Española*, April 1, 1932, 177; Villegas, *No hay enemigos a la derecha*, 97, 107, 109.

141. Israel Gershoni and James Jankowski, *Confronting Fascism in Egypt: Dictatorship versus Democracy in the 1930s* (Stanford, CA: Stanford University Press, 2009), 251.

142. José Vasconcelos, "Otro fantasma," *Timón,* May 4, 1940; José Vasconcelos, "La inteligencia se impone," *Timón,* June 8, 1940, both in Itzhak M. Bar-Lewaw, ed., *La Revista "Timón" y José Vasconcelos* (Mexico: Edimex, 1971), 138, 152–54.

143. Matteo Pasetti, "Il progetto corporativo della società senza classi e le tendenze populiste dell'ideologia fascista" (paper presented at the XIII Conference of the Asociacion de Historia Contemporanea, University of Castilla-La Mancha, Albacete, September 2016); Griffin, *Nature of Fascism,* 41, 42, 32, 124, 178.

144. See Peter Wien, "Arabs and Fascism: Empirical and Theoretical Perspectives," *Die Welt des Islams* 52 (2012): 345; Hofmann, *Fascist Effect,* 39, 74.

145. Dan Stone, *Histories of the Holocaust* (Oxford: Oxford University Press, 2010), 264; Michael Wildt, *Hitler's Volksgemeinschaft and the Dynamics of Racial Exclusion* (New York: Berghahn, 2012); Aristotle Kallis, *Genocide and Fascism: The Eliminationist Drive in Fascist Europe* (London: Routledge, 2008), 312.

146. Dylan Riley, *The Civic Foundations of Fascism in Europe: Italy, Spain, and Romania 1870–1945* (Baltimore: Johns Hopkins University Press, 2010), 5.

147. Ernesto Laclau, *Politics and Ideology in Marxist Theory: Capitalism Fascism—Populism* (1977; repr. London: Verso, 2011), 111, 142, 153; Slavoj Žižek, "Against the Populist Temptation," *Critical Inquiry* 32, no. 2 (2006): 556–59, 567.

148. Steven Levitsky and Lucan Way, *Competitive Authoritarianism: Hybrid Regimes after the Cold War* (New York: Cambridge University Press, 2010); Andreas Schedler, *The Politics of Uncertainty: Sustaining and Subverting Electoral Authoritarianism* (Oxford: Oxford University Press, 2013).

149. See Finchelstein, *Origins of the Dirty War,* 28. On fascism and dictatorship, see also Paul Corner, "Italian Fascism: Whatever Happened to Dictatorship?" *Journal of Modern History* 74, no. 2 (2002): 325–51.

150. I thank Andrew Arato for sharing his thoughts on this matter.

151. This early Latin American form of postfascism anticipates the European cases of the National Front in France and the Italian Social Movement and Alleanza Nazionale in Italy, which much later turned from neofascist forms to more clearly postfascist populist formations. For the European debates on postfascism, see Roger Griffin, "The 'Post-fascism' of the Alleanza Nazionale: A Case Study in Ideological Morphology" *Journal of Political Ideologies* 1, no. 2 (1996): 123–45; Tamir Bar-On, *Where Have All the Fascists Gone?* (Aldershot: Ashgate, 2007), 137; Gian Enrico Rusconi, *Resistenza e postfascismo* (Bologna: Il Mulino, 1995); Michael Löwy and Francis Sitel, "Le Front national dans une perspective européenne," *Contretemps* (October 17, 2016), www .contretemps.eu/fn-europe-fascisme/; and Enzo Traverso, *Las nuevas caras de la derecha* (Buenos Aires: Siglo Vientiuno, 2018).

2. WHAT IS POPULISM IN HISTORY?

1. Pierre Rosanvallon, *La Contrademocracia. La política en la era de la Desconfianza* (Buenos Aires: Manantial, 2007), 260–61.

2. For a treatment of these questions, see Raanan Rein, "From Juan Perón to Hugo Chávez and Back: Populism Reconsidered," in *Shifting Frontiers of Citizenship*, ed. Mario Sznajder, Luis Roniger, and Carlos Forment (Boston: Brill, 2012); Carlos de la Torre, *Populist Seduction in Latin America* (Athens: Ohio University Press, 2010); and the essays in Carlos de la Torre, ed. *The Promise and Perils of Populism: Global Perspectives* (Lexington: University Press of Kentucky, 2015). See also my books: *Transatlantic Fascism* (Durham, NC: Duke University Press, 2010); and *The Ideological Origins of the Dirty War: Fascism, Populism, and Dictatorship in Twentieth Century Argentina* (Oxford: Oxford University Press, 2014).

3. On this topic see Federico Finchelstein and Fabián Bosoer, "Is Fascism Returning to Europe?," *New York Times*, December 18, 2013.

4. See Benjamin Moffitt, *The Global Rise of Populism: Performance, Political Style, and Representation* (Stanford. CA: Stanford University Press, 2016); Benjamin Moffitt, "Contemporary Populism and 'The People' in the Asia-Pacific Region: Thaksin Shinawatra and Pauline Hanson," in de la Torre, *Promise and Perils of Populism;* Danielle Resnick,

"Varieties of African Populism in Comparative Perspective," in de la Torre, *Promise and Perils of Populism*.

5. This chapter further elaborates on my historical research on populism. For my recent work on populism, see especially chapter 4 of my book *The Ideological Origins of the Dirty War*. Historians who are important exceptions in their engagement with populism are Loris Zanatta, Raanan Rein, Alberto Spektorowski, and Alan Knight. See Loris Zanatta, *El Populismo* (Buenos Aires: Katz Editores, 2014); Raanan Rein, "From Juan Perón to Hugo Chávez and Back: Populism Reconsidered," in *Shifting Frontiers of Citizenship*, ed. Mario Sznajder, Luis Roniger, and Carlos Forment; Alberto Spektorowski, *The Origins of Argentina's Revolution of the Right* (Notre Dame, IN: University of Notre Dame Press, 2003); Alan Knight, "Populism and Neo-Populism in Latin America, Especially Mexico," *Journal of Latin American Studies* 30, no. 2 (1998): 240.

6. See the classic text by Isaiah Berlin, "Russian Populism," *Encounter* 15, no. 1 (1960): 13–28. See also Berlin, *The Power of Ideas* (Princeton, NJ: Princeton University Press, 2013), 127–29. On Russian populism, see also Franco Venturi, *Roots of Revolution: A History of the Populist and Socialist Movements in Nineteenth Century Russia* (New York: Knopf, 1966). For the United States, see Michael Kazin, *The Populist Persuasion* (Ithaca, NY: Cornell University Press, 1995); and Ritchie Savage, "A Comparison of 'New Institutionalized' Populism in Venezuela and the USA," *Constellations* 21, no. 4 (2014).

7. Isaiah Berlin, "To Define Populism," *Government and Opposition* 3, no. 2 (1968): 175. See also Gino Germani, *Política y sociedad en una época de transición: De la sociedad tradicional a la sociedad de masas* (Buenos Aires: Paidós, 1962); Torcuato S. Di Tella, "Populismo y Reforma en América Latina," *Desarrollo Económico* 4, no. 16 (1965): 391–425; Gino Germani, Torcuato Di Tella, and Octavio Ianni, *Populismo y contradicciones de clase en Latinoamérica* (México: Ediciones Era, 1973).

8. Berlin, "To Define Populism," 174, 177.

9. See Zeev Sternhell, *The Anti-enlightenment Tradition*, trans. David Meisel (New Haven, CT: Yale University Press, 2009); Sandra McGee Deutsch, *Las Derechas. The Extreme Right in Argentina, Brazil, and Chile 1890–1939* (Stanford, CA: Stanford University Press, 1999); Guy Hermet,

Les populismes dans le monde: Une histoire sociologique, XIXe-XXe siècle (Paris: Fayard, 2001) 167–204.

10. On Peronism and fascism, see Paul H. Lewis, "Was Perón a Fascist? An Inquiry into the Nature of Fascism," *Journal of Politics* 42, no. 1 (1980): 242–56; Cristián Buchrucker, *Nacionalismo y Peronismo* (Buenos Aires: Sudamericana, 1987); Alberto Spektorowski, *Argentina's Revolution of the Right.*

11. On Wast, see David Rock, *Authoritarian Argentina: The Nationalist Movement, Its History and Its Impact* (Berkeley: University of California Press), 137; Loris Zanatta, *Perón y el mito de la nación católica: Iglesia y Ejército en los orígenes del peronismo, 1943–1946* (Buenos Aires: Sudamericana, 1999), 104–15.

12. See James W. McGuire, *Peronism without Perón: Unions, Parties, and Democracy in Argentina* (Stanford, CA: Stanford University Press, 1997), 52.

13. Robert Potash, "Las fuerzas armadas y la era de Perón," in *Los años peronistas (1943–1955)*, ed. Juan Carlos Torre (Buenos Aires: Sudamericana, 2002), 92–94. On this topic, see also Leonardo Senkman, "Etnicidad e inmigración durante el primer peronismo," *E.I.A.L* 3, no. 2 (1992).

14. See Juan Carlos Torre, Introduction in *Los años peronistas (1943–1955)*, ed. Juan Carlos Torre (Buenos Aires: Sudamericana, 2002).

15. See Raanan Rein, *In the Shadow of Perón* (Stanford, CA: Stanford University Press, 2008), 2. On Peronism, see also Juan Carlos Torre, "Interpretando (una vez más) los orígenes del peronismo," *Desarrollo Económico* 28, no. 112 (1989): 525–48; Juan Carlos Torre, ed., *Los años peronistas;* Miguel Murmis and Juan Carlos Portantiero, *Estudios sobre los orígenes del peronismo* (Buenos Aires: Siglo Veintiuno Editores, 1971); Tulio Halperín Donghi, *La larga agonía de la Argentina peronista* (Buenos Aires: Ariel, 1994); Mathew Karush and Oscar Chamosa, eds., *The New Cultural History of Peronism* (Durham, NC: Duke University Press, 2010); Loris Zanatta, *Breve historia del peronismo clásico* (Buenos Aires: Sudamericana, 2009).

16. See Eric Hobsbwam, *The Age of Extremes: The Short Twentieth Century 1914–91* (London: Michael Joseph, 1994)

17. New forms of populism have belatedly emerged in Mexico in our new century since the demise of the one-party state. The most

important example is Andrés Manuel López Obrador. See Carlos Illades, "La izquierda populista mexicana," *Nexos*, September, 1, 2016. ww.nexos.com.mx/?p=29483#ftn5. López Obrador has also been attacked in antipopulist ways that symptomatically opposed populism to the Mexican liberal status quo as the only two choices available in Mexican politics. See Enrique Krauze, "López Obrador, el mesías tropical," *Letras Libres,* June 30, 2006.

18. See Steve Stein, "The Paths to Populism in Peru" in *Populism in Latin America*, ed. Michael L. Conniff, 2nd ed. (Tuscaloosa: University of Alabama Press, 1999), 97–116; Carlos de la Torre, *Populist Seduction*, 15; Steve Stein, *Populism in Peru* (Madison: University of Wisconsin Press, 1980); Martin Bergel, "Populismo y cultura impresa: La clandestinidad literaria en los años de formación del Partido Aprista Peruano," *Ipotesi* I 17, no. 2 (2013); 135–46; Víctor Raúl Haya de la Torre, *Obras Escogidas* (Lima: Comisión del Centenario del Nacimiento de Víctor Raúl Haya de la Torre, 1995), 2:77, 92, 131.

19. On Bonapartism, see, for example, Domenico Losurdo, *Democrazia o bonapartismo: Trionfo e decadenza del suffragio universale* (Turin: Bollati Boringhieri, 1993). On the relationship between early populism and antisemitism, see the important work of Michele Battini, *Socialism of Fools: Capitalism and Modern Anti-Semitism* (New York: Columbia University Press, 2016).

20. See Thomas Skidmore, "Las dimensiones económicas del populismo en Argentina y Brasil" in *La democratización fundamental. El populismo en América Latina,* ed. Carlos M. Vilas (Mexico: Consejo Nacional para la Cultura y las Artes, 1994), 245, 257; Thomas Skidmore, *Politics in Brazil* (New York: Oxford University Press, 1967), 74, 75, 132, 133; Francisco Weffort, "El populismo en la política brasileña" in *Populismo y Neopopulismo en América Latina: El problema de la cenicienta,* ed. Maria M. Mackinnon and Mario A. Petrone (Buenos Aires: Eudeba, 1998), 136–43

21. Paradoxically, the dictatorship of General Gustavo Rojas Pinilla (1953–57) was profoundly inspired by Perón's own accession to power from dictatorial origins to elected candidate in free elections. Rojas wanted to create his own "third-way" party by mobilizing workers, bureaucrats, and even former followers of Gaitán, but he faced the opposition of the two traditional parties (Liberal and Conservative),

as well as that of the emerging student movement, which he antagonized through repression. After failing in his plans to turn his dictatorship into a populist democracy, Rojas returned to politics, now perhaps in more Brazilian *varguista* fashion, under the ANAPO Party, and he again attempted to attract citizens who did not feel represented by the two parties. He ran for president in 1962. He ran again in 1970, when he lost in a highly contested election. See César Augusto Ayala Diago, *Resistencia y oposición al establecimiento del Frente Nacional: los orígenes de la Alianza Nacional Popular, ANAPO: Colombia, 1953–1964* (Bogota: Universidad Nacional de Colombia,1996); Herbert Braun, *The Assassination of Gaitán: Public Life and Urban Violence in Colombia* (Madison: University of Wisconsin Press, 1985), 37, 57, 92, 108–9, 121; Daniel Pécaut, "El populismo Gaitanista," in *La Democratización Fundamental: El populismo en América Latina*, ed. Carlos M. Vilas (Mexico: Consejo Nacional para la Cultura y las Artes, 1995), 501, 505, 515; John W. Green, *Gaitanismo, Left Liberalism, and Popular Mobilization in Colombia* (Gainesville: University Press of Florida, 2003); Enrique Peruzzotti, "Populismo y representación democrática," in *El retorno del pueblo: El populismo y nuevas democracias en América Latina*, ed. Carlos de la Torre and Enrique Peruzzotti (Quito: Flacso, 2008), 97–125.

22. See de la Torre, *Populist Seduction*, 28–79. On Peronism and Ibarra, see Loris Zanatta, *La internacional justicialista: Auge y ocaso de los sueños imperiales de Perón* (Buenos Aires: Editorial Sudamericana, 2013), 44, 295, 346. On Gaitán and Peronism, see Zanatta, *La internacional justicialista*, 156, 161.

23. Tulio Halperin Donghi, *Historia contemporánea de América Latina* (Buenos Aires: Alianza, 1994), 485.

24. See Laura Gotkowitz, *Revolution for Our Rights: Indigenous Struggles for Land and Justice in Bolivia, 1880–1952* (Durham, NC: Duke University Press, 2007), 287, as well as 15, 164–66, 172–73, 289; Víctor Paz Estenssoro, *Pensamiento Político de Paz Estenssoro: Compilación*, ed. Ramiro Antelo León (La Paz, Bolivia: Plural Editores, 2003), 107. Also see Loris Zanatta, "The Rise and Fall of the Third Position: Bolivia, Perón and the Cold War, 1943–1954," *Desarrollo Económico* 1 (2006): 76–84; Zanatta, *La internacional justicialista*, 30–32; Donghi, *Historia contemporánea de América Latina*, 440–44; 502–6, Herbert Klein, *Bolivia: The Evolution of a*

Multi-ethnic Society (New York: Oxford University Press, 1982), 219–20, 225–26, 244–45; Christopher Mitchell, *The Legacy of Populism in Bolivia, From the MNR to Military Rule* (New York: Praeger, 1977).

25. Like Peronism, Acción Democrática was also toppled by an antipopulist military dictatorship. When Acción Democrática returned to power in 1959–69, it moved further to the right but always in an antidictatorial mode. In fact, Rómulo Betancourt was a strong advocate against the military dictatorships of the region. For Frédérique Langue, Betancourt's populism was of a much more moderate bent than other classic examples, especially Peronism. Frédérique Langue, "Rómulo Betancourt: Liderazgo democrático versus personalismo en tiempos de celebraciones," *Araucaria: Revista Iberoamericana de Filosofía, Política y Humanidades* 21 (2009), 226–38. On Betancourt and Acción Democrática, see also Steven Ellner, "El Populismo en Venezuela, 1935–1948: Betancourt y Acción Democrática," in *La Democratización Fundamental*, ed. Carlos M. Vilas, 419–34; Manuel Caballero, *Rómulo Betancourt, político de nación* (Caracas: Alfadil-FCE, 2004).

26. See my extensive analysis of these topics in my books *Transatlantic Fascism* and *The Ideological Origins of the Dirty War*.

27. See Étienne Balibar, *We, the People of Europe? Reflections on Transnational Citizenship* (Princeton, NJ: Princeton University Press, 2004), 2.

28. Knight notes that, "There is also a tautological tendency to impute populism (or anything else) to 'crisis,' as if 'crisis' were a discernible cause, when, in fact, it is often a loose description of a bundle of phenomena which need to be disaggregated. Disaggregation sometimes reveals that it was not 'crisis' which generated populism (or mobilisation, rebellion, etc.), but rather populism (or mobilisation, rebellion, etc.) which generated crisis" ("Populism and Neo-populism," 233). For a critique of static "historicist" notions of populism, see also Francisco Panizza, introduction to *Populism and the Mirror of Democracy*, ed. Francisco Panizza (London: Verso, 2005), 3.

29. Knight, "Populism and Neo-Populism," 233.

30. Ibid., 237.

31. To a lesser extent, some scholars of Latin American populism downplay the relevance of European populism.

32. Remarks by Isaiah Berlin at the conference To Define Populism at the London School of Economics, May 1967, Isaiah Berlin Virtual Library, 5–6, accessed October 14, 2014, http://berlin.wolf.ox.ac.uk /lists/bibliography/bibᴍbLSE.pdf. The edited conference papers were published in the influential book by Ghita Ionescu and Ernest Gellner, eds., *Populism: Its Meaning and National Characteristics* (London: Weidenfeld and Nicolson, 1969). On this debate, see also Maria M. Mackinnon and Mario A. Petrone, eds., *Populismo y Neopopulismo en América Latina* (Buenos Aires: Eudeba, 1998).

33. See Margaret Canovan, *The People* (Cambridge: Polity, 2005); Pierre Rosanvallon, *Democracy Past and Future* (New York: Columbia University Press, 2006).

34. See Rosanvallon, *La Contrademocracia*, 257.

35. See Rosanvallon, *La Contrademocracia*, 257; Margaret Canovan, *Populism* (London: Junction, 1981), 12, 13, 15, 148, 169, 229–30, 294, 298. For Canovan, Peronism was a "populist dictatorship." More recently she argued, "Outside Europe, more or less dictatorial populist leaders have been particularly common in Latin America" (Canovan, *People*, 71). She mentions Juan and Eva Perón and Hugo Chávez as examples. See also Canovan's "Trust the People! Populism and the Two Faces of Democracy," *Political Studies* 67, no. 3 (1999): 2–16; and "Populism for Political Theorists?," *Journal of Political Ideologies* 9, no. 3 (2004): 241–52.

36. See Rosanvallon, *La Contrademocracia*, 262, 263, 264.

37. For them, "Due to its restricted morphology, populism necessarily appears attached to other concepts or ideological families, which normally are much more relevant than populism on its own" (Cas Mudde and Cristóbal Rovira Kaltwasser, "Populism," in *The Oxford Handbook of Political Ideologies*, ed. Michael Freeden and Marc Stears [New York: Oxford University Press, 2013], 508–9). See also Cas Mudde and Cristóbal Rovira Kaltwasser, *Populism: A Very Short Introduction* (Oxford: Oxford University Press, 2017), 5–6; Cristóbal Rovira Kaltwasser, "The Ambivalence of Populism: Threat and Corrective for Democracy," *Democratization* 19, no. 2 (2012); Cas Mudde, *On Extremism and Democracy in Europe* (London: Routledge, 2016); Matthijs Rooduijn, "The Nucleus of Populism: In Search of the Lowest Common Denominator," *Government and Opposition* 49, no. 4 (2014); Pierre-André

Taguieff, "Le Populisme et la science politique du mirage conceptuel aux vrais problèmes," *Vingtième Siècle: Revue d'histoire 56*, no. 1 (1997): 4–33. An expanded and updated version of Taguieff's article can be found in his book, *L'Illusion populiste: De l'archaïque au médiatique* (Paris: Berg, 2002).

38. De la Torre states, "Populists do not view citizens as a body with a plurality of opinions that deliberate in the public sphere." But he also adds, "Yet populists are not fully authoritarian because their policies redistribute resources and could potentially empower the poor" ("The People, Democracy, and Authoritarianism in Rafael Correa's Ecuador," *Constellations* 21, no. 4 [2014], 463).

39. Carlos de la Torre, "Populism and the Politics of the Extraordinary in Latin America," *Journal of Political Ideologies* 21, no. 2 (2016): 131.

40. See Carlos de la Torre, "The Contested Meanings of Populist Revolutions in Latin America," in *Transformations of Populism in Europe and the Americas: History and Recent Tendencies,* ed. John Abromeit, Bridget Maria Chesterton, Gary Marotta, and York Norman (London: Bloomsbury, 2016), 332.

41. De la Torre notes,

The empowerment of indigenous people is evidenced in the symbolic changes in the Bolivian political landscape. Indigenous rituals are performed in the Presidential palace, previously a center of white power. The cultural and symbolic inclusion of indigenous people is carried with populist understandings of rivals as enemies. The authoritarian specter is present in small communities and at the national level. For example, after learning the results of the 2005 presidential election in the small village of Quilacollo an indigenous leader affirmed: 'in our community there was one vote for Tuto Quiroga (Morales rival in the election), we are going to investigate who this is because we cannot tolerate betrayals by our own comrades.' This undemocratic view of opponents as enemies characterizes the president and vice-president's worldviews and speeches. ("Contested Meanings," 338)

See also Fernando Mayorga, "Movimientos Sociales y Participación Política en Bolivia," in *Ciudadanía y Legitimidad Democrática en América Latina,* ed. Isidoro Cheresky (Buenos Aires: Prometeo, 2011).

42. See Jan-Werner Müller, "Getting a Grip on Populism," *Dissent,* September 23, 2011, accessed October 14, 2014, www.dissentmagazine .org/blog/getting-a-grip-on-populism.

43. See Paul Taggart, *Populism* (Buckingham: Open University Press, 2000); Paul Taggart, "Populism and the Pathologies of Representative Politics," in *Democracies and the Populist Challenge*, ed. Yves Meny and Yves Surel (Oxford: Palgrave, 2002); Benjamin Arditi, *La política en los bordes del liberalismo: diferencia, populismo, revolución, emancipación*, 2nd augumented ed. (Buenos Aires: Gedisa, 2014).

44. Jan-Werner Müller, "Populists and Technocrats in Europe's Fragmented Democracies," *World Politics Review*, March 31, 2016, www.worldpoliticsreview.com/articles/18928/populists-and-technocrats-in-europe-s-fragmented-democracies. See also Müller, *What Is Populism?* (Philadelphia: University of Pennsylvania Press, 2016), 102.

45. See Slavoj Žižek, "Against the Populist Temptation," *Critical Inquiry* 32, no. 2 (2006): 551–74. See also Žižek, "Una aclaración con respecto al populismo," *Público,* April 27, 2015, http://blogs.publico.es /otrasmiradas/4501/una-aclaracion-con-respecto-al-populismo/. For the conceptual history of totalitarianism, see Enzo Traverso, *El totalitarismo: Historia de un debate* (Buenos Aires: Eudeba, 2001); and Simona Forti, Il *totalitarismo* (Rome-Bari: Laterza, 2005).

46. For examples of this confusion, see generic scholar Pierre-André Taguieff's *La révanche du nationalisme: Néopopulistes et xénophobes à l'assaut de l' Europe* (Paris: PUF, 2015). See also Andreas Pantazopoulos, "The National-Populist Illusion as a 'Pathology' of Politics: The Greek Case and Beyond," *Telos Scope,* March 25, 2016, www.telospress.com/the-national-populist-illusion-as-a-pathology-of-politics-the-greek-case-and-beyond/; Pierre-André Taguieff, "The Revolt against the Elites, or the New Populist Wave: An Interview," *Telos Scope,* June 25, 2016, www.telospress.com/the-revolt-against-the-elites-or-the-new-populist-wave-an-interview/#notes.

47. Alexandros Kioupkiolis, "Podemos: The Ambiguous Promises of Left-Wing Populism in Contemporary Spain," *Journal of Political Ideologies* 21, no. 2 (2016); Luis Ramiro and Raul Gómez, "Radical-Left Populism during the Great Recession: Podemos and Its Competition with the Established Radical Left," *Political Studies* (June 2016); Nicolás Damín, "Populismo entre Argentina y Europa: Sobre la transnacionalización de un concepto," *Revista Cuestiones de Sociología* 4, no. 2 (2015): 61; Iñigo Errejón Galván, "También en Europa: posibilidades populistas

en la política europea y Española," *Viento Sur* 115, no. 3 (2011): 105, 109, 111, 113; Pablo Iglesias, *Una nueva transición* (Madrid: Akal, 2015); Jesús Jaén "Un debate con el populismo," *Viento Sur* July 14 (2015), http://vientosur.info/spip.php?article10293; Pablo Iglesias," Guerra de trincheras y estrategia electoral, *Público*, May 3, 2015, http://blogs.publico.es/pablo-iglesias/1025/guerra-de-trincheras-y-estrategia-electoral/.

48. See Giorgos Katsambekis, "Radical Left Populism in Contemporary Greece: Syriza's Trajectory from Minoritarian Opposition to Power," *Constellations* 23, no. 3 (2016): 391–403. Yannis Stavrakakis and Giorgos Katsambekis, "Left-Wing Populism in the European Periphery: The Case Of SYRIZA," *Journal of Political Ideologies* 19, no. 2 (2014); 119–42; Giorgos Katsambekis "'The People' and Political Opposition in Post-democracy: Reflections on the Hollowing of Democracy in Greece and Europe," in *The State We're In: Reflecting of Democracy's Troubles*, ed. Joanna Cook, Nicholas J. Long, and Henrietta L. Moore (Oxford: Berghahn, 2016): 144–66.

49. See Antonio Gramsci, *Il Risorgimento* (Rome: Editori Riuniti, 1979): 197–98.

50. For an analysis of *kirchnerismo*, see Beatriz Sarlo, *La audacia y el cálculo: Kirchner 2003–2010* (Buenos Aires: Sudamericana, 2011). For the Five Stars Movement, see Roberto Biorcio and Paolo Natale, *Politica a 5 stelle: Idee, storia e strategie del movimento di Grillo* (Milan: Feltrinelli, 2013).

51. For the propopulist idea of Latin America, see Javier Lorca, "'Hay que latinoamericanizar Europa': Entrevista a la politóloga Chantal Mouffe," *Página 2*, October 21, 2012.

52. On Macri, see Beatriz Sarlo, "Macri es un neopopulista de la felicidad," *La Nación*, October 14, 2016.

53. See Enzo Traverso, "La Fabrique de la haine xénophobie et racisme en Europe," *Contretemps* 9 (2011).

54. See Nadia Urbinati, "The Populist Phenomenon," *Raisons politiques* 51, no. 3 (2013): 137–54.

55. Urbinati argues that "Populist and plebiscitarian phenomena are incubated within democratic diarchy as a longing to overcome the distance between will and opinion and achieve unanimity and homogeneity, an idealization that has characterized democratic communi-

ties since antiquity" (*Democracy Disfigured: Opinion, Truth, and the People* [Cambridge: Harvard University Press, 2014], 27).

56. See Finchelstein, *Transatlantic Fascism*.

57. The recent history of Venezuelan populism is a clear exception to this Latin American pattern.

58. Ernesto Laclau, *On Populist Reason* (London: Verso, 2005), especially 68–77, 110, 117–121, 154, 156, 224. See also Ernesto Laclau, "Populism: What's in a Name," in *Populism and the Mirror of Democracy*, ed. Francisco Panizza (London: Verso, 2005), 32–49.

59. Andrew Arato, *Post Sovereign Constitutional Making: Learning and Legitimacy* (Oxford: Oxford University Press, 2016), 281–89; Urbinati, *Democracy Disfigured*.

60. See the excellent analysis of Laclau by Nicolás Damín, in "Populismo entre Argentina y Europa," 56.

61. See Yannis Stavrakakis, "The Return of "the People," *Constellations* 21, no. 4 (2014).

62. See Jacques Rancière, "L'introuvable populisme," in *Qu'est-ce qu'un peuple?*, ed. Alain Badiou, Pierre Bourdieu, Judith Butler, Georges Didi-Huberman, Sadri Khiari, Jacques Rancière (Paris: La Fabrique, 2013), 137. See also Marco D'Eramo, "Populism and the New Oligarchy," *New Left Review* 58 (2013): 8; Ezequiel Adamovsky, "¿De qué hablamos cuando hablamos de populismo?," *Revista Anfibia*, June 19, 2015, www.revistaanfibia.com/ensayo/de-que-hablamos-cuando-hablamos-de-populismo-2/.

63. See Jacques Rancière, *Hatred of Democracy* (London: Verso, 2006), 73, 79, 80.

64. Jean Comaroff, "Populism and Late Liberalism: A Special Affinity?," *Annals AAPSS*, 637 (2011): 100, 101, 103.

65. See Étienne Balibar, "Our European Incapacity," *Open Democracy*, May 16, 2011, www.opendemocracy.net/etienne-balibar/our-european-incapacity; Yannis Stavrakakis, "The Return of 'the People,'" 512–14. See also, Étienne Balibar "*Europe: l'impuissance des nations et la question 'populiste,'*" *Actuel Marx* 2, no. 54 (2013): 2, 13–23. On Balibar's reflections on Laclau, see Étienne Balibar, *Equaliberty* (Durham: Duke University Press, 2014), 187–95.

66. Cristóbal Rovira Kaltwasser, "The Ambivalence of Populism: Threat and Corrective for Democracy," *Democratization* 19, no. 2 (2012): 185.

67. "Investigaciones empíricas revelan que la gran mayoría de los individuos tienen actitudes populistas que se encuentran en un estado de latencia, vale decir, están dormidas y solo son activadas frente a ciertas situaciones contextuales. En otras palabras, casi todos tenemos un 'pequeño Hugo Chávez' al interior nuestro, pero éste se encuentra en un lugar oculto y, por lo tanto, no define nuestras preferencias políticas." See Cristóbal Rovira Kaltwasser, "Explicando el populismo," *Agenda Pública,* May 30, 2016, http://agendapublica.es /explicando-el-populismo/. See also Agnes Akkerman, Cas Mudde, and Andrej Zaslove, "How Populist Are the People? Measuring Populist Attitudes in Voters," *Comparative Political Studies* 47, no. 9 (2014). On populism as pathology, see Cas Mudde, "Populist Radical Right Parties in Europe Today," in *Transformations of Populism in Europe and the Americas: History and Recent Tendencies,* ed. John Abromeit, Bridget Maria Chesterton, Gary Marotta, and York Norman (London: Bloomsbury, 2016).

68. Cristóbal Rovira Kaltwasser argues that empirical data could be used along with Cas Mudde's "minimal definition" of populism, which Rovira Kaltwasser understands "as a distinct ideology that conceives society to be separated into two antagonistic camps: 'the pure people' versus 'the corrupt elite'" ("The Ambivalence of Populism: Threat and Corrective for Democracy," *Democratization* 19, no. 2 [2012]: 185, 192–96, 200). See also Kaltwasser's "Latin American Populism: Some Conceptual and Normative Lessons," *Constellations* 21, 4 (2014); and his "Explicando el populismo."

69. For Mudde, as for many other observers, Trump was a transitory phenomenon of the early primary season. For him, Trump was more in line with American conservatism than populism. To be sure, Mudde noted that populism was "underlying some of the support" for Trump, but he stressed the need to exclude Trump from studies of populism. See Cas Mudde, "The Trump Phenomenon and the European Populist Radical Right," *Washington Post,* August 26, 2015, www .washingtonpost.com/blogs/monkey-cage/wp/2015/08/26/the-trump-phenomenon-and-the-european-populist-radical-right/; Cas Mudde,

"The Power of Populism? Not really!," *Huffington Post,* February 13, 2016, www.huffingtonpost.com/entry/the-power-of-populism-not_b_9226736.

70. See Dominick LaCapra, *History in Transit: Experience, Identity, Critical Theory* (Ithaca, NY: Cornell University Press, 2004), 156.

71. See Carl Schmitt, *The Crisis of Parliamentary Democracy* (Cambridge, MA: MIT Press, 1994). For a criticism of Laclau's reading and his use of Schmitt, see Arato, *Post Sovereign Constitution Making,* 269–70, 281. For an example of Laclau's recuperation of Sorel's theory of political myth in terms of the construction of political subjectivity, see Ernesto Laclau, *The Rhetorical Foundations of Society* (New York: Verso, 2014).

72. This criticism does not apply to many scholars working on Latin America. Among the more suggestive, I would like to mention the key works of Kurt Weyland, "Clarifying a Contested Concept: Populism in the Study of Latin American Politics," *Comparative Politics* 34, no. 1 (2001): 1–22; and Carlos de la Torre, *Populist Seduction in Latin America.*

73. Gino Germani, *Authoritarianism, Fascism and National Populism* (New Brunswick, NJ: Transaction Books, 1978).

74. Ibid., vii.

75. See Tulio Halperín Donghi, *Testimonio de un observador participante: Medio siglo de estudios latinoamericanos en un mundo cambiante* (Buenos Aires: Prometeo, 2014), 23.

76. Tulio Halperín Donghi, "Del fascismo al peronismo," *Contorno* 7–8 (1958).

77. Finchelstein, *Origins of the Dirty War,* chapter 4.

78. On populism and delegation, see Olivier Dabene, "Un pari néo-populiste au Vénézuéla" *Critique internationale* 4 (1999), 38. On delegative democracy, see the influential essay by Guillermo O'Donnell, "Delegative Democracy," *Journal of Democracy* 5, no. 1 (1994): 55–69.

79. Perón, quoted in Cristián Buchrucker, *Nacionalismo y Peronismo,* 325.

80. Finchelstein, *Origins of the Dirty War,* 90–91.

81. Tulio Halperín Donghi, *Argentina en el callejón* (Buenos Aires: Ariel, 1995), 30.

82. Ibid., 35.

83. See Ertug Tombus, "The Tragedy of the 2015 Turkish Elections," *Public Seminar,* November 11, 2015, www.publicseminar.org /2015/11/the-tragedy-of-the-2015-turkish-elections/#.V5oZqOgrLIU.

84. Benjamin Moffitt, *Global Rise of Populism,* 63, 81–83, 148–149; Moffitt, "Contemporary Populism," 293–311.

85. Hobsbwam, *Age of Extremes,* 133, 135; Eric Hobsbwam, *How to Change the World: Marx and Marxism* (London: Little, 2011), 270–71.

86. As Michael Kazin notes in *The Populist Persuasion,* this migration of populist rhetoric from left to right happened in the context of the emerging Cold War and the New Deal, as well as of the red scares of the 1950s and 1960s. This was the context when most white Americans "came to regard themselves as middle-class consumers and taxpayers, the booming growth of evangelical churches whose political leanings were as conservative as their theology" (4). Kazin defines populism as a "persistent yet mutable style of political rhetoric" (5). He observes that populism had deep roots in the nineteenth century when it was progressive whereas in the second half of the century, it became predominantly rightist. It is very clear that Kazin's "definition" of populism is almost exclusively presented in terms of American history. But there are many convergences between American and others historical developments of populism. See also Kazin, "Trump and American Populism," *Foreign Affairs,* October 6, 2016, www.foreignaffairs.com/articles /united-states/2016–10–06/trump-and-american-populism; and the insightful recent discussions by Charles Postel, Gary Marotta, and Ronald Formisano, in *Transformations of Populism in Europe and the Americas,* ed. John Abromeit, Bridget Maria Chesterton, Gary Marotta, and York Norman. See also Charles Postel, *The Populist Vision* (New York: Oxford University Press, 2008), where he defends the thesis of populism as being exclusively on the left.

87. Regarding Perot, Ronald Formisano argues, "Although Perot was a conservative former Republican whose career had benefited from political connections, he attracted largely independents or weak party identifiers motivated by frustration and anger with professional politicians and fed up with 'politics as usual.' Perot appealed strongly to working- and middle-class Americans who felt left behind by the Reagan bonanza for millionaires of the 1980s, and threatened by

corporate downsizing and elite (and bipartisan) policies such as NAFTA. Before writing off Perot as a conservative or reactionary populist, historians should look first at the range of his support, as well as some of the progressive reforms favored by many of his supporters" ("Populist Movements in U.S. History: Progressive and Reactionary," in *Transformations of Populism in Europe and the Americas,* ed. John Abromeit, Bridget Maria Chesterton, Gary Marotta, and York Norman. 144).

88. Ronald Formisano, "Populist Movements," 145. See also his book *The Tea Party: A Brief History* (Baltimore: Johns Hopkins University Press, 2012); and Vanessa Williamson, Theda Skocpol, and John Coggin, "The Tea Party and the Remaking of Republican Conservatism," *Perspectives on Politics* 9, no. 1 (2011): 33, 34, 35.

89. Virginia Hale, "Le Pen: Trump's Win 'Victory of the People Against the Elites,'" *Breitbart,* November 13, 2016, www.breitbart.com/london/2016/1w1/13/le-pen-trumps-win-victory-people-elites/; "Far-Right Hopeful: French Election 'Choice of Civilization,'" *Breitbart,* February 5, 2017, www.breitbart.com/news/far-right-hopeful-french-election-choice-of-civilization/. See also Thomas D. Williams, "Italian Leftist Media in Meltdown Over Trump's Populist Victory," *Breitbart,* November 9, 2016, www.breitbart.com/london/2016/11/09/italian-leftist-media-meltdown-trumps-populist-victory/; Chris Tomlinson, "European Populist Candidates to Benefit from 'Trump Effect,'" Breitbart, November 9, 2016, www.breitbart.com/london/2016/11/09/european-populist-candidates-benefit-trump-effect/; Donna Rachel Edmunds, "Emboldened by Trump's Success, Italian Populist Parties Circle Prime Minister Renzi," *Breitbart,* November 10, 2016, www.breitbart.com/london/2016/11/10/emboldened-trumps-success-italian-populist-parties-circle-prime-minister-renzi/.

90. See Antonio Costa Pinto, "Donald Trump, com e sem populismo," *Público.* September 3, 2016.

91. Andreas Kalyvas and Ira Katznelson, *Liberal Beginnings: Making a Republic for the Moderns* (Cambridge: Cambridge University Press, 2008), 4–5, 14, 16, 93, 96, 98–99.

92. Andreas Kalyvas, "Popular Sovereignty, Democracy, and the Constituent Power," *Constellations* 12, no. 2 (2005): 224. As Kalyvas

argues, a similar position on the undemocratic potential of sovereignty was taken by a variety of authors as diverse from each other as Hans Kelsen and Michel Foucault.

93. Jason Frank, *Constituent Moments: Enacting the People in Postrevolutionary America.* (Durham, NC: Duke University Press, 2010), 5.

94. Pierre Bourdieu, "You said 'popular'?," in *What Is a People?*, ed. Alain Badiou, Pierre Bourdieu, Judith Butler, et al. (New York: Columbia University Press, 2016), 32–48.

95. On this topic see Alain Badiou, "Twenty-Four Notes on the Uses of the Word 'People,'" in *What Is a People?*, ed. Alain Badiou, Pierre Bourdieu, Judith Butler, 21–22.

96. Federico Finchelstein and Pablo Piccato, "Donald Trump May Be Showing Us the Future of Right-Wing Politics," *Washington Post,* February 27, 2016.

97. See "Desde los balcones de la Casa de gobierno despidiéndose de los trabajadores concentrados en la Plaza de Mayo: Octubre 17 de 1945," in Coronel Juan Perón, *El pueblo ya sabe de qué se trata: Discursos* (Buenos Aires: 1946), 186. See also Dirk Moses, Federico Finchelstein, and Pablo Piccato, "Juan Perón Shows How Trump Could Destroy Our Democracy without Tearing It Down," *Washington Post,* March 22, 2017.

98. See Tomás Eloy Martínez, *Las vidas del General* (Buenos Aires: Aguilar, 2004), 2.

99. Hans Vorländer, "The Good, the Bad, and the Ugly: Über das Verhältnis von Populismus und Demokratie—Eine Skizze," *Totalitarismus und Demokratie* 8, no. 2 (2011), 187–194.

100. See Fabián Bosoer and Federico Finchelstein, "Populism and Neoliberalism: The Dark Sides of the Moon," *Queries* 3 (2014), accessed October 14, 2014, www.queries-feps.eu/populism-and-neoliberalism-the-dark-sides-of-the-moon/. See also Fabián Bosoer and Federico Finchelstein, "Russia Today, Argentina Tomorrow," *New York Times,* October 21, 2014. On populism and technocracy, see Christopher Bickerton and Carlo Invernizzi Accetti, "Populism and Technocracy: Opposites or Complements?," *Critical Review of International Social and Political Philosophy* 20, no. 2 (2017): 182–206; Müller, *What Is Populism?*, 93–99. For Latin America, see Carlos de la Torre, "Technocratic Populism in Ecuador," *Journal of Democracy* 24, no. 3 (2013): 33–46. On the

notion of elites and the current populism, see Hugo Drochon, "Between the Lions and the Foxes," *New Statesman,* January 13–19, 2017.

101. See Nancy Postero, "El Pueblo Boliviano, de Composición Plural: A Look at Plurinationalism in Bolivia," in de la Torre, *Promise and Perils of Populism,* 398–423; Östen Wahlbeck, "True Finns and Non-True Finns: The Minority Rights Discourse of Populist Politics in Finland," *Journal of Intercultural Studies* 37, no. 6 (2016): 574–88.

102. See Étienne Balibar, "Brexit: A Dismantling Moment," *Open Democracy,* July 14, 2016, www.opendemocracy.net/can-europe-make-it/etienne-balibar/brexit-anti-grexit. On populism as a protest movement, see Hans Vorländer, Maik Herold, and Steven Schäller, *PEGIDA: Entwicklung, Zusammensetzung und Deutung einer Empörungsbewegung* (Wiesbaden: Springer, 2016).

103. See Jacques Rancière, *Hatred of Democracy,* 96–97. See also by Rancière, "Non, le peuple n'est pas une masse brutale et ignorante," *Libération,* January 3, 2011.

104. Neoliberalism represents a "steady disciplining of policy and politics by the logic of the market and an ongoing realignment of social structure toward the functional imperatives of liberal market capitalism." See the following works by Wolfgang Streeck: "Small-State Nostalgia? The Currency Union, Germany, and Europe: A Reply to Jürgen Habermas," *Constellations* 21, no. 2 (2014): 214, 218; "Markets and Peoples," *New Left Review* 73 (2012): 64, 67; "L'egemonia tedesca che la Germania non vuole," *Il Mulino* 4 (2015): 608.

105. Finchelstein and Bosoer, "Is Fascism Returning?"; Andreas Kalyvas and Federico Finchelstein, "Fascism on Trial: Greece and Beyond," *Public Seminar,* October 10, 2014.

106. See Finchelstein and Bosoer, "Populism and Neoliberalism."

107. See, for example, Cristóbal Rovira Kaltwasser, "Explaining the Emergence of Populism" in de la Torre, *Promise and Perils of Populism,* 212–13.

108. Juan Domingo Perón, *El gobierno, el estado y las organizaciones libres del pueblo, La comunidad organizada: Trabajos, alocuciones y escritos del general Juan Domingo Perón que fundamentan la concepción justicialista de la comunidad* (Buenos Aires: Editorial de la Reconstrucción, 1975), 76; "La gira del arco iris," *La Nación,* April 5, 1998.

3. POPULISM BETWEEN DEMOCRACY
AND DICTATORSHIP

1. See for example, Alain Rouquié, *A la sombra de las dictaduras: La democracia en América Latina* (Buenos Aires: Fondo de Cultura Económica, 2011), 114–15, 119–34, 251–59. Maria Victoria Crespo analyzes populism and dictatorship in "Entre Escila y Caribdis: Las democracias constitucionales contemporáneas de América Latina" (paper presented at the Academic Meeting of the Feria Internacional del Libro, Guadalajra, December 4–5, 2014).

2. On the notion of modern dictatorship presented here, I have relied on the pathbreaking work of Andrew Arato, "Conceptual History of Dictatorship (and Its Rivals)," in *Critical Theory and Democracy*, ed. E. Peruzzotti and M. Plot (London: Routledge, 2013), 208–81. See also Carl Schmitt, *Dictatorship* (Cambridge: Polity Press, 2013); Ernst Fraenkel, *The Dual State* (Oxford: Oxford University Press, 1941); Norberto Bobbio, *Democracy and Dictatorship* (Minneapolis: University of Minnesota Press, 1989).

3. Andrew Arato, "Dictatorship before and after Totalitarianism," *Social Research*, no. 2 (2002), 473–503; Thomas Vormbaum, *Diritto e nazional-socialismo: Due lezioni* (Macerata: EUM, 2013), 44–45. See also Andrew Arato, "Good-bye to Dictatorship?," *Social Research* 67, no. 4 (2000): 926, 937. See also Andreas Kalyvas, "The Tyranny of Dictatorship: When the Greek Tyrant Met the Roman Dictator," *Political Theory* 35, no. 4 (2007); Hannah Arendt, *The Origins of Totalitarianism* (New York: Meridian, 1959).

4. See Federico Finchelstein, *The Ideological Origins of the Dirty War: Fascism, Populism, and Dictatorship in Twentieth Century Argentina* (Oxford: Oxford University Press, 2014), 1–12.

5. For a discussion of the notion of *dictablanda*, see also Paul Gillingham and Benjamin Smith, eds., *Dictablanda: Politics, Work, and Culture in Mexico, 1938–1968* (Durham, NC: Duke University Press, 2014).

6. See Paul Corner, *The Fascist Party and Popular Opinion in Mussolini's Italy* (Oxford: Oxford University Press, 2012). See also by Paul Corner, "Italian Fascism: Whatever Happened to Dictatorship?," *Journal of Modern History* 74 (2002): 325–51.

7. On Borges, see Federico Finchelstein, *El Mito del Fascismo: De Freud a Borges* (Buenos Aires: Capital intellectual, 2015). See also Gino Germani, *Authoritarianism, Fascism and National Populism* (New Brunswick, NJ: Transaction Books, 1978), vii. On the general context of European antifascism, see Enzo Traverso, *Fire and Blood: The European Civil War 1914–1945* (New York: Verso, 2016).

8. Eva Perón, "Discurso pronunciado el 22 de agosto de 1951, en la asamblea popular, que se constituyó en el Cabildo Abierto del Justicialismo en la Avenida 9 de Julio," in Eva Perón, *Mensajes y discursos* (Buenos Aires: Fundación pro Universidad de la Producción y del Trabajo: Fundación de Investigaciones Históricas Evita Perón, 1999), 333:254.

9. See Carl Schmitt, *Dictatorship.*

10. On constitutional reform in Latin America, see Gabriel Negretto, *Making Constitutions: Presidents, Parties, and Institutional Choice in Latin America* (Cambridge: Cambridge University Press, 2013); Nicolás Figueroa García-Herreros, "Counter-hegemonic Constitutionalism: The Case of Colombia," *Constellations* 19, no. 2 (2012); Angélica M. Bernal, "The Meaning and Perils of Presidential Refounding in Latin America," *Constellations* 21, no. 4 (2014). See also Andrew Arato, *Post Sovereign Constitutional Making: Learning and Legitimacy* (Oxford: Oxford University Press, 2016), 289–98.

11. Fujimori eventually called for a reform of the constitution, and a new electoral process, to legitimize his rule, turning again to a hybrid populist rule after the coup. In 1995, he was re-elected to a second term.

12. See Danielle Resnick, "Varieties of African Populism in Comparative Perspective," in *The Promise and Perils of Populism: Global Perspectives,* ed. Carlos de la Torre (Lexington: University Press of Kentucky, 2015), 317–48.

13. Nic Cheeseman and Miles Larmer, "Ethnopopulism in Africa: Opposition Mobilization in Diverse and Unequal Societies," *Democratization* 22, no. 1 (2015): 22–50.

14. See Danielle Resnick, "Varieties of African Populism," 317–48.

15. David Roberts, *Fascist Interactions: Proposals for a New Approach to Fascism and Its Era, 1919–1945* (New York: Berghahn Books, 2016), 6;

António Costa Pinto and Aristotle Kallis, eds., *Rethinking Fascism and Dictatorship in Europe* (New York: Palgrave, 2014).

16. Dani Filc, *The Political Right in Israel: Different Faces of Jewish Populism* (New York: Routledge, 2010), 70–75; 103–23; Zeev Sternhell, "The Extreme Right Turned Israel into an Anachronism," *Haaretz*, April 1, 2011; Gidi Weitz, "Signs of Fascism in Israel Reached New Peak during Gaza Op, Says Renowned Scholar," *Haaretz*, August 13, 2014; Ishaan Tharoor, "On Israeli Election Day, Netanyahu Warns of Arabs Voting 'in Droves'," *Washington Post*, March 17, 2015; "Livni: Netanyahu Is Harmful to Israel, but He Isn't an Enemy of Israel," *Jerusalem Post*, March 19, 2015; "Israel Has Been Infected by the Seeds of Fascism, Says Ex-prime Minister Ehud Barak," *Haaretz*, March 20, 2016; Zeev Sternhell, "The Leadership Must Stop Pandering," *Haaretz*, June 17, 2016; Uri Ram, *The Globalization of Israel: McWorld in Tel-Aviv, Jihad in Jerusalem* (New York: Routledge, 2008). Unlike the neoliberal Likud party, which in Latin American fashion combined exclusionary and participatory dimensions, Lieberman's populism was more typical of European xenophobic populist parties. For Filc, Lieberman's extreme notion of a homogenous ethnic community; his antiliberalism and anti-pluralism; and an idea of the vertical leader of the people that is radically opposed to the "oligarchy," the judiciary, and ethnic minorities made it a "clear example of exclusionary populism" (*Political Right in Israel*, 103).

17. Filc, *Political Right in Israel* 74.

18. Kurt Weyland, "Neopopulism and Neoliberalism in Latin America: How Much Affinity?," *Third World Quarterly* 24, no. 6 (2003): 1102. See also by Weyland: "A Paradox of Success? Determinants of Political Support for President Fujimori," *International Studies Quarterly* 44, no. 3 (2000): 481–502; Kenneth Roberts. "Neoliberalism and the Transformation of Populism in Latin America," *World Politics* 48 (1995): 82–116. On Menem see also Marcos Novaro, "Menemismo, pragmatismo y romanticism," in *La Historia Reciente: Argentina en Democracia*, ed. Marcos Novaro and Vicente Palermo (Buenos Aires: Edhasa, 2006), 199–221.

19. Kurt Weyland, "Neoliberal Populism in Latin America and Eastern Europe," *Comparative Politics* 31, no. 4 (1999): 379–401.

20. Nadia Urbinati, *Democracy Disfigured: Opinion, Truth, and the People* (Cambridge: Harvard University Press, 2014), 14; Angelo Ventrone,

Il Nemico Interno: Immagini, parole e simboli della lotta politica nell'Italia del Novecento (Rome: Donzelli, 2005), 59, 312; Loris Zanatta, *El Populismo* (Buenos Aires: Katz Editores, 2014), 36, 43, 110, 250; Enzo Traverso, "Après le spectacle, la débacle," *Regards* (2011): 12, 43–47; Andrea Mammone, *Transnational Neofascism in France and Italy* (Cambridge: Cambridge University Press, 2015), 245; Paul Ginsborg and Enrica Asquer, eds., *Berlusconismo: Analisi di un sistema di potere* (Rome: Laterza, 2011); Nicola Tranfaglia, *Populismo: Un carattere originale nella storia d'Italia* (Rome: Castelvecchi, 2014); Perry Anderson, *L'Italia dopo L'Italia* (Rome: Castelvecchi, 2014); "Il populismo continentale secondo Perry Anderson," *Il Manifesto,* March 4, 2015.

21. When, in a typical cycle of populism-technocracy, a center-left coalition called "La Alianza" replaced Menemism in 1999, while still following its neoliberal economic ideology, its main advisors were known as the more elitist "Sushi Group." Without the culinary metaphors in Italy, Berlusconismo was eventually replaced by a center-left that left behind neoliberal populism to engage simply with technocratic neoliberalism.

22. Carlos Saúl Menem, *Discurso del presidente Dr. Carlos Saúl Menem desde los balcones de la Casa de Gobierno* (Buenos Aires: Secretaría de Prensa y Difusión, Presidencia de la Nación, República Argentina, 1989), 1–5.

23. See *Diario de sesiones de la Cámara de Diputados,* vol. 2 (Buenos Aires: Congreso Nacional, 1989), 1070.

24. "El día que Cristina reclamó votar a favor de la privatización de YPF," *Clarín,* April 4, 2012; "Personajes," *Noticias,* June 15, 1996; "Cristina criticó a la izquierda por una movilización," *La Nación,* March 28, 2013; "Menem va por su reelección de senador con apoyo kirchnerista," *La Razón,* March 23, 2011.

25. Juan Perón, "En la ciudad de Santa Fe: 1 de Enero de 1946," in Juan Domingo Perón, *Obras Completas* (Buenos Aires: Docencia, 1998), 8:18.

26. Folleto, "Dijo el Coronel Perón," Archivo Cedinci.

27. Juan Domingo Perón, "Aspiramos a una sociedad sin divisiones de clase: En el Cine Park, 12 de agosto de 1944," in Juan Perón, *El pueblo quiere saber de qué se trata* (Buenos Aires: 1944), 149; Juan Domingo Perón, *Obras Completas,* vol. 17 (Buenos Aires: Docencia, 1998), 215.

28. Jorge Eliécer Gaitán, *Discurso-Programa del Doctor Jorge Eliécer Gaitán en la proclamación de su candidatura a la presidencia de la República* (Bogota: 1945), 4–6, 8, 10, 12–13, 30–31.

29. See Rómulo Betancourt, *Selección de escritos políticos (1929–1981)* (Caracas: Fundación Rómulo Betancourt, 2006), 121, 144, 147, 150, 153, 158–159, 162, 163, 169, 172, 175, 178, 191, 195, 214, 216.

30. Jorge Eliécer Gaitán, "Arenga a los venezolanos" (1946); and "Parte de Victoria" (1947), both in *Gaitán el orador*, ed. Julio Roberto Galindo Hoyos (Bogota: D.C Alvi Impresores 2008), 151–53; 154–69.

31. Juan Domingo Perón, *Los Vendepatria: Las pruebas de una traición* (Buenos Aires: Liberación, 1958), 220, 228. Some years later Perón stated the Peronist movement had "enemies from within and from without. The one that does not fight against the enemy and for the cause of the people is a traitor. The one who fights against the enemy and for the cause of the people is a compañero [i.e., Peronists]. And the one who fights against a compañero is an enemy or a traitor" (Juan Domingo Perón, *Obras Completas*, vol. 23:461).

32. Juan Perón, *Latinoamerica, ahora o nunca* (Montevideo: Diálogo, 1968), 52.

33. "Chávez: 'Yo soy peronista de verdad,'" *La Nación*, March 6, 2008; "Mesa: La frase 'quien no es chavista no es venezolano' incita al odio," *El Universal*, June 27, 2012; Juan Domingo Perón, "Ante los ferroviarios," in Juan Domingo Perón, *Obras Completas* (Buenos Aires: Docencia, 1998), 6:406.

34. See Andreas Kalyvas, *Democracy and the Politics of the Extraordinary: Max Weber, Carl Schmitt, Hannah Arendt* (Cambridge: Cambridge University Press 2008). This interpretation of Kalyvas' work with respect to populism is presented by Carlos De la Torre in "Populism and the Politics of the Extraordinary in Latin America." *Journal of Political Ideologies* 21, no. 2 (2016).

35. See Jorge Eliécer Gaitán, *Discurso-programa del doctor Jorge Eliécer Gaitán: En la proclamación de su candidatura a la presidencia de la república* (Bogota: 1945), 5; Daniel Pécaut, *Orden y Violencia: Evolución socio-política de Colombia entre 1930 y 1953* (Bogotá: Norma, 2001), 441. See also the discussion among Herbert Braun, Rubén Darío Acevedo, and Ricardo

Arias, in "La oratoria de Jorge Eliécer Gaitán," *Revista de Estudios Sociales* 44 (2012): 207–11.

36. On delegative democracy, see the influential essay by Guillermo O'Donnell, "Delegative Democracy," *Journal of Democracy* 5, no. 1 (1994).

37. Perón's speech is cited in Raanan Rein, *In the Shadow of Perón* (Stanford, CA: Stanford University Press, 2008), 107.

38. Cas Mudde and Cristóbal Rovira Kaltwasser, *Populism: A Very Short Introduction* (Oxford: Oxford University Press, 2017), 44, 64.

39. Jack, Montgomery, "France First," *Breitbart,* February 7, 2017, www.breitbart.com/london/2017/02/07/french-first-marine-le-pen-hits-islamism-financial-globalisation/; "Le Pen se présente en candidate du 'peuple' *Le Figaro,* February 4, 2017, www.lefigaro.fr/elections/presidentielles/2017/02/04/35003-20170204LIVWWW00039-en-direct-le-fil-politique-du-week-end.php.

40. I thank Natalia Mehlman Petrzela for her comments on this topic. See also Rick Perlstein, *Before the Storm: Barry Goldwater and the Unmaking of the American Consensus* (New York: Hill and Wang, 2001), 433–34.

41. During the 2016 campaign, Trump also suggested that progun activists could use their weapons against her or her Supreme Court nominee if she were elected president. Nick Corasaniti and Maggie Haberman, "Donald Trump Suggests 'Second Amendment People' Could Act against Hillary Clinton," *New York Times,* August 9, 2016; Alexander Burns and Maggie Haberman, "Trailing Hillary Clinton, Donald Trump Turns to Political Gymnastics," *New York Times,* September 1, 2016; Patrick Healy and Jonathan Martin, "Personal Attacks in the Forefront at Caustic Debate," *New York Times,* October 10, 2016.

42. Juan Domingo Perón, *Obras Completas,* 22:83.

43. Michael D. Shear, "Reading between the Lines of Trump's Interview with *Times,*" *New York Times,* March 24, 2017; Rebecca Harrington, "TRUMP: 'A Global Power Structure' Is Trying to Take Down My Campaign," *Business Insider,* October 13, 2016, www.businessinsider.com/donald-trump-global-power-structure-palm-beach-speech-2016-10.

44. Harrington, "TRUMP"; Juan Doming Perón, *Política y estrategia: (no ataco, critico),* in Juan Domingo Perón, *Obras Completas,* 11:100.

45. See Boris Fausto, *Getúlio Vargas: O poder e o sorriso* (São Paulo: Companhia das Letras, 2006), 196–99. See also the ironically argued, cogent reading by Tulio Halperin Donghi, *Historia contemporánea de América Latina* (Buenos Aires: Alianza, 1994), 470.

46. Eva Perón, *Mensajes y discursos,* 2:62. Eva Perón died just six months after the reelection of her husband and after her surgery at the Hospital President Perón in Avellaneda. According to Perón, she refused to cease working for the people until the very end of her life. On Eva Perón's death, see Tulio Halperín Donghi, *Argentina en el callejón* (Buenos Aires: Ariel, 1995), 162; Marysa Navarro, *Evita* (Buenos Aires : Edhasa, 2005), 333; Loris Zanatta, *Eva Perón: Una biografía política* (Soveria Mannelli: Rubbettino, 2009), 297

47. Ernesto Laclau, "El legado de Néstor Kirchner," *Página 12,* November 4, 2010. See also "'Scioli no es Cristina,' dijo el filósofo Laclau," *La Voz del Interior,* September 21, 2013.

48. Ignacio Ramonet, "Chávez en campaña," *Le Monde Diplomatique en Español,* August 2012; "Sin Hugo Chávez, Venezuela enfrenta un futuro dividido," *La Nación,* March 6, 2013.

49. "Cristina Fernández crea la secretaría del Pensamiento Nacional," *El País,* June 5, 2014; "Venezuela inaugura un ministerio de la Felicidad," *Clarín,* October 24, 2013.

50. Beatriz Sarlo, *La audacia y el cálculo: Kirchner 2003–2010* (Buenos Aires: Sudamericana, 2011), 146, 153, 155. On Laclau and Argentina, see Nicolás Damín, "Populismo entre Argentina y Europa: Sobre la transnacionalización de un concepto," *Revista Cuestiones de Sociologia* 4, no. 2 (2015); Omar Acha, "Del populismo marxista al postmarxista: La trayectoria de Ernesto Laclau en la Izquierda Nacional (1963–2013)," *Archivos de historia del movimiento obrero y la izquierda* 2, no. 3 (2013); Enrique Peruzzotti, "Conceptualizing Kirchnerismo," *Partecipazione e conflitto* 10, no. 1 (2017): 47–64.

51. Ricardo Forster, "El nombre del kirchnerismo," *Página 12,* May 18, 2014.

52. Ernesto Laclau, "Populism: What's in a Name," in *Populism and the Mirror of Democracy,* ed. Francisco Panizza (London: Verso, 2005), 40.

53. "La ultima entrevista de Ernesto Laclau," *La Nación*, April 13, 2014; "Kirchner fue un populista a medias," *Clarín*, October 29, 2010; "Para Laclau, el Estado argentino es hoy más democrático que en 2003," *Perfil*, November 7, 2013.

54. "Fútbol gratis por diez años en TV abierta," *Página 12*, August 21, 2009.

55. Andrew Arato, *Post Sovereign Constitutional Making*, 269–270.

56. "Vamos a una polarización institucional," *Página 12*, May 17, 2010; "Hay que seguir su combate," *Página 12*, October 7, 2015. Like Laclau, Mouffe had opposed the Kirchners to "a series of interests that are against the democratization of the country." See "Entrevista con la politóloga belga Chantal Mouffe," *Página 12*, September 5, 2010; "Claroscuros de la razón populista," *Clarín*, April 4, 2014; Fabián Bosoer, "Los debates y los combates abiertos," *Clarín*, April 4, 2014.

57. Ernesto Laclau, "El legado de Néstor Kirchner," *Página 12*, November 4, 2010.

58. See "Cristina rindió un homenaje a Laclau," *La Nación*, April 15, 2014; Ernesto Laclau, *The Rhetorical Foundations of Society* (New York: Verso, 2014).

59. "Hay que seguir su combate," *Página 12*, October 7, 2015. Like Laclau, Mouffe had opposed the Kirchners to "a series of interests that are against the democratization of the country." See "Entrevista con la politóloga belga Chantal Mouffe"; "Claroscuros de la razon populista"; Bosoer, "Los debates y los combates abiertos."

60. "Plazas, puentes y calles reflejan el culto a Kirchner," *La Nación*, March 6, 2011; "Kirchner para todos: Se multiplican los lugares públicos con su nombre," *Clarín*, October 2, 2011.

61. "Woody Guthrie Wrote of His Contempt for His Landlord, Donald Trump's father," *New York Times*, January 25, 2016.

62. See Michael Kazin, *The Populist Persuasion* (Ithaca, NY: Cornell University Press, 1995), 232, 233. On Wallace, see also Joseph Lowndes, "From Founding Violence to Political Hegemony: The Conservative Populism of George Wallace," in Panizza, *Populism and the Mirror*, 144–71

63. Andrew Kaczynski and Jon Sarlin, "Trump in 1989 Central Park Five interview: "Maybe Hate Is What We Need," *CNN*, October 10 2016, www.cnn.com/2016/10/07/politics/trump-larry-king-central-

park-five/; Roberto Gargarella, *Castigar al prójimo: Por una refundación democrática del derecho penal* (Buenos Aires: Siglo XXI, 2016).

64. "'Tutti con Silvio,' il discorso integrale di Berlusconi," *Secolo d'Italia,* March 23, 2013, www.secoloditalia.it/2013/03/tutti-con-silvio-il-discorso-integrale-di-berlusconi/.'Siamo tutti Berlusconi"; "Il Pdl con le maschere di SilvioGalleria fotográfica," *Repubblica,* August 14, 2013, www.repubblica.it/politica/2013/08/04/foto/manifestazione_pdl_le_maschere_di_berlusconi-64280320/1/#7.

65. Juan Domingo Perón, *Obras Completas,* 18:215.

66. "Marine Le Pen dénonce les 'totalitarismes' qui 'menacent' la France," *Mediapart,* February 5, 2017, www.mediapart.fr/journal/france/050217/marine-le-pen-denonce-les-totalitarismes-qui-menacent-la-france; Mark Landler, "Trump Under Fire for Invoking Nazis in Criticism of U.S. Intelligence," *New York Times,* January 11, 2017; "The Turkish President Has Just Called the Netherlands 'Nazi Remnants' and 'Fascists,'" *Quartz,* March 11, 2017, https://qz.com/930584/turkish-president-recep-tayyip-erdogan-lashed-out-at-the-netherlands-calling-them-nazi-remnants-and-fascists/.

67. George Wallace quoted in John Judis, *The Populist Explosion* (New York: Columbia Global Reports, 2016), 35; Juan Perón, "¿Por qué el gobierno argentino no es fascista?," in Juan Domingo Perón, *Obras Completas,* 6:571.

68. See Hugo Chávez Frías, *La democracia poderosa y el liderazgo* (Caracas: Ministerio para el Poder Popular para la Comunicación y la Información, 2008), 14; "Chávez ganó la reforma y lanzó ya su candidatura para el 2012," *Clarín,* February 16, 2009; "Chávez diz que vitória em referendo consolida socialismo na Venezuela," *Folha de S. Paulo,* February 16, 2009; "Chávez: Si fuera gobernador de Miranda estaría todos los días en la calle," *El Universal,* July 28, 2012.

69. See Juan Domingo Perón, *Política y estrategia, 230.* See also Finchelstein, *Origins of the Dirty War,* 82.

70. See Pablo Piccato, Fabián Bosoer, and Federico Finchelstein, "In Trump's America, the Independent Press Would Become the Enemy," *Open Democracy,* November 1, 2016, www.opendemocracy.net/pablo-piccato-fabian-bosoer-federico-finchelstein/why-president-trump-will-target-independent-media.

71. On the history of populist right-wing media, see Nicole Hemmer, *Messengers of the Right: Conservative Media and the Transformation of American Politics* (Philadelphia: University of Pennsylvania Press, 2016).

72. "Trump Uses Policy Speech to Attack Media, Promises to Sue Accusers," *Reuters,* October 23, 2016, www.reuters.com/article/us-usa-election-idUSKCN12MoQ J?feedType=RSS&feedName=topNews&utm_source=twitter&utm_medium=Social.

73. Sarlo, *La audacia y el cálculo,* 71.

74. See Silvio Waisbord, *Vox Populista: Medios, Periodismo, Democracia* (Buenos Aires: Gedisa, 2013), 17, 28–29, 166, 187.

75. Jean Comaroff, "Populism and Late Liberalism: A Special Affinity?," *Annals of the American Academy of Political and Social Science* 637 (2011): 102.

76. Umberto Eco, "UR-Fascism," *New York Review of Books,* June 22, 1995.

77. For a different view that presents populism as being in the process of substantially changing because of the new media landscape, see Benjamin Moffit, *The Global Rise of Populism: Performance, Political Style, and Representation* (Stanford. CA: Stanford University Press, 2016), 3.

78. See Fondo Documental Secretaria Técnica, Legajo 484, Mensajes Presidenciales, Clase dictada por el EXCMO Señor Presidente de la Nación, General Juan Perón en la Escuela Superior Peronista, Julio 2, de 1953, 62/70, Archivo General de la Nación, Argentina (AGN); Fondo Documental Secretaria Técnica Legajo 484, Mensajes Presidenciales editados en libreto, Folleto, *"No queremos hacer el proletariado campesino: Queremos hacer agricultores felices" dijo Perón a los hombres del campo* (Buenos Aires: Presidencia de la Nación, 1953) (June 11. 1953), 11, AGN.

79. "La navidad de Perón," *La Vanguardia,* December 24, 1946.

80. See Finchelstein, *Origins of the Dirty War,* 78–82

81. See José Pedro Zúquete, "'Free the People': The Search for 'True Democracy' in Western Europe's Far-Right Political Culture," in De la Torre, *Promise and Perils of Populism,* 236; Daniel Pécaut, "El populismo Gaitanista," in *La Democratizacioon Fundamental,* ed. Carlos M. Vilas, 501.

82. Juan Domingo Perón, *Los Vendepatria,* 228.

83. See "Chávez agradeció estar vivo para sentir el rugir de las multitudes," *El Universal,* July 14, 2012; "Chávez en campaña," *Le Monde*

diplomatique en español, August, 2012; "Chávez lloró y le pidió a Dios: "No me lleves todavía," *La Nación,* April 6, 2012; "Chávez promete volver 'con más vida' de Cuba," *El Mundo,* February 25, 2012.

84. De la Torre, "Politics of the Extraordinary."

85. "Chávez será velado siete días más," *Página 12,* March 7, 2013; "Maduro: Somos los apóstoles de Chávez," *El Universal,* March 18, 2013; "Maduro inscribió su candidatura rodeado de una multitud de chavistas," *Clarín,* March 11, 2013.

86. "Italy's Silvio Berlusconi Changes His Party's Tune— Literally," *Christian Science Monitor,* December 30, 2009.

87. Private communication from Ertug Tombus. See also "Sólo hay que tenerle miedo a Dios ... y un poquito a mí," *Clarín,* September 7, 2012; and Benjamin Moffitt, *Global Rise of Populism,* 63. For the role of clericalism in Central and Eastern European populism, see Andrea Pirro, "Populist Radical Right Parties in Central and Eastern Europe: The Different Context and Issues of the Prophets of the Patria," *Government and Opposition* 49, no. 4 (2014), 612, 613.

88. "Trump, as Nominee, Vows: 'I Am Your Voice,'" *New York Times,* July 22, 2016.

89. When he was asked "Who is God to you?" Trump responded, "Well I say God is the ultimate. You know you look at this? Here we are on the Pacific Ocean. How did I ever own this [a golf course]? I bought it fifteen years ago. I made one of the great deals they say ever. I have no more mortgage on it as I will certify and represent to you. And I was able to buy this and make a great deal. That's what I want to do for the country. Make great deals. We have to, we have to bring it back, but God is the ultimate. I mean God created this and here's the Pacific Ocean right behind us. So nobody, no thing, no there's nothing like God" (Denver Nicks, " Here's What Donald Trump Thinks about God." *Time,* September 2015, http://time.com/4046620/donald-trump-god-ultimate/). See also "Trump on God: 'Hopefully I Won't Have to Be Asking for Much Forgiveness,'" *Washington Post,* June 8, 2016, www.washingtonpost.com/news/acts-of-faith/wp/2016/06/08/trump-on-god-hopefully-i-wont-have-to-be-asking-for-much-forgiveness/; "Trump Predicts Winning the Presidency Will Get Him into Heaven," *Politico* August 11, 2016, www.politico.com/story/2016/08

/trump-heaven-president-pastors-226923#ixzz4H89vfgFO. For the connections between populism and capitalism in American history, see Bethany Moreton, *To Serve God and WalMart: The Making of Christian Free Enterprise* (Cambridge, MA: Harvard University Press, 2009); and Julia Ott, *When Wall Street Met Main Street: The Quest for Investor Democracy* (Cambridge, MA: Harvard University Press, 2011).

90. Chiara Bottici, "The Mass Psychology of Trumpism: Old and New Myths," *Public Seminar,* November 17, 2016, www.publicseminar.org/2016/11/the-mass-psychology-of-trumpism/#.WH954hsrLIW. For Bottici's key work on political myth, see *Philosophy of Political Myth* (Cambridge: Cambridge University Press, 2007).

91. Judith Butler, "Reflections on Trump," Hot Spots, *Cultural Anthropology* website, January 18, 2017, https://culanth.org/fieldsights/1032-reflections-on-trump.

92. I thank Aaron Jakes for this last point.

93. See Lahouari Addi, "De la permanence du populisme algérien," *Peuples méditerranéens* (1990): 37–46. See also his book *L'impasse du populisme* (Alger: Entreprise nationale du livre, 1991); and more recently "Sociologie politique d'un populisme autoritaire," *Confluences Méditerranée* 2, no. 81 (2012): 27–40. See also Olivier Roy, *The Failure of Political Islam* (Cambridge, MA: Harvard University Press, 1994), 10, 83; Kaveh L. Afrasiabi, "Islamic Populism," *Telos,* June 20, 1995: 97–125; Vedi R. Hadiz, *Islamic Populism in Indonesia and the Middle East* (Cambridge: Cambridge University Press, 2016).

94. See Fondo Documental Secretaria Técnica, Mensajes presidenciales Clase dictada por el EXCMO Señor Presidente de la Nación, General Juan Perón en la Escuela Superior Peronista, Julio 2, de 1953, 61, 91, AGN; "La familia en el pensamiento vivo de Perón," *Mundo Peronista,* January, 1952, 5. See also Silvia Sigal, "Intelectuales y peronismo," in *Los años peronistas, 1943–1955,* ed. Juan Carlos Torre (Buenos Aires: Sudamericana, 2002), 518.

95. See Cas Mudde and Cristóbal Rovira Kaltwasser, "Vox populi or vox masculini? Populism and Gender in Northern Europe and South America," *Patterns of Prejudice* 49, nos. 1–2 (2015). Mudde and Rovira argue that "The stereotypical populist strongman is more likely to be attractive to people in societies with a more traditional

and machismo culture, while entrepreneur-populists will probably be attractive in more capitalist and materialist societies." See Mudde and Kaltwasser, *Populism,* 77.

96. David Farehnthold, "Trump Recorded Having Extremely Lewd Conversation about Women in 2005," *Washington Post,* October 8, 2016; "Tape Reveals Trump Boast about Groping Women," *New York Times,* October 8, 2016; "Don't Just Listen to Donald Trump Boast about Sexual Assault: Listen to the Women Who've Accused Him," *Quartz,* October 8, 2016, http://qz.com/804486/the-women-whove-accused-donald-trump-of-sexual-assault/; "Biden Accuses Trump of 'Sexual assault,'" *Politico,* October 8, 2016.

97. Duterte said, "As you know, I'm fighting with [US Secretary of State John Kerry's] ambassador. His gay ambassador, the son of a whore. He pissed me off" ("Philippines' Rodrigo Duterte Insults US Envoy with Homophobic Slur," *Guardian,* August 10, 2016, www.theguardian .com/world/2016/aug/10/philippines-leader-calls-us-ambassador-gay-son-of-a-whore-prompting-summons); "El Trump filipino: Duterte, el hombre fuerte que llega con recetas polémicas, *La Nación,* June 5, 2016, www.lanacion.com.ar/1905827-el-trump-filipino-duterte-el-hombre-fuerte-que-llega-con-recetas-polemicas; "Silvio Berlusconi: 'My Passion for Women Is Better Than Being Gay,'" *Telegraph,* November 2, 2010; "Donald Trump Makes His Penis a Campaign Issue during Debate," March 4, 2016, *NBC News,* www.nbcnews.com/politics/2016-election/donald-trump-makes-his-penis-campaign-issue-during-debate-n531666; "Duterte Tells Obama Not to Question Him about Killings," Associated Press, September 5, 2016, http://bigstory.ap.org/article /cd9eda8d34814aedabb9579a31849474/duterte-tells-obama-not-question-him-about-killings; "Obama anula una reunión con Duterte porque le llamó 'hijo de puta,'" *El País,* September 6, 2016.

98. "Philippines' Duterte Likens Himself to Hitler, Wants to Kill Millions of Drug Users," Reuters, October 1, 2016, www.reuters.com /article/us-philippines-duterte-hitler-idUSKCN1200B9.

99. "¡Marisabel, prepárate, que esta noche te voy a dar lo tuyo!" See "Las mujeres y Chávez, un vínculo intenso," *La Nación,* March 10, 2013; "Chávez manda oposição venezuelana 'tomar Viagra,'" *Folha de S.Paulo,*

December 10, 2001; "'Vou descontaminar o Mercosul,' afirma Chávez na chegada," *Folha de S.Paulo,* January 19, 2007.

100. See Carlos de la Torre, *Populist Seduction in Latin America* (Athens: Ohio University Press, 2010), 109, 105, 107. On this topic, see also the essays in Karen Kampwirth, ed., *Gender and Populism in Latin America* (University Park: The Pennsylvania State University Press, 2010).

101. Federico Finchelstein and Pablo Piccato, "A Belief System That Once Laid the Groundwork for Fascism," *New York Times,* December 10, 2015, www.nytimes.com/roomfordebate/2015/12/09/donald-trumps-america/a-belief-system-that-once-laid-the-groundwork-for-fascism.

102. Nicola Tranfaglia, "Trump e il populismo fascista," *Articolo 21,* March 2, 2016, www.articolo21.org/2016/03/trump-e-il-populismo-fascista/; "Entrevista a Carlos de la Torre 'El populismo de Le Pen es un fascismo disfrazado de democracia,'" *ABC,* June 29, 2016, www.abc.es /espana/abci-populismo-fascismo-disfrazado-democracia-201606290918_noticia.html.

EPILOGUE

1. "Le Pen: Trump's Win 'Victory of the People against the Elites,'" *Breitbart,* November 13, 2016, www.breitbart.com/london/2016/11/13 /le-pen-trumps-win-victory-people-elites/. See also Fernando Scolnik, "La particular visión de Cristina Kirchner sobre el triunfo de Donald Trump," *La Izquierda Diario,* November 11, 2016.

2. See Eva Perón, "Palabras pronunciadas el 29 de Mayo de 1951, en el acto organizado por la colectividad japonesa residente en el país, en el Salón blanco de la Casa de Gobierno," in Eva Perón, *Mensajes y discursos* (Buenos Aires: Fundación pro Universidad de la Producción y del Trabajo: Fundación de Investigaciones Históricas Evita Perón, 1999), 3:244.

3. See Dylan Riley, *The Civic Foundations of Fascism in Europe: Italy, Spain, and Romania 1870–1945* (Baltimore: Johns Hopkins University Press, 2010), for insightful and provocative analyses of fascism and civil society.

4. Ibid., 212.

5. Legajo 20, Sala VII 2596, Carpeta recortes s/n, Archivo General de la Nación, Argentina, Archivo Uriburu.

6. See Juan Domingo Perón, "En la Bolsa de Comercio: 25 de agosto de 1944," in Coronel Juan Perón, *El pueblo quiere saber de qué se trata* (Buenos Aires: 1944).

INDEX

Made in the USA
Las Vegas, NV
02 August 2022

52578630R00215